PINKS, PANSIES, AND PUNKS

THE RHETORIC OF MASCULINITY
IN AMERICAN LITERARY CULTURE

James Penner

INDIANA UNIVERSITY PRESS   *Bloomington & Indianapolis*

This book is a publication of

Indiana University Press
601 North Morton Street
Bloomington, Indiana 47404-3797 USA
iupress.indiana.edu

Telephone orders   800-842-6796
Fax orders   812-855-7931
Orders by e-mail   iuporder@indiana.edu

Library of Congress Cataloging-in-Publication Data

Penner, James, [date]
  Pinks, pansies, and punks : the rhetoric of masculinity
in American literary culture / James Penner.
     p. cm.
  Includes bibliographical references and index.
  ISBN 978-0-253-35547-8 (cloth : alk. paper) — ISBN 978-0-253-22251-0 (pbk. :
alk. paper) 1. American literature—20th century—History and criticism.
2. American literature—Male authors—History and criticism. 3. Men in literature.
4. Masculinity in literature. 5. Social classes in literature. 6. Gender identity in
literature. 7. Literature and society—United States—History—20th century. I. Title.
  PS173.M36P46 2011
  810.9'3521—dc22
                                                                    2010017543

1   2   3   4   5   16   15   14   13   12   11

TO SHIRLEY MORI

DIONYSUS   I give you sober warning, fools:
           place no chains on me.

PENTHEUS   But *I* say: chain him.
           And I am the stronger here.

DIONYSUS   You do not know the limits of your strength.
           You do not know what you do.
           You do not know who you are.

EURIPIDES, *THE BACCHAE,*
TRANS. WILLIAM ARROWSMITH

Contents

Acknowledgments

The road to *Pinks, Pansies, and Punks* has been a long one. Since the project's inception, I have received support and encouragement from many people at various institutions. I would like to begin by thanking my wonderful mentors at Brown University: Spencer Golub, David Savran, Arnold Weinstein, and Don Wilmeth. Each of them helped me to hone my craft, and each has had a profound influence on my intellectual development. Arnold taught me how to compress my ideas onto a single page and how to talk about my ideas in front of a large audience (no small feat). Don has been a great friend and mentor and has given me valuable advice about publishing my work. I am indebted to Spencer for teaching me a great deal about writing, creativity, and the importance of rejecting the established way of thinking about texts, authors, and literary periods. I am grateful to David for first introducing me to the idea of writing about masculinity and its role in American literary culture. David's study *Taking It Like a Man* was a seminal text for my project. I would also like to thank Nancy Armstrong for reading and commenting on the earliest version of my 1950s chapter ("Highbrows and Lowbrows"). Her enthusiastic reading and writing seminar helped me reconceptualize my 1950s chapter.

I am also grateful to my many academic mentors at the University of Southern California: Joseph Boone, Alice Echols, Tim Gustafson, Anthony Kemp, Rebecca Lemon, Tania Modleski, and Bruce Smith. I thank Tony for being a great friend and colleague and for pointing me to Otto Weininger's *Sex and Character*, a crucial text for my early chapters and my conception of soft masculinity. I thank Alice for recommending several important historical studies and for carefully reading and critiquing the earliest versions of my chapter on the 1960s. I would also like to thank the Department of English at USC for awarding me a dissertation fellowship for the academic year of 2002–2003, and the graduate school at USC for awarding me a final year fellowship during 2004–2005.

My project benefited from a rigorous, yet generous, doctoral committee. I want to thank Dana Polan for his expertise in French critical theory and his vision, insight, and professionalism; Dana stuck with the project during a move to New York City and provided excellent advice about getting my manuscript published. I thank David Román for being an extraordinary mentor throughout my time at USC. David urged me to write about Clifford Odets and Tennessee Williams and always provided excellent advice about my project and academic career. When I was baffled, he was especially good at demystifying academic culture. Last, I thank my dissertation chair, Leo Braudy, for being an expert reader and my harshest critic. Leo was generous with his time and always open to obscure authors and crackpots whom other scholars would prefer to ignore. Best of all, he taught me to curb my didactic tendencies and to let the authors and texts speak for themselves. Leo's erudition has been a source of great inspiration to me. I also want to thank him for helping me to prepare my book proposal and guiding me through the maze of academic publishing.

I also thank my friends and fellow graduate students at USC, who provided encouragement and a creative intellectual environment: Vidhu Aggarwal, Memo Arce, Ruth Blandón, Tanya Heflin, Christian Hite, Jennifer Kwon-Dobbs, Sun Hee Lee, Marci McMahon, Samuel Park, Jeff Solomon, and Annalisa Zox-Weaver. I am grateful to Vidhu for generosity and enthusiasm and for never offering easy praise; to Memo for reading my earliest chapters and for steering me through the most challenging periods of the project; to Christian for urging me to include the hard/soft binary chart in the introduction; to Annalisa for editorial finesse and for helping me turn the Sontag section into a full-length article; and, finally, to Jeff for taking detailed and copious notes on each of my chapters and for helping me to sharpen my prose. Jeff also taught me a great deal about an extremely rich genre: the author photo. Our monthly meetings at Groundworks were absolutely crucial to the project.

The assistance of numerous librarians was also essential to this book. I thank the expert librarians at Doheny Library at USC (especially the incomparable Ross Scimeca) and at the Literature Department of the Los Angeles Public Library in downtown LA. I am grateful to Liz Phillips of UC Davis's Special Collections, who diligently sifted through Gianfranco Mantegna's Living Theatre archive and found remarkable production stills from *The Brig* and *Paradise Now.* I am deeply indebted to Julie Herrada of the Special Collections Library at the University of Michigan, who found in the Labadie Collection some wonderful, unpublished photos of Michael Gold on Ernest Hemingway's boat in 1929–1930, which appear on the cover of *Pinks, Pansies, and Punks.* I thank the Library of Congress for granting permission to use the author photos of Allen Ginsberg, Ernest Hemingway, and Walt Whitman. Finally, I thank Erica MacDonald of *Rolling Stone* for granting permission to reproduce the amazing Eldridge Cleaver image. This book would not be the same without it.

I would also like to thank the very supportive faculty in the English Department at Dickinson College: Lynn Johnson, Carol Ann Johnston, David Kranz, Wendy Moffat, Ash Nichols, and Bob Winston. I thank Carol and David for interviewing me and inviting me to Dickinson for a campus visit. As a visiting professor, I was given the opportunity to teach my first upper-division course, "The Politics of Gender and American Literary Culture," and several courses on American drama and performance. My students at Dickinson helped me to find new ways to talk about my scholarship, and their influence can be seen in the final version of this book.

My colleagues in the English Department at the University of Puerto Rico, Rio Piedras, have provided a supportive environment for my scholarship; I am grateful to Ángel Arzán, Ada Haiman, Madeleine Hudders, Illia Aixa Madrazo, George Noble, Nadjah Rios, Janine Santiago, Dorsia Smith, Luz Miriam Tirado, Madeleine Vala, and Mark Wekander. In the fall of 2009, I was pleased to be awarded a TARE (Research Grant) from the College of General Studies, which enabled me to complete the final draft of *Pinks, Pansies, and Punks*. I am especially grateful to Luz Miriam for meeting me at the airport when I first arrived in San Juan and for helping me to find a beautiful, quiet apartment at UPR's Residencias de la Facultad. The Finca has become my home and a pleasant place to write.

Portions of this book were previously published in different form. Some of the material on the 1960s was published as "Gendering Susan Sontag's Criticism in the 1960s: The New York Intellectuals, the Counter Culture and the *Kulturkampf* over 'the New Sensibility,'" *Women's Studies* 37.8 (December 2008): 921–41. Portions of the section on the Living Theatre were published as "The Living Theatre and Its Discontents: Excavating the Somatic Utopia of *Paradise Now*," *Ecumenica: Journal of Theatre and Performance* 2.1 (Spring 2009): 17–36. I would like to thank Carolyn Roark for reading early drafts of the latter article and for encouraging me to submit it to *Ecumenica*.

I am deeply indebted to the staff of Indiana University Press. Jane Behnken has been a wonderful editor. She championed the project from the beginning and has offered expert advice and wise counsel at each stage of the march to publication. It has been a pleasure to work with her. I also want to thank Scott Herring. Scott was a brilliant and generous reader of my manuscript; his insightful commentary guided my final rewrite of *Pinks, Pansies, and Punks*, and I can't say enough about his contribution. I would like to thank Merryl Sloane; I have been extremely impressed with her peerless editing and professionalism. This book has certainly benefited from Merryl's remarkable critical eye. Last, I would also like to thank Marvin Keenan for his editorial expertise, and for guiding the manuscript through the final stages of the printing process.

Finally, I thank my mother, Marilyn Penner, for always supporting my academic endeavors and my desire to be a scholar. I would also like to thank my father, L. C. Penner, who passed away a few years before this manuscript was completed, and my brothers and sisters; their humor, encouragement, and support have meant a great deal to me. Several close friends have helped me during my periods of geographic readjustment: Giovanni Di Simone, Christoph Greger,

Fernando Jimenez, Mark Landsman, Oliver X., David Ralicke, José Manuel Roque, George Skarpelos, Charlie Staveley, Rias van den Doel, and Gabby Villanueva. I want to thank Oliver for first introducing me to Eldridge Cleaver's vicious attack on James Baldwin in *Soul on Ice*. We were both 16 or 17 at the time, and it was my first authentic encounter with a new literary genre: macho criticism. In retrospect, I believe Cleaver's vivid and arresting language had a strong effect on me: it made me aware of the sheer visceral power of macho criticism and its unspoken influence on American literary culture. Since our undergraduate days at Berkeley, Christoph has been a wonderful friend, an intellectual mentor, and an enthusiastic reader of my work. Many of the probing conversations I have had with David about creativity, dream interpretation, and Jungian psychoanalysis have seeped into the heart of this book. Last, I would like to express my deepest gratitude to Shirley Mori. Since we first met, she has been a vital source of enchantment and awe. During the writing of this book, she has often made my life wonderful.

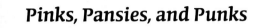

Pinks, Pansies, and Punks

Introduction: A Short History
of Macho Criticism

In 1928, Michael Gold, an aspiring Marxist critic, wrote a review of Ernest Hemingway's *Men Without Women* (1927) for the *New Masses.* Gold had not yet published *Jews Without Money* (1930), the working-class memoir that would make him an important literary figure during the Depression. The review of Hemingway might have been entirely forgotten except for Gold's novel approach to literary criticism. He makes no references to the short stories collected in *Men Without Women.* Instead, Gold is interested in the masculine fantasies that are communicated in Hemingway's literary works. Consider Gold's analysis of H. L. Mencken, Sherwood Anderson, and Ernest Hemingway and the respective audiences they attract:

> Mencken, Hemingway, Sherwood Anderson all the bourgeois modern American writers, whom do they write for? Not for workingmen, and not for the bankers of Wall Street. They write for and they express the soul of, the harried white-collar class. . . . Sherwood Anderson expressed the soft daydreams of this class, an epicene's dream of escape, without will, without vigor. Hemingway offers the daydreams of a man. Liquor, sex, and sport are his three chief themes, as they are in the consciousness of the American white-collar slave today. ("Hemingway—White Collar Poet" 159–60)

Gold's gendered analysis introduces the literary virility test. His scale is based on what could be termed the hard/soft binary. Anderson's fiction is soft in the sense that it is associated with effeminacy ("epicene's dream") and feckless impotence ("without will, without vigor"). In contrast, Hemingway's fiction is hard because it celebrates traditional masculine concerns and phallic potency: "liquor, sex, and sport." In Gold's reading, men's literature becomes a collection of masculine wish-fulfillment fantasies, and the assumed audience is male. Gold also describes how the hard fantasies of Hemingway are specifically designed for the repressed white-collar middle classes:

> The young American "liberal" writes advertising copy meekly all day, then at night dreams of Hemingway's irresponsible Europe, where everyone talks literature, drinks fine liqueurs, swaggers with a cane, sleeps with beautiful and witty British aristocrats, is well-informed in the mysteries of bullfighting, has a mysterious income from home. That is why Hemingway is suddenly popular. He has become the sentimental storyteller to a whole group of tired, sad, impotent young Americans, most of whom must work in offices every day. (160)

Gold's approach to literary criticism—ignoring the text and mocking the author's readers—was provocative in the 1920s, and Gold quickly made a name for himself in bohemian and left-wing circles. Unlike other Marxists in the 1920s, Gold's Marxist literary criticism is unique in that he is specifically interested in identifying and analyzing the gender myths to which the various literary audiences respond. Much of Gold's criticism rests on the premise that one's social class is necessarily reflected in one's masculine identity. Gold's gender-inflected Marxism also posits that one's masculine identity and persona are necessarily linked to one's social class and the labor one performs. The ideal of masculine toughness is personified in the working-class male who performs hard labor and possesses robust vitality. By the same token, a man of the leisure classes is considered less manly because he rarely works with his hands and does not perform "real" labor.

The success of *Jews Without Money* and Gold's gender-laden critiques of Hemingway and Thornton Wilder quickly established his literary reputation in the 1930s. It could be argued that Gold's linking of social class and gender identity in his early writings was an early example of a new genre of literary criticism: macho criticism. Gold was certainly not the first author to exhibit an interest in masculinist concerns. However, his literary reviews are a good place to start because he is the genre's most avid and vociferous practitioner. In his critical arsenal, the vilest insults are softness, effeminacy, and impotency, and these sins often go hand in hand. As a macho critic, Gold is adept at policing the literary text and uncovering any effete references. For Gold, the effete, in aesthetic terms, connotes a penchant for poetic verbosity and emotional excess while the masculine is associated with economy and restraint: "[Hemingway] deserves recognition; he is powerful, original. . . . he has technical control of his material as sure as a locomotive engineer. . . . he has led American writing back to the divine simplicities of the prosaic" (159). For Gold, the ideal of a "locomotive engineer" is suitable because it deflects the concept of leisure-culture effeteness by turning the male writer into a Marxist ideal: a technician who performs socially useful labor.

In the end, Hemingway passes the test of hardness and virility, but Gold is suspicious of the "impotent" white-collar audience that his fiction attracts. The authors (John Steinbeck, Richard Wright, James T. Farrell, Sinclair Lewis) who write about the working class and the class struggle tend to be the writers who pass the virility test and receive Gold's blessing. Gold's strategy is to use gender concerns to promote his own class issues; thus, he mocks Hemingway's readers in an attempt to nudge Hemingway in the proletarian direction. It could be argued that this strategy did work: Hemingway's novel *To Have and Have Not* (1937) was his first attempt at a proletarian novel.[1] Gold's success in literary circles in the 1930s highlights the salience of gender myths as a political weapon in the Depression and the notion that the reader's understanding of literature is often rooted in various gender fantasies.

During the 1930s, Gold's class-based criticism was popular because the literary establishment had begun to shift to the left during the Depression.[2] Literary editors sought him out because he was a leading authority on proletarian art and a bridge to a nascent working-class audience of readers, and it is clear that Gold relished playing the role of literary ruffian, a proletarian bull in the china shop of American literary culture. Gold was also an important figure in the ongoing revolt against the genteel tradition of American letters, which maintained that literature should respect decorum and the polite social dictates of upper-class society. Deriding the genteel tradition was a popular cause in the teens and twenties, and many writers (Hemingway, Sherwood Anderson, Mencken, Malcolm Cowley, Lewis, Theodore Dreiser) shared Gold's contempt for the polite and "prissy" sensibility that often characterized some American literary magazines during the pre–World War I era.[3] For a male writer of the 1920s and 1930s, attacking the genteel tradition was not only a question of literary sensibility, but also a way of foregrounding one's masculine identity in the world of literary culture.

Franco La Cela, an Italian cultural anthropologist and a contemporary scholar of machismo in various cultures, points out that visibility is a crucial trope for the male who desires to reaffirm his masculinity in the public realm:

> Males in order to show that they are real men, must produce rowdy noise and make scenes—the roar of a Harley Davidson, popping wheelies on a Vespa, a certain tone of voice. Otherwise, their "sex" remains invisible. As a Mexican proverb points out, either you are a macho, or you simply are nothing: *El macho vive mientras el corbarde quiere.*[4] This is to say there is no zero degree of masculinity: it is always excessive, hypertrophic, emphatic. Machismo, then, is the only way men can be seen. (39)

The theme of making oneself visible is especially relevant to literary culture because the written word is not a form of visual culture. Unlike art or film, the literary male body is not readily visible or embodied in print culture because it must be imagined by the reader. The end result of the process of mediation—the author's use of language, imagery, and subtext to foreground a particular gendered presence—is, in many cases, an excessive or hyperbolic version of maleness. Similarly, the critics who indulge in gender critiques and literary "gay bashing" employ a variety of techniques and approaches. Some, like Gold in the 1920s and 1930s and Eldridge Cleaver in the 1960s, opt to be hyperbolic and direct while other authors favor innuendo and subtext; the latter know that a well-placed phrase in a review can plant suspicion in the mind of the reader. Because homosexuality was considered unspeakable in certain literary circles at different points in American history (e.g., 1930s, 1940s, and 1950s), indirection was often the preferred approach in American letters.

For many authors, the most effective way to assert their masculinity was through excess or hypermasculine display. However, positing the existence of hypermasculinity does not imply that there is some normative quotient of masculinity upon which we can all readily agree during any particular historical moment. That said, hypermasculinity is often easy to spot because it usually calls attention to itself.

RAHV'S "PALEFACE AND REDSKIN" AND AMERICAN LITERARY CULTURE IN THE 1930S

In the 1930s, the imaginary norm was often the brawny masculinity of the salt-of-the-earth proletarian. Philip Rahv's classic essay "Paleface and Redskin" (1939) has its roots in Gold's masculinist reading of American literature. Unlike Gold—who leans toward the party line and Stalinism—Rahv is a Trotskyite critic. In 1934, Rahv and William Phillips founded the *Partisan Review*. At the time, the influential magazine was the literary companion to the *New Masses*.[5] Rahv was often highly critical of generic proletarian literature (i.e., propaganda), and his erudite criticism was decidedly less vituperative than Gold's brand of Marxism.[6] In "Paleface and Redskin," Rahv's binary phrase foregrounds the masculine antipodes of the American literary tradition. The designation "paleface" suggests an Anglo-Saxon lineage and, more important, the notion that these upper-class writers spend much of their time in libraries, drawing rooms, and literary salons. Thus, they are "patricians" and "highbrows," and their pale skin denotes an abundance of leisure culture and their exclusion from backbreaking labor. For Rahv, Henry James is the author who best exemplifies the paleface tradition of American letters, and the epithet carries with it a tacit connotation of effeteness and fastidiousness: James is described as "genteel, snobbish and pedantic" (4).

Rahv's rhetoric also suggests the theme of sickliness. The paleface lacks energy and robustness. In another passage, Rahv even hints at the paleface's impotence: "[the paleface writer creates] products of cultivation that remain abstract because they fall short on evidence drawn from the sensuous and material world" (5). In this case, the lack of sexual experience ("evidence") suggests that the paleface author lacks masculine vigor and phallic proficiency. Although Rahv does not directly state that Henry James was impotent, the association is easy to make, given James's status as a lifelong bachelor. After James's death, it was rumored that James became impotent during an accident that occurred when he was a young man.[7] Regardless of the specifics of James's sexual orientation, the rumor itself has influenced how readers understand and read James's body, his masculine image, and his fiction. Although Rahv's rhetoric is critical of the paleface tradition, it should be pointed out that he also has great admiration for Henry James and his fiction ("incomparable narratives").

In stark contrast to the Jamesian paleface, the "redskin" writers are virile figures who possess "aggression" and "lived experience." Rahv notes that "the redskin deserves the epithet 'lowbrow,' not because he is badly educated—which he might or might not be—but because his reactions are primarily emotional, spontaneous, and lacking in personal culture" (3). Their red skin indicates that they are comfortable outdoors and that many of them have rubbed shoulders with fellow workers and spent time on the frontier; their skin coloration also suggests that they possess richness and vigor, precisely the qualities that the paleface lacks. For Rahv, Walt Whitman is the classic redskin who exemplifies the "open-air" approach to literature. In the paleface/redskin dialectic, James embodies refined "sensibility" whereas Whitman is linked to "energy." In this case, "sensibility" suggests refinement and devotion to decorum whereas the redskin writers are somewhat hostile to decorum because it often implies overcivilization. Like Twain's robust heroes, the redskin writers must always resist the feminizing forces of civilization and refinement.

Rahv's concluding paragraphs also allude to another problem. In a striking passage, Rahv suggests that the Jew and the paleface share a penchant for overrefinement: "As for the paleface, in compensation for backward cultural conditions and a lost religious ethic, he has developed a supreme talent for refinement, just as the Jew, in compensation for adverse social conditions and a lost national independence, has developed a supreme talent for cleverness" (6). Rahv's insight should not be viewed as mere self-congratulation for his own Jewishness. Although Rahv is clearly fond of high culture and refinement, he is also troubled by it. He even warns male writers about the perils of overrefinement: "Now this peculiar excess of refinement is to be deplored in an imaginative writer, for it weakens his capacity to cope with experience and induces in him a fetishistic attitude toward tradition" (ibid.). Rahv's suggestion that Jews are often inclined toward excessive refinement is a veil over a thorny topic: the association of the Jew with effeminacy and leisure culture.[8] Rahv's advice to aspiring writers encourages them to seek out experience and become hypermasculine as a strategy of avoiding the afflictions of overrefinement and effeteness.

Although Rahv is evenhanded in his criticisms of both traditions in American literature, it is clear to the reader that the redskin model is a more desirable form of manliness, if not artistry. The paleface model, with its connotations of sickliness and impotence, is presented as a brilliant albeit antiquated style of literature. Although Rahv praises the up-and-coming redskin writers, he yearns for a synthesis of the two opposing ideas.

Rahv's "Paleface and Redskin" can also be read as a veiled commentary on race and whiteness. Henry James's sickly white body, his withdrawal from healthy outdoor life, and his perceived lack of sexual experience illustrate the symptoms of a familiar obsession of the nineteenth century: overcivilization. James, a product of inherited wealth and luxury, epitomizes the overcivilized man of letters who haunts American literary culture in the early twentieth century. In racial terms, James signifies the white, upper-class, "literary" body that is desperately in need of renewal and vigor. In the nineteenth and early twentieth centuries, upper-class whiteness was often stigmatized because it was associated with neurasthenia ("nervous exhaustion").[9] In contrast, Whitman's healthy and robust redskin body is the imaginary solution and antidote to paleface whiteness.[10] The connection to Native American culture ("redskin") symbolically conveys a return to nature and the embrace of an active outdoor life. Whitman's iconic image—a healthy body, sunburn, beard, and long hair—is offered as proof of his vitality while James's effete body is a symbol of the waning genteel tradition and the obsolete refined literary culture of the nineteenth century. Rahv, under the spell of Marxist dialectics, proposes that a synthesis of the two traditions will emerge in the future.

Rahv's "Paleface and Redskin" is fascinating because it imagines the male body in relation to literary creation. The body of the leisure class produces one mode of fiction and the robust working-class body another. In short, the American literary text is indelibly marked by the body type that produces it. In Rahv's physiological view of literary production, the crucial dichotomy is leisure-culture impotence and working-class energy, which emphasizes the notion that certain bodies (hard/soft, young/old) produce particular styles of prose (masculine/effete) and genres of literature (the Jamesian novel, social realism, etc.).

Rahv's decision to highlight Whitman's body as a literary model is an interesting choice, given Whitman's bisexuality. Apart from Whitman, Rahv's male redskin writers are primarily rough-and-tumble heterosexuals: Hemingway, James Fenimore Cooper, Dreiser, Lewis, Anderson, Wolfe, Carl Sandburg, Erskine Caldwell, Steinbeck, Farrell, and William Saroyan.[11] Rahv's selection of Whitman is also interesting because it indicates that same-sex passion is not wedded to effeminacy; moreover, he suggests that Whitman is an open and generous spirit who is forever "plunging with characteristic impetuosity into the turbulent, formless life of the frontier and big cities, accept[ing] experience in its total ungraded state" (13). Thus, Whitman embodies energy and porousness. Rahv's conception of Whitman's body is insightful because it untangles manliness from the hard body and makes the "masculine" signify experiential knowledge in general.

This book begins with Gold's and Rahv's criticism because their essays demonstrate how the male body becomes a reflection of class identity and masculine persona in the 1930s. In this study, I write an intellectual and cultural history of the politics of masculinity in American literary culture from the Depression to the tail end of the sexual revolution (1975). I will demonstrate how the rhetoric of masculinity has often played a crucial role in the practice and production of literary culture—how, both as a subtext and as a central concern, masculinity cannot be divorced from the important literary and political debates of the various decades (e.g., class struggle in the 1930s, anti-Communism in the 1950s).

While I am writing a history of the rhetoric of masculinity in American literature, I am mindful of the fact that literary culture often occupies an elevated status within the cultural imagination.

Literary endeavors and the publication of the written word often epitomize refinement and civility in the sphere of culture, and success in literary culture can provide an author with considerable cultural capital. For many, the creation of the written word signifies a preference for the "life of the mind" and an exclusive status within the rarefied realm of high culture.

However, within literary culture itself, there is also a counternarrative to the rhetoric of literary refinement and high culture. Paradoxically, literary prestige is, in some cases, obtained through aggression and literary expressions of masculine domination. As authors jockey for power and respect in the literary marketplace, the intense struggle for literary recognition and fame fosters the desire to assail and lash out at one's competition. Thus, in *Pinks, Pansies, and Punks,* literary culture often resembles a vicious cockfight. Within the genre of literary fights, the preferred mode of attack is the gendered critique (or virility test). While social class was the bête noire of the nineteenth century, the gendered critique became an extremely viable form of attack in the mid-twentieth century. Hence, the male writer must always be on guard and prepared to defend himself from the hated charge of effeminacy. When evaluating an author's work, age-old questions about literary merit can quickly morph into macho criticism and the question of whether an author is sufficiently masculine. A macho critic can create a literary scandal by attacking an author's creation (e.g., an effeminate or soft literary character), or the author's sexuality or sexual preference.

A crucial aspect of this book will be the writer's relationship to other authors in the public sphere. In many cases, a writer's masculine or feminine image is a negotiation of sorts. Through publicity materials, frontispieces, author photos, and carefully chosen biographical anecdotes, the author consciously situates his/her gender image in relation to other writers. The writer's masculine image has a strong effect on the reader. For example, photos of Hemingway with a shotgun and African big game become an essential part of the mythic construction of masculinity. If one never bothers to read Hemingway's fiction, one may still be familiar with the author's mythic masculine image. It is often difficult to divorce an author from his/her gender myth and body type, and we, as readers, often have gender preconceptions that we superimpose on the author whom we are reading.

Another important part of literary culture is literary criticism; much of my discussion of literary culture will focus on literary critics who are concerned with the business of policing texts for feminine and effete motifs and references. My brief history of macho criticism will include the genre's most adept practitioners (Michael Gold, Leslie Fiedler, Eldridge Cleaver). However, I realize that many critics might object to being labeled "macho." Therefore, I use the term very loosely; it connotes that the writer or critic is keenly aware of the gendered aspects of literature and how literary figures reproduce or contradict certain masculine myths. I am mindful of the fact that macho criticism often functions on both conscious and unconscious levels; thus, the term "macho" should not be read simply as a term of abuse. My study includes some writers and critics who are deeply concerned about the "feminization" of American literature (Malcolm Cowley, John Crowe Ransom). There are also literary critics (Irving Howe, Philip Rahv) who are not openly macho; nonetheless, whether they admit it or not, their understanding of literature foregrounds various masculinist obsessions.

Historically, the promulgation of a tough masculine persona in print often emerges as a response to the cutthroat competition of the literary marketplace. For the male writer, masculine identity is often inextricably linked to the act of writing in American culture; it influences the writer's worldview, how the writer perceives himself in society, and, above all, his understanding of literary expression as a pitched battle that must be fought in the public realm that is the written word. In *Making It* (1967), Norman Podhoretz points out how the act of publication and the establishment of a literary reputation were masculine rituals for what he calls "the family" (the New York intellectuals of the 1950s). In his memoir, Podhoretz reveals how he gained his manhood when he attacked Saul Bellow's new novel *The Adventures of Augie March* in a review for *Commentary* in the early 1950s. Podhoretz's dissenting view of Bellow's much-praised second novel caused a minor literary scandal among New York intellectuals. Podhoretz notes that the event resembled a "bar mitzvah ceremony which signified, like that ancient Jewish rite itself, that I had finally come of age"; Podhoretz also vividly recalls the moment when Philip Rahv uttered "Today, you are a man" at a cocktail party that Podhoretz attended after the publication of his scathing review (166–67). This anecdote from Podhoretz's autobiography reveals the importance of masculine identity in the act of writing and how an attack in print, and publication itself to this day, resemble a pugilistic contest in which one's literary performance is often perceived as an external expression of one's virility and propensity for masculine domination.

Like Rahv's allusion to the Jew in "Paleface and Redskin," Podhoretz's anecdote also brings up the importance of Jewishness in my study. Many of the key figures discussed in *Pinks, Pansies, and Punks* (Gold, Rahv, Podhoretz, Norman Mailer, Howe, Fiedler) are Jewish. During the period (1930–1975) that this book covers, Jewish literary critics and authors dominated New York literary culture and thus figure prominently in my study of American literary culture. In the case of the New York Jewish intellectuals, one question quickly becomes central: how is their literary masculinity informed by their identity and status as Jews? To address this complex question, my study will draw from scholarship that examines the theme of the feminized and so-called soft Jew, who is often stereotypically linked to leisure-culture effeminacy by the majority culture.[12] According to historian George Mosse, the notion that male Jews are effeminate was prevalent in Europe in the late nineteenth and early twentieth centuries.[13]

Otto Weininger's writings are especially illuminating on this subject. In *Sex and Character* (1906), Weininger, a Viennese Jew and contemporary of Freud, argues that Jews are inherently feminine: "The Jewish race [Judentum] is pervasively feminine. The femininity comprises those qualities that I have shown to be in total opposition to masculinity. The Jews are much more feminine than the Aryans . . . and the manliest Jew may be taken for a female" (409). In other passages of *Sex and Character,* although Weininger was "unwilling to argue for the complete identification of the Jew with Woman, he argued that the two types shared many attributes."[14] Weininger, a self-hating Jew, represents a hyperbolic point of view. However, his paranoid perspective demonstrates that the cultural association of Jewishness with femininity was a popular obsession in certain European cultural milieus at the turn of the twentieth century. After Weininger committed suicide in 1903, his racist writings found an audience in right-wing and nationalist circles in Germany and Austria.[15]

In *Tough Jews: Political Fantasies and the Moral Dilemma of American Jewry* (1990), Paul Breines discusses the link of Jewishness and effeminacy in relation to American culture in the twentieth century. Breines identifies two familiar stereotypes—the gentle Jew and the Jewish weakling. For Breines, both stereotypes can also be described as "the Woody Allen figure": "the schlemiel: the pale, bespectacled, diminutive vessel of Jewish anxieties who cannot, indeed, must not, hurt a flea and whose European forebears fell by the millions to Jew-hating savagery" (3). Breines argues that, in the era after the 1973 Yom Kippur War, "the images of Jewish wimps and nerds are being supplanted by those of the hardy, bronzed kibbutznik, the Israeli para-trooper, and the Mossad (Israeli Intelligence) agent" (ibid.). Breines's analysis of Jewish stereotypes is important because my study focuses on the 1930s, 1940s, and 1950s, eras when ethnic stereotypes were more widespread in American literary culture. Thus, this book examines a few crucial questions about Jewishness: How does rebellion against the stereotype of Jewish softness play out in the arena of literary culture? How does the literary Jew strive to make his masculinity visible in literary culture? My study also contrasts American Jewish critics with non-Jewish critics (Malcolm Cowley, Granville Hicks, T. S. Eliot, John Crowe Ransom) who present their own particular brand of literary machismo. This project also examines how African American literature reproduces the rhetoric of the hard/soft binary. In the 1930s, Richard Wright's "Blueprint for Negro Writing" (1937) scorned the effete writing of the Harlem Renaissance and endorsed social realism, the preferred genre of hard writers. Hardness will also play a crucial role in the rhetoric of the Black Power movement of the late 1960s and early 1970s and in Eldridge Cleaver's *Soul on Ice*.[16]

THE APOLLONIAN AND THE DIONYSIAN

In order to discuss the hard/soft dichotomy, we need to examine how hardness and softness relate to the "masculine" and the "feminine." My conception of softness has two distinct sources: the Dionysian feminine and the mythic cultural feminine. The Dionysian feminine is borrowed from Friedrich Nietzsche's *The Birth of Tragedy* (1872). For Nietzsche, the Dionysian represents ecstasy, the irrational, and the cult of the primitive. The polar opposite of the Dionysian is the Apollonian, Nietzsche's conception of the mythic cultural masculine; the Apollonian signifies rationality and the principles of order, control, form, and restraint. For Nietzsche, music is the highest form of human culture because it, in its ideal form, possesses a perfect equilibrium of the Apollonian and the Dionysian. However, it is important to note that Nietzsche's conceptualization of the Dionysian is not necessarily connected to the female body itself, and certainly not to the theme of feminine submission. Hence, the Dionysian flood of impulse, passion, and instinct is that which cannot be controlled by reason and logic. The term "Dionysian masculinity" will have specific relevance in my discussion of the Beats in the 1950s and the counterculture in the 1960s. In contrast, the mythic cultural feminine could be compared to D. H. Lawrence's neoprimitivism. In Lawrence's gender essentialism, the mythic cultural feminine is venerated because it signifies a turning away from rationality and an embrace of the will of the body—passion, intuition, spontaneity. In literary culture, the mythic cultural feminine is therefore intimately connected with the affective dimension. In contrast to the Dionysian feminine, the mythic cultural feminine is rooted in the symbolism of the feminine body and the ideal of somatic openness and porousness. When the mythic cultural feminine is transferred to the masculine body, the implication is that the male body becomes porous and capable of being penetrated, and this conception is not limited to a sexual act. In the American literary tradition, Allen Ginsberg perhaps best personifies the open and porous spirit of transformative masculinity. His celebration of the affective dimension of literature and his emphasis on the primacy of feeling in the act of poetic creation are essential to the soft masculinities that emerge in the 1950s and 1960s. For these reasons, he is often seen as the crucial link between the Beats and the hippies.

The final twist in the genealogy of alternative masculinities is the mythic cultural feminine's association with mutability. Otto Weininger was obsessed with the idea that femininity is necessarily linked to mutability and that this particular association can explain the differences between the sexes. In *Sex and Character*, Weininger provocatively argues that women do not possess a true autonomous self, and he thus assumes that women's natural state is "infinitely porous, infinitely malleable, and infinitely open to external influences" (Sengoopta 11). Weininger also maintains that women's personalities are elaborate simulacra that reflect the desire to win male approval. Weininger's misogynist theories were an attempt to solve the "woman question" of the late nineteenth century and to present a case for why women cannot be trusted with political autonomy. In my discussion of American literary culture, Weininger and his masculinist conception of women are relevant *not* because he had a strong influence on American critics—he definitely did not—but because his writings coherently and succinctly theorize the attempt to link the feminine to mutability. Weininger went to great lengths to link his antifeminist theories to physiology and science; thus, menstruation was offered as a biological explanation for women's chameleon-like persona. *Sex and Character* is a classic masculinist text that attempts to connect women's biology—gestation and menstruation—to women's psychological makeup. Hence, in Weininger's gender essentialism, men embody stasis and rationality while women signify emotionalism and mutability. At the root of Weininger's paranoid theories is a fear of male softness and the spectacle of the feminized Jewish male.

Weininger's gender theories are also relevant because various American literary critics in the twentieth century—consciously and unconsciously—share his anxieties; Leslie Fiedler and John Crowe Ransom remain fixated with the supposed link between femininity and mutability and the notion that American literature is becoming feminized.

If softness is inevitably wedded to mythic notions of femininity, my conception of hardness is linked to what could be described as the mythic cultural masculine. In contrast to the mythic cultural feminine, the mythic cultural masculine is often associated with the opposing qualities: intellect or reason rather than nature, rationality rather than emotion, stasis rather than mutability, and, above all else, a propensity for aggression rather than passivity. Thus, hypermasculinity is often characterized as excess aggression. In some historical epochs, aggression is thought to be desirable and advantageous while in other epochs it is a handicap and a serious social problem.[17] Sexual metaphors have also profoundly influenced the historic conception of masculinity. The hard masculine body is associated with phallic dominance. In somatic terms, the masculine body is conceived of as hard, solid, rigid, or that which cannot be penetrated. In my conception of hard masculinity, the ideal of a hard body has certain recurring themes, including a propensity for rationality and a reserved or laconic mode of expression. The hard-shell masculine figure is not entirely comfortable with the expression of emotion, nor with the spectacle of the male body being put on display. Conversely, the soft male is less afraid of expressing emotion and of embracing feminine allure.

When discussing constructions of masculine identity, I have, whenever possible, chosen to avoid the phrase "masculinity in crisis." This catchphrase, which is popular in the media and academic studies, is often misleading because it implies that one form of masculinity is approaching its end and that a new form of masculinity will somehow emerge and replace the previous form of masculinity. However, it is a foregone conclusion that the crisis in masculinity will never end. Hence, the phrase is often inappropriately used as a blanket term for describing opposing types of masculinity that co-exist in the same historical moment. In my estimation, the phrase is entirely inadequate for describing specific gender formations or understanding complex historical situations. Ultimately, we need a more nuanced way of discussing the fissures in masculine identity that exist both in the present and in the cultural past.

In lieu of "masculinity in crisis," *Pinks, Pansies, and Punks* refers to the "hard/soft binary" to chart the contrasting representations of masculinity that emerge in different historical moments. This is a highly flexible mythic system that allows the reader, cultural critic, or historian to examine the so-called crisis with greater specificity.[18] The hard/soft binary is crucial to the male socialization process: to be male is to encounter, confront, and internalize its dictates (whether one likes it or not).

Hardness is not merely a phallic fantasy. Culturally and psychologically, hardness functions as a powerful structuring mechanism that shapes and influences male behavior and masculine gender norms. Hardness is tacitly encouraged and understood as a social ideal while softness is overtly stigmatized.

The need to project and promote the mythology of hardness becomes an idée fixe for many writers of the American mid-century. Thus, *Pinks, Pansies, and Punks* will examine the various forms of macho criticism and their attack on leisure-culture effeminacy—the most familiar and overt form of softness. Although softness appears to be thoroughly discredited in the 1930s and much of the 1940s, it will demonstrate great resilience in subsequent decades; the affective and porous male body will become a repressed ideal for the subcultures of the 1950s (the hipsters and Beats) and the counterculture of the 1960s and 1970s.

THE HARD/SOFT BINARY[19]

Hard	Soft
Solid	Porous
Rational	Attracted to the irrational
Impervious to affect	Embraces affect
Emotionally closed	Emotionally open
Aggressive	Empathic/Sympathetic
Hard-shell	Pliable/Malleable
Fixed/Static	Mutable
Penetrator	Penetrated/Receptive
Reticent/Laconic	Expressive
Labor/Breadwinner	Leisure culture/Idle
Reserved/Not on display	On display/Alluring/ "To-be-looked-at-ness"[20]

In my discussion of American literary culture, I will examine how various writers and critics have often been obsessed with promulgating a particular masculine identity and style at different moments in U.S. history. My discussion of masculinity, with few exceptions, often revolves around men and the male body. However, I am not suggesting that masculinity is exclusively the property of men and male writers, nor am I positing that femininity is the exclusive property of women. As Judith Halberstam has noted, masculinity should not be "reduce[d] down to the male body and its effects."[21] The project of recognizing female masculinity is an important one because it is a primary way of unraveling the myths of gender essentialism. That said, because my project focuses on hypermasculine and macho texts, for fairly obvious reasons I often gravitate toward male authors. However, my study does include second wave feminists (Kate Millett, Valerie Solanas) who have offered critiques of hypermasculinity. Moreover, my chapter on the 1960s analyzes Susan Sontag's conception of the "new sensibility" and argues that it contains a somewhat veiled critique of the "egghead" masculinity of the Old Left.

It is important to note that the politics of masculinity in literary culture exist for women as well as men. For example, the aspiring female author can gain admittance to masculine literary culture by performing toughness in the arena of literary criticism. Many female writers who had success in the 1950s and 1960s (Mary McCarthy, Diana Trilling, Elizabeth Hardwick) were aware that a scathing review of another author's work was often the best way to advance in the macho world of literary culture. Moreover, for women authors, the worst sin of all was to be labeled a literary lightweight. Although I have only peripherally addressed the role of the female author in the literary marketplace, I believe that when more studies of the politics of masculinity in literary culture emerge in the coming years—especially work that focuses on the female authors who wrote in the masculine literary world of the 1950s and 1960s—these issues will be even more salient.[22]

PINKS, PANSIES, AND PUNKS AND MASCULINITY SCHOLARSHIP

A great many books on masculinity have come out in the 1990s and 2000s. Many of them have focused on analyzing disturbing trends in masculine identity (hypermasculinity, angry white males, homophobia, etc.). At the beginning of my project, I examined various forms of hypermasculinity; I was interested in analyzing how hypermasculinity is represented in literary texts and in the broader world of literary culture (especially literary fights and attacks). While doing this research, I encountered Susan Jeffords's *The Remasculinization of America: Gender and the Viet Nam War* (1989). Jeffords's important study examines how Hollywood filmmakers of the Reagan era reimagined masculine identity through the lens of the Vietnam conflict and how masculinity was central to mythic constructions of nationalism. I was immediately drawn to Jeffords's use of the term "remasculiniza-tion." By invoking this term, Jeffords seems to be tacitly implying that, at a certain point in the 1970s, the traditional way of defining masculinity was no longer valid or viable, that it had to be mythically put back together ("remasculinization"). What exactly was being put back together? What social forces (the Vietnam War, second wave feminism) had dismantled the prevailing myths of masculinity?

When I looked for answers to these questions, I found that a con-troversial figure like Timothy McVeigh—or a fictional character like Rambo—cannot be understood simply by studying the immediate political landscape of the 1990s. To really understand the social forces that created McVeigh, one has to understand the gender upheavals of the 1960s and 1970s. The sexual revolution, second wave feminism, and gay liberation had turned our society's understanding of gender and masculine identity upside down. In literary culture, the struggle that interested me the most was the conflict between the fathers who grew up during the Depression (the Old Left) and their children (the New Left and the counterculture). When examining the "culture wars" of the 1960s, most historians focus on the so-called lifestyle differences (rock music, long hair, sexual promiscuity, psychedelic drugs), while *Pinks, Pansies, and Punks* posits that the kulturkampf was not merely a generational struggle, but a profound clash over gender sensibility and, ultimately, gender ideology. Unlike previous works of cultural and literary history, my critical study attempts to theorize the split between the Old Left and the New Left/counter-culture in terms of gender and masculine identity.

While many books (see Jeffords 1989 and 1994, Savran 1998, Robinson 2000, Kimmel 2008, to name a few) have attempted to ac-count for masculine identity in the 1980s, 1990s, and 2000s, few books have attempted to cover exclusively the crucial period between the 1930s and the 1970s.[23] Using American literary culture as my canvas, *Pinks, Pansies, and Punks* will provide a cultural history between the Depression and the sexual revolution, an extremely diverse and rich period for gender studies because it concludes with the emergence of second wave feminism and gay liberation.

This study of literary culture and masculinity begins in the 1930s. The Depression era is important to my book because historians and literary critics, for fairly obvious reasons, have often focused on economic and social issues (unemployment, working-class struggles, poverty, etc.) when discussing literary works of the Depression. In most literary accounts of the 1930s, gender inevitably takes a backseat to the economic and social issues. Thus, when I reread the literature of the 1930s, I attempted to uncover the gender attitudes of this era, which have often been ignored by other scholars, and I will demonstrate how class identity was often rooted in gender myths (i.e., the upper classes are effete and sickly while the working classes are tough and virile). I also found that the 1930s are an ideal vantage point for viewing the cultural changes that emerge in the 1960s. The social and gender rebels of the 1960s are best understood when we examine the cultural values and gender attitudes of their parents who, in many cases, inherited and absorbed the weltanschauung of the Depression era.

Last, two major historical studies of masculinity in the first part of the twentieth century—George Chauncey's *Gay New York: Gender, Urban Culture, and the Making of the Gay Modern World 1890–1940* (1994) and Gail Bederman's *Manliness and Civilization: A Cultural History of Gender and Race in the United States, 1880–1917* (1995)—both end roughly where my project begins. *Pinks, Pansies, and Punks* was written with these important studies in mind.[24] In many respects, my study follows the trajectory that both Bederman and Chauncey have carefully mapped out. For example, in Bederman's *Manliness and Civilization,* the neurasthenic body of the upper-class male is a major concern in late nineteenth- and early twentieth-century medical discourse. Although neurasthenia, as a medical theory, is largely discredited by the 1910s and 1920s, many of the stereotypes it identified—based on the notion that hypercivilized refinement in the upper classes is a social problem that needs to be remedied—continue to circulate widely within American culture. In the twentieth century, many of the symptoms of neurasthenia are increasingly projected onto the body of the homosexual male and the effete man of letters (e.g., the Gold-Wilder scandal of 1930). In short, literary culture is often concerned with not only the literary text, but also fantasies about the body—virile, effeminate, or otherwise—that produced it. *Pinks, Pansies, and Punks* will explore how and why various American authors on the literary Left become obsessed with the notion of rooting out leisure-culture effeminacy during the height of the Depression.

In *Gay New York,* Chauncey explores how the "pansy craze" of the 1920s is increasingly pushed underground in the 1930s. Chauncey notes that, in the 1930s, "a powerful backlash to the Prohibition-era pansy craze developed . . . [and] the anti-gay reaction gained force [and] became part of a more general reaction to the cultural experimentation of the Prohibition years and to the disruption of gender arrangements by the Depression" (331). With Chauncey's argument in mind, my study analyzes how the backlash against the "pansy craze" is vividly expressed in the literary culture of the Depression.

In *Pinks, Pansies, and Punks,* I have avoided relying on one particular methodological approach. That said, my project is fundamentally an attempt to demystify the various masculine myths that are prevalent in literary culture; in doing so, this book incorporates insights from several critical approaches: psychoanalysis, feminism, Marxism, and queer studies. My theoretical eclecticism is a tactical choice that is based on the premise that previous scholarship on specific literary authors has been hindered by the attempt to see literature through the prism of one particular critical approach. For example, the plays of Clifford Odets are uniformly read as social protest literature that documents the struggles of the lower-middle class and the working class during the Depression. However, this particular approach often ignores how gender politics and masculine identity are crucial to Odets's plays. The end result of this critical approach is the erection of a theoretical firewall between class and gender concerns. Instead, my study demonstrates how masculine identity is, more often than not, constructed at a point where class and gender myths intersect. Moreover, as Michael Gold's work suggests, the mythic intersection is often a reflection of the popular belief that class identity and masculine identity are one.

In a theoretical sense, my project also has been influenced by Eve Kosofsky Sedgwick's *Epistemology of the Closet* (1990) and the attempt to deconstruct the social and cultural foundations of the homo/hetero binary. My task is to examine the rhetoric of American literary culture in the middle of the twentieth century. Although much of the hypermasculine rhetoric that is discussed tends to reinforce sharp distinctions between virile heterosexual writers and effeminate homosexuals, my study will demonstrate how a counter-tradition of hard same-sex passion also coexists within American literary culture in the twentieth century. Hard or macho same-sex passion can be found in the works of Clifford Odets (Eddie Fuseli of *Golden Boy*) and Gore Vidal (Jim Willard of *The City and the Pillar*), in Kinsey's anonymous sex histories (1940s), and in the Beat movement of the 1950s (Jack Kerouac, William Burroughs, Allen Ginsberg). My study also traces how hard-bodied same-sex passion morphs into gay macho, a full-fledged social movement and highly visible subculture, with the emergence of gay liberation in the late 1960s and early 1970s.[25] The reoccurrence of hard-bodied same-sex passion in a wide range of literary texts suggests that masculine-identified homosexuality should not be viewed as an anomaly, but as a viable parallel tradition in modern U.S. sex/gender systems; uncovering and recognizing the marginalized hard gay tradition is important in that it undermines the stereotypical association of homosexuality and effeminacy that is ubiquitous in American literary culture in the mid-twentieth century.

Many of the formations of masculine identity (macho, hard, soft, hyper, robotic, egghead, transformative, Dionysian, etc.) that are discussed in my survey of literary masculinities feature anomalies that stand outside the assumptions of the various masculinist theories (some macho writers admire soft male authors and vice versa). In the end, these anomalies are worth noting because they suggest that the range of masculine identities is far more diverse and pluralistic than we have realized; they also suggest that the various monolithic and static conceptions of masculinity that existed before second wave feminism and gay liberation often depended on denying that these contradictions exist.

In this study of hyperbolic literary masculinities, my use of the term "literary culture" is fairly broad, and it includes novels, plays, poetry, diaries, journals, manifestos, essays, literary criticism, journalism, nonfiction, essays from psychology and sociology, and screenplays that have been turned into Hollywood films. My study includes some nonfiction writers who are not literary in the traditional sense of the word. My choice of Timothy Leary, for instance, may seem curious to some. However, Leary, a Harvard psychologist, enjoyed great popularity in the 1960s and early 1970s, and his writings—especially

The Politics of Ecstasy (1968)—were very influential for the counterculture and American literary culture during that time. His writings
are also relevant because they succinctly articulate the rhetoric of
Dionysian masculinity. For similar reasons, my study also includes
many writings by sociologists, psychologists, and social scientists; it
analyzes nonfiction works by Lewis Terman and Catharine Miles,
Talcott Parsons, Philip Wylie, Samuel A. Stouffer, Edward Strecker,
David Riesman, William H. Whyte, C. Wright Mills, Alfred C. Kinsey, Wilhelm Reich, and R. D. Laing. Since my project is essentially a
history of mythic conceptions of masculinity within literary culture,
these so-called empirical texts were particularly useful and, in some
cases, extremely revealing. The works of nonfiction offer a snapshot
of gender attitudes in various historical moments. In some cases, they
are more useful than literary texts because the authors are speaking
concretely and specifically about their understanding of gender and
gender formations. This is not always the case in literary texts.

I want to caution against crude and monolithic interpretations
of the hard/soft binary (i.e., the American male of the 1930s was hard
and the hippies were soft). By using the hard/soft dichotomy, I am
merely suggesting that certain popular trends existed within various
cultural moments and decades. The terms "hardness" and "softness"
merely imply a metaphorical understanding of how the male body
is framed and imagined in literary texts in particular epochs. While
some may feel that soft masculinity is preferable to hard masculinity,
Dionysian soft masculinity can also be morally problematic. My examination of the Living Theatre's *Paradise Now* in my chapter on the
1960s will explore the ethical limitations of soft masculinity. It is also
a mistake to assume that the term "soft male" necessarily implies a
more enlightened or progressive view of women and the female body.
My chapters on the 1960s will explore the ethical blind spots within
the New Left's gender politics and the subsequent rise of second wave
feminism and gay liberation.

CHAPTER OVERVIEWS

My study of the politics of masculinity in American literary culture
begins in the Depression because the decade is dominated by the
masculine cult of virility and the overthrow of the so-called effete

genteel tradition, the two antipodes of the hard/soft dichotomy. The first chapter examines Michael Gold's attack on Thornton Wilder and how that literary scandal establishes the gender parameters of the literary class struggle of the 1930s. I also include a detailed discussion of Lewis Terman and Catharine Miles's *Sex and Personality* (1936), a work in applied psychology that documents the notion of hard-shell masculinity, and what I have termed the hypermasculine ideal. The work of Terman and Miles reveals that the hard-shell ideal was an important intellectual and cultural trend in the Depression era. Chapter 1 also includes an analysis of "tough-guy" literature—especially the hard-boiled novels of James M. Cain, which represent, in many respects, the apogee of literary machismo in the 1930s. This chapter also examines how the construction of masculine identity is crucial to the social realist plays of Clifford Odets, the most popular American playwright of the era.

The second chapter surveys World War II American culture, the various attempts to harness hypermasculine myths to the war effort, and how the cult of hardness becomes a recurring theme in American cultural life and in the anti-Communist crusade. I trace the evolution of the hard/soft dichotomy in its mythic guises and examine how the stigmatization of effeminacy is reflected in various gendered epithets—doughface, egghead, softie—that first appear in the 1940s. This chapter also pays attention to the conflicting trends that emerge in the 1940s: a greater openness to same-sex passion (Gore Vidal's *The City and the Pillar*, 1948) and homoeroticism (Leslie Fiedler's "Come Back to the Raft Ag'in, Huck Honey!" 1948) in literary culture, and a countertrend of anti-homosexual discourse that is often rooted in a hysterical critique of American mothers ("momism"). Chapter 2 ends with a queer reading of the Hiss-Chambers trial (1949), a cultural event that could be described as the soft trial of the century.

The chapter on the 1950s is concerned with the various youth cultures that emerge in the age of anti-Communism; it examines how the hard/soft dichotomy informs the rise of various youth cultures: the squares, Beats, hipsters, and white Negroes. My analysis of the literature of "squareness" looks back at two important American plays from the 1940s: Tennessee Williams's *The Glass Menagerie* (1945) and Arthur Miller's *Death of a Salesman* (1949). Chapter 3 also examines how the hard/soft dichotomy informs the literature of the hipsters and white Negroes (Norman Mailer), the Beats (Allen Ginsberg, Jack Kerouac), and the New Critics (John Crowe Ransom). My reading of the New Critics focuses on the fear of feminine contamination that underpins their critique of the affective tradition of American literature. The chapter also includes a reading of T. S. Eliot's "Tradition and the Individual Talent" (1917), a foundational text for New Criticism.

My survey of the 1960s begins with the cultural debates between Irving Howe of the Old Left and Susan Sontag, a proponent of the new sensibility and the intellectual darling of the New Left and the counterculture.[26] Chapter 4 includes a cultural genealogy of Dionysian masculinity, its intellectual roots (Norman O. Brown, R. D. Laing), and its leading practitioners and adherents (William S. Burroughs, Timothy Leary, the Living Theatre). Specifically, this chapter examines the Living Theatre's controversial production of *Paradise Now* and how the production stages and enacts a utopian critique of aggressive masculinity and the rigidity of the hard body. Finally, chapter 5 (the late 1960s and early 1970s) examines the revival of hardness (Eldridge Cleaver's *Soul on Ice*, 1968), assesses the cultural significance of gay liberation and the women's movement, and looks at how the latter two liberation movements challenge hegemonic forms of masculinity and foster a more pluralistic conception of male identity.

Credit for the phrase "pinks, pansies, and punks" goes to Senator Joseph McCarthy. He used it in an attempt to discredit Adlai Stevenson's campaign staff in 1952, and thus it conveys the American right wing's discomfort with bohemians, homosexuals, progressives, and a particular sector of the American leisure class that gravitated toward left-wing politics in the 1940s and 1950s ("pinks"). Though McCarthy represents a paranoid aspect of American culture, his suspicions about Communism and the suggestion that America was being subverted from within resonated with many people in mainstream society in the early 1950s; his message was also successful because he tapped into the popular culture's distrust for intellectuals, book learning, and—I would argue—literary culture itself.[27] In this study of authors and literary culture, I explore how the American writer and the intellectual are often mindful of popular culture's anxieties and suspicions. Hence, for many writers and macho critics the act of writing itself becomes an elaborate attempt to deflect the charge of leisure-culture effeminacy.

"Healthy Nerves and Sturdy Physiques": Remaking the Male Body of Literary Culture in the 1930s

Nearly a year after the stock market crash of 1929, Michael Gold, a young radical Communist and author of the much-acclaimed *Jews Without Money* (1930), attacked Thornton Wilder in the book review column of the *New Republic*. In a particularly damning passage, Gold labels Wilder "the Emily Post of culture" who writes novels that are "a synthesis of all the chambermaid literature, Sunday-school tracts and boulevard piety" ("Wilder: Prophet of the Genteel Christ" 200). A proponent and theorist of proletarian fiction, Gold dubs Wilder a poet of the "parvenu" leisure classes:

> Mr. Wilder remains the poet of the small sophisticated class that has recently arisen in America—our genteel bourgeoisie. . . . Thornton Wilder is the perfect flower of the new prosperity. He has all the virtues [Thorstein] Veblen said the leisure class would demand: the air of good breeding, the decorum, priestliness, glossy high finish as against intrinsic qualities, conspicuous inutility, caste feeling, love of the archaic, etc. (ibid., 201–202)

In another passage, Gold mockingly describes Wilder's *The Bridge of San Luis Rey* (1928) as "a homosexual bouquet" (198). Gold's class baiting, inflammatory rhetoric, and explicit references to Wilder's supposed effeteness and homosexuality were obvious breaches of literary decorum. These affronts to good taste were deliberate because Gold, a working-class revolutionary, certainly did not want to be thought of as a "gentleman." Gold's attempt to *épater les bourgeois* was successful in the sense that he created a scandal: his scathing review generated an outpouring of vitriolic letters that astounded the staff of the liberal publication. The literary controversy lasted for several weeks, and Edmund Wilson, then an editor at the *New Republic,* noted that two literary camps quickly emerged: "The people who applauded Gold seemed to be moved by a savage animus; those who defended Wilder protested or pleaded in the tone of persons who had been shocked by the desecration of a dearly beloved thing. Strange cries from the depths arose, illiterate and hardly articulate" ("The Literary Class Struggle" 535). Wilson also described the Gold-Wilder case as one of the "most violent controversies which the literary world has lately known" (ibid.). After seven weeks of vituperative letters, the editors published a statement: "[The] Gold-Wilder controversy is hereby called on account of darkness. No further letters on this subject will be published."[1] Recalling the scandal a few years later, Wilson argued that the Gold-Wilder controversy demonstrated that "the economic crisis would be accompanied by a literary one" (539). The implication was clear: the literary world could no longer ignore the reality of the class struggle and no writers were impervious to attack.

Wilder's biographers and some scholars of the literary Left have noted the importance of the scandal and how it altered the subject matter of Wilder's future work and reflected the emerging class conflicts in the literary culture of the 1930s.[2] However, literary historians have generally focused on the political aspects of the Gold-Wilder controversy and have paid less attention to the gendered aspects of Gold's rhetoric and the various explicit references to Wilder's homosexuality and effete masculinity, for example: "it is a newly fashionable literary religion that centers around Jesus Christ, the First

British Gentleman. It is a pastel, pastiche, and dilettante religion, without the neurotic blood and fire, a daydream of homosexual figures in graceful gowns moving archaically through the lilies. It is Anglo-Catholicism, that last refuge of the American Literary snob" ("Wilder: Prophet of the Genteel Christ" 200). In this passage, Gold again places great emphasis on the male body. Wilder's supposedly effeminate body is linked to Cardinal Newman's Oxford movement ("a daydream of homosexual figures in graceful gowns moving archaically through the lilies"). Gold's critique of Wilder also extends to the literary style that his body produces: "Mr. Wilder strains to be spiritual; but who could reveal any real agonies and exaltations of spirit in this neat, tailor-made rhetoric? It is a great lie. It is death. Its serenity is that of the corpse. Prick it, and it will bleed violet ink and *aperitif*" (ibid.). In Gold's rhetoric, Shylock's famous speech is transformed into homophobic mockery: the homosexual author ("violet ink") is linked to death, decay, and leisure-culture symbols of the nouveaux riches (*"aperitif"*). Gold also uses unveiled invective to "out" Thornton Wilder and thus discredit his fiction and, by extension, his presumed political point of view. Wilder, who regarded his sexuality as a private matter, opted not to respond to Gold's vicious attacks.

It is significant that literary style suddenly becomes a political issue during the Depression. In Gold's hypermasculine imaginary, the homosexual author reveals himself through literary refinement, decorous language, impeccable grammar, and a fondness for classical references (Wilder was a prep school teacher who taught Latin and Greek). In a column in the *New Masses*, Gold even goes so far as to associate "perfect English with effeminacy" (qtd. in Aaron 256). In a telling phrase, Gold describes Wilder's prose as "diluted Henry James." Thus, Gold's criticism prefigures Rahv's "Paleface and Redskin" dichotomy.[3] By making Wilder a crude symbol of leisure-culture decadence, Gold aligns himself with the muscular redskin tradition of American literary culture and suggests that Wilder's literary milieu mystifies the true source of his class's wealth: "[Wilder's fiction] helps the parvenu class forget its lowly origins in American industrialism. It yields them a short cut to the aristocratic emotions" ("Wilder: Prophet of the Genteel Christ" 202). Thus, in Gold's rhe-

torical scheme, the homophobic attack ultimately reinforces his particular ideological thesis: the moral and spiritual bankruptcy of the
leisure classes.

Gold's contempt for Wilder and the leisure classes can be juxtaposed with his adoration of Walt Whitman, the populist poet of the
nineteenth century. In Gold's "Towards Proletarian Art," Whitman
is considered to be the grandfather of proletarian literature. Whitman's literary brilliance stems from his ability to embrace the masses:
"Walt dwelt among the masses, and from them he drew his strength.
From the obscure lives of the masses he absorbed those deep affirma-
tions of their instinct that are his glory" (68). For Gold, the explicitly
social dimension of Whitman's literary works is conveyed through
the absorption of working-class energy ("instinct") and manliness. If
Gold was aware of Whitman's bisexuality, he chose to look the other
way because the explicitly social character of Whitman's verse negated the supposed association between homosexuality and leisure
culture. The irony of Gold, the classic homophobe, adoring Whitman is familiar in macho criticism. When one scratches the surface,
one discovers that the apparently water-tight gender theories that
conflate class and masculine type often contain an ideological leak.

I have begun my discussion of the 1930s with the Gold-Wilder
controversy to problematize the traditional way of approaching the
literature of that era. Many literary scholars of the Depression focus on the theme of social protest and how the political and social
struggle of the 1930s is mirrored in the novels and plays from that
era.[4] For example, Steinbeck's *The Grapes of Wrath* (1939) is correctly
read as a social protest novel. However, in many cases, this particular
genre classification tends to emphasize class and political issues and
marginalize gender themes. Thus, a gendered reading of *The Grapes
of Wrath* might emphasize how the author is attempting to legitimize
"feminine" responses (pity and sympathy) to human suffering and, in
some cases, to criticize certain aggressive forms of masculinity—the
violence of vigilante groups or police brutality—that are presented as
antisocial and fascist. Given that we cannot separate gender from the
representation of certain political ideas, we need to examine carefully
how the binary of the masculine/feminine is central to several of the
most popular literary genres of the 1930s—particularly, social protest
fiction and political drama.

The critical tendency to overlook gender concerns in Depression literature is linked to the 1930s itself. During that time, writers and politicians considered class issues to be more legitimate than gender concerns. Paula Rabinowitz, a feminist literary critic, notes that for the Left of the 1930s "gender was not recognized as a salient political category" (4). Rabinowitz's study *Labor & Desire: Women's Revolutionary Fiction in Depression America* (1991) is an important work of scholarship on the revolutionary literature of the Depression because it demonstrates how class and gender identity were ideologically connected in the left-wing literature of the time. Following Rabinowitz's work, I argue that the gendered aspects of the Gold-Wilder controversy are crucial to our understanding of literature in the 1930s. In contrast to how Gold is traditionally read—as a leftist critic with eccentric ideas about masculinity—I argue that his conception of masculine identity is not a bizarre anomaly, but an important part of the Old Left's nascent political vision.[5] As the Depression progresses, leftist writers increasingly idealize the "healthy nerves and sturdy physiques of working men."[6] Moreover, the fascination with the hard body of the working-class male, which often borders on the homoerotic, is a familiar feature of New Deal public murals and literary texts. Much like Rahv's "Paleface and Redskin" dichotomy, the working class—and especially its virile male representatives—personifies energy, virtue, and potency while the upper classes are typically associated with sterility and sickliness. The dichotomy of working-class virility and leisure-culture impotence becomes a central trope for the American Left of the 1930s: the movement often imagines itself—and its future—through the robust male body.

THE ORIGINS OF GOLD'S MASCULINIST RHETORIC

Gold's heavily gendered readings of literature are largely based on his misreading of Thorstein Veblen's *The Theory of the Leisure Class* (1899), a book that appeared a few years after the Oscar Wilde trials. Veblen's original notion of "conspicuous consumption" suggested that the newly emerging middle classes were wasting their earnings on "useless" luxury goods that merely advertised their class status to the outside world. In the coming decades, and especially during the boom of the 1920s, Veblen's critique of the conformist leisure classes and their moral smugness became extremely popular in left-wing circles. Along similar lines, it was generally believed that conspicuous consumption and leisure culture have a feminizing effect on the upper classes; thus, leisure culture inevitably produces overcivilized men who lack vitality and virility, traits the working class possesses in abundance. In Gold's literary criticism, the images of conspicuous consumption and extravagance are quickly attached to a mythical idle homosexual; the nonnormative male subject becomes the personification of Veblen's notion of "conspicuous inutility" because he supposedly does not produce wealth or offspring, but lives only for idleness, pleasure, and beauty. Thus, the homosexual is a parvenu, an upper-class phenomenon and the degenerate product of a corrupt economic system.

However, Gold's suggestion that leisure culture somehow produces effeminacy and homosexuality is not evident in Veblen's work. If anything, Veblen takes great pains to emphasize the aggressive side of the leisure class. In the chapter "The Modern Survivals of Prowess," he argues that the leisure class's "addiction to sports is a trait that [it] shares with lower-class delinquents" (271). In this chapter, Veblen also debunks the so-called manly virtues that are often associated with sports and in turn argues that sports and other leisure activities actually produce "barbarian traits"—ferocity and astuteness. In other chapters, Veblen highlights the bellicosity of the upper classes and their penchant for dueling, a decidedly macho activity. Since Veblen makes no reference to the effeminate male body in his study of the leisure classes, it is clear that Gold's homophobic obsessions are a phenomenon of the 1920s and 1930s and not of Veblen's era.

Gold singled out Wilder for attack because he felt that the novelist exemplified the American leisure class's obsession with high culture and worldly sophistication. The son of a diplomat, Wilder had a privileged background and was urbane and well-spoken. In literary culture, he was often described as the American version of Marcel Proust. For Gold, the comparison was not a compliment because Proust embodied his idée fixe—the "idle homosexual" who writes about the splendors of leisure-culture life. At the time of the Gold-Wilder controversy, Gold was considered the leading proponent and theorist for the genre of proletarian realism. On September 30, 1930, just a month before the infamous Wilder book review, Gold published an article in the *New Masses* that attempts to codify his literary theories and his conception of proletarian realism:

> Proletarian fiction deals with real conflicts of men and women who work for a living. . . . The worst example and the best of what we do not want to do is the spectacle of Marcel Proust, the master-masturbator of bourgeois fiction. We know the suffering of hungry, persecuted and heroic millions is enough of a theme for anyone, without inventing these precious silly little agonies. ("Proletarian Realism" 206)

The critique of Proust also extends to style as the French novelist's ornate and decorous style is scorned as effeminate; Gold's objection to modernism's penchant for literary experimentation ("we are not interested in the verbal acrobats—this is another form of bourgeois idleness") is matched with a preference for lean and masculine prose: "swift action, clear form, the direct line, cinema in words" (207).

Gold's animus toward Marcel Proust, which verges on the obsessive, is also revealing in that it can be read as an expression of Gold's desire to anticipate and negate the image and stereotype of the effeminate leisure-culture Jew. Proust's homosexuality makes him doubly suspicious. Thus, Gold's slice-of-life, coming-of-age novel, *Jews Without Money* (1930), is a conscious rejoinder to Proust's *Remembrance of Things Past* and the French novelist's status as the moneyed Jew who adores leisure culture. Gold's "tough Jew" persona, which stems from his working-class upbringing on the Lower East Side, is presented as the masculine alternative to the Proustian male. Hence, Gold's attacks on Wilder and Proust are essentially about literary masculinities and how literature cannot be separated from the male body that produces it. In Gold's macho criticism, it is a given that Proust's effeminate and bedridden body can produce only unhealthy literature.

In contrast to Proust's leisure-culture body, Gold recommends a new hybrid of working-class masculinity and bold social criticism. In an essay that was written for the *New Masses* in 1926, Gold describes his ideal:

> O Life, send us a great literary critic. . . . It is unfashionable to believe in human progress. It is unfashionable and unsophisticated to follow in the footsteps of Tolstoi, of Dickens, Shelley, Blake, Burns, Whitman, Trotsky. Send us a critic. Send us a giant who can shame our writers back

to their task of civilizing America. Send us a soldier who has studied history. Send us a strong poet who loves the masses, and their future. Send
someone who does not give a damn about money. Send one who is not
a pompous liberal, but a man of the street. Send no mystics—they give
Americans the willies. Send no coward. Send no pedant. Send us a man
fit to stand up to skyscrapers. A man of art who can match the purposeful
deeds of Henry Ford. Send us a joker in overalls. Send us no saint. Send
an artist. Send a scientist. Send a Bolshevik. Send a man. ("America
Needs a Critic" 138–39)

In this passage, Gold's masculinist rhetoric, which today evokes
the campy excess of disco anthems ("Send a man"), conveys a fascination with utilitarian function ("overalls," "skyscrapers," "Henry
Ford") and the attempt to spawn an American version of the Soviet
cult of the New Man. Gold traveled to Moscow in the 1920s and was
deeply impressed by Vsevolod Meyerhold's constructivist theatre
productions, which attempted to wed the human form with industrial technology. By praising and emphasizing art's usefulness, Gold
attempts to pry artistic expression away from the "boudoir bards"
and "minor Oscar Wildes" who insist that "art is never useful" (133).
Hence, Gold's rhetoric attempts to masculinize art by mocking the
aesthetes and their feminine interest in beauty for its own sake; the
masculine is efficacious and utilitarian while the feminine is merely
conspicuous consumption. Much of Gold's and the Left's homophobia is therefore less about homosexual acts than about the enervating
spectacle of leisure culture. With the arrival of the economic crisis,
the homosexual of the 1930s becomes especially suspect because he
is stereotyped as a person who supposedly exempts himself from
useful employment.

The association of homosexuality with leisure culture did not
begin in the 1930s. Most historians of gender point to the 1890s as the
key turning point. In *The Wilde Century: Effeminacy, Oscar Wilde and
the Queer Moment*, Alan Sinfield persuasively argues that the public
figure of Oscar Wilde is central to the creation of the stereotypical
image of the homosexual in Anglo-American literary culture: "The
Wilde Trials helped to produce a major shift in perceptions of the
scope of single sex passion. At that point, the entire, vaguely discon-
certing nexus of effeminacy, leisure, idleness, immorality, luxury,
insouciance, decadence, and aestheticism, was transformed into a
brilliantly precise meaning" (3). In contrast to the aristocratic notion

that a gentleman does not perform labor, the emerging and growing British middle class of the nineteenth century differentiated itself from the aristocracy by frowning on excessive displays of wealth and championing social utility and moral uprightness; its conceptions of manliness were linked to industry, sobriety, and respectability. Since industry and purposefulness were defined as manly virtues, the feminine was often associated with idleness and the finer things in life—art, poetry, music, furniture, fashion—which were the rewards of masculine labor. Thus, with the rise of the middle class in British and American society at the end of the nineteenth century, effeminacy in men was often linked to idleness, immorality, and decadence; all these vices were considered to be the vestiges of aristocratic leisure culture. In the post-Wildean era, the union of homosexuality, idleness, and leisure culture becomes the dominant stereotype that envelops discussions of masculinity in literary culture. The fact that Wilde, a prolific author, was anything but idle had little bearing on the stereotype that developed in the wake of the scandal. While the myth of the idle homosexual became something of an ingrained stereotype in the aftermath of the Wilde trials, the notion that literary culture was inherently feminine became embodied in what is now known as the "genteel tradition."[7]

In the 1930s, the literary Left launched an all-out frontal attack on all writers who were associated with the genteel tradition. The Left's critique of the genteel tradition during the Depression is crucial for understanding the literature of the 1930s because it informs the populist shift toward genres that were considered anti-elitist (the social protest novel, proletarian fiction, hard-boiled fiction). What is particularly striking about the Left's critique of the genteel tradition is its explicitly masculinist rhetoric.

The phrase "genteel tradition" implies the elevated status of the literary author as a custodian of ethical values and moral character. Hence, the genteel critic thought of himself as a purveyor of good taste and decency. In the nineteenth century, some of the authors associated with the genteel tradition were magazine editors (William Dean Howells) who promoted decorum and the suppression of literature that was derogatory to religious ideals and moral standards. Today, the genteel tradition is primarily remembered for its Victorian prudery. Howells, the author of *The Rise of Silas Lapham* (1885) and the editor of the *Atlantic Monthly* from 1866 to 1881, advocated censoring indecent passages and bowdlerizing the classics if circumstance demanded it:

> The worst of the literature of past times, before an ethical conscience began to inform it, or the advance of the race compelled it to decency, is that it leaves the mind foul with filthy images and base thoughts.... at the end of the ends such things do defile, they do corrupt.... I hope the time will come when the beast-man will be so far subdued and tamed in us that the memory of him in literature shall be left to perish; that what is lewd and ribald in the great poets shall be kept out [of] such editions as are meant for general reading. (*My Literary Passions; Criticism and Fiction* 42)

For Howells, the modern author has a moral responsibility to slay the "beast-man" in his/her fiction through the practice of self-censorship. Howells's defense of literary prudishness was also based on the premise that most readers of novels were women, who must be protected from indelicate exhibitions. Howells's distaste for gross and vulgar subjects was extreme in that he even sought to restrict the representation of sexual passion in literature.[8]

The censorious side of the genteel tradition was matched by its didactic interest in fostering moral character. Hence, the literary author assumed an exalted, quasi-religious function in society. Henry Van Dyke, a contemporary of Howells, perhaps best embodies the union of the didactic and the literary. Van Dyke was a pastor and a professor at Princeton, and his literary criticism is peppered with sermons about manliness and the proper moral behavior for aspiring young authors:

> The best way to improve a manly stock is to eat what you like if it agrees with you, to spend as much time as possible in the open air, to have a sport that amuses you and a work that engages your best powers, to love one woman and to make as many friends as you can without capitulation, and finally to believe that Some One wiser and better than you is governing the universe. (317)

Van Dyke's passage contains many salient genteel attitudes. Since Van Dyke was also worried about the perils of too much leisure culture, he recommends outdoor activities, vigorous sport, and fruitful labor. The chaste ideal ("love one woman") is offered as an antidote to fin de siècle degeneracy. The genteel tradition was concerned with promoting religious beliefs ("Some One wiser and better than you is governing the universe"), but also the notion that literature should be essentially optimistic: whenever possible, it should avoid philosophical pessimism and skepticism. In the rhetoric of the Victorian age, manliness is distinct from masculinity, which is a more neutral term. Thus, we should not use the two terms interchangeably. Manliness is explicitly concerned with building moral character. As Gail Bederman has noted, the virtues of Victorian manliness were "sexual self-restraint, a powerful will, and strong character" (18).[9] Masculinity has no attendant moral connotation; it simply implies maleness in a neutral sense (masculine dress, masculine habits), and, in a general sense, all men qualify as masculine.

The promotion of manly virtues—including censoriousness and the advocacy of stern Victorian morality—ultimately presented a problem for the genteel critics: it allowed their literary opponents to label them "prissy," "old-maidish," and a host of other epithets for effeminacy. The genteel tradition is crucial to the literature of the 1890s and 1900s in that it inspires a fervent counterreaction and prompts some male writers—Jack London, Theodore Dreiser, Frank Norris—to adopt masculine poses that attempt to deny the popular notion that literary culture is feminizing. When London is not writing about gold mining in Alaska, he creates working-class literary heroes like Martin Eden, who challenge the effete and corrupt literary establishment.

The rebellion against the genteel tradition continues well into the twentieth century, and in the 1920s and 1930s the debate resurfaces frequently. Apart from the Gold-Wilder controversy, the most popular reference to the debate is probably Sinclair Lewis's Nobel address of 1930, "The American Fear of Literature." The controversy began when Henry Van Dyke publicly stated that Lewis was unworthy of the Nobel Prize because he frequently scoffed at American institutions in his fiction and, thus, the Nobel committee and the Swedish Academy had gravely insulted America by honoring the novelist. Lewis responded by mocking Van Dyke and Howells in his address.

Sinclair Lewis's speech offers a persuasive indictment of the genteel tradition and the enervating effect it has had on American literature. For Lewis, Theodore Dreiser is the chief opponent of

the genteel tradition: "Dreiser, more than any other man, march-
ing alone, usually unappreciated, often hated, has cleared the trail
from Victorian and Howellsian timidity and gentility in American
fiction to honesty and boldness and passion of life" (7). For my gender
analysis, Dreiser is a key figure because his crude subject matter and
his cumbersome prose style are interpreted as distinctly anti-genteel
and, for many readers, as the antithesis of leisure-culture refinement.
Lewis's speech also contains some carefully placed gender-inflected
metaphors: "Mr. Howells was one of the gentlest, sweetest, and most
honest of men, but he had the code of a pious old maid whose greatest delight was to have tea at the vicarage" (15). While the effeminacy
of the genteel tradition certainly appalled Lewis, he, unlike Gold,
does not indulge in homophobic jousts. His long list of praiseworthy
American writers includes both Thornton Wilder and Michael Gold,
and it is perhaps not a coincidence that they are both mentioned
in the same paragraph.[10] Thus, in 1930 some critics could be anti-
effeminate without being homophobic, but this distinction would
become increasingly blurred as the 1930s progressed.

Following Lewis's lead, Malcolm Cowley's *After the Genteel Tradition* (1936) also contains gendered readings of American literature.
Cowley notes that "fortunately...the younger generation [of American writers] has untied itself from their stepmotherly apronstrings.
A whole new literature has come of age, a literature that tries to express the sweep and strength and beauty in ugliness of the American
empire as it is today" (6). Cowley's famous work also argues that
American literature became feminized during the reign of the genteel
critics:

> Every cultural object that entered the home was supposed to express
> the highest ideals and aspirations. Every book or magazine intended to
> appear on the center table in the parlor was kept as innocent as milk.
> American women of all ages, especially the unmarried ones, had sud-
> denly become more than earthly creatures; they were presented as the
> milk-white angels of art and compassion and culture. (10)

Cowley's domestic images stress the theme of feminine readership
and the idea that an author's subject matter formerly was geared
toward womanly concerns. In genteel literature, the crude and
unseemly, as well as explicit descriptions of the female body, were
strenuously avoided.

The literary Left's political rhetoric often reinforces its own manliness by employing specific gendered terms that connote effeminacy ("sissy," "priggish," "pussy foot"); the Left was also fond of specific code words for effeteness ("delicate," "florid," "fastidious," "squeamish," "overly refined," "blue-blood," "stuffed-shirt," "decorous"), and, in some cases, certain adjectives become loaded phrases that evoke the homosexual ("callow," "immature," "sentimental"). The latter suggest the notion that homosexuality is a form of "arrested development" (i.e., the idea that the homosexual has not progressed to the final stage of normal adulthood—heterosexual desire). In leftist discourse of the 1930s, the use of French words becomes a code that signifies the notion of leisure-culture degeneracy. Thus, when Gold labels Wilder "a veteran *cocette* [*sic*]," the feminizing phrase carries added rhetorical weight.

Gold's vituperative criticism and the literary Left's masculinist crusade against the genteel tradition highlight the problem of the American male in relation to literary culture. The writer with an artistic sensibility and literary refinement was a source of great anxiety. Hence, both Gold and the literary Left posit that the male writer—and, by extension, American literary culture—must undergo a thorough process of remasculinization. For the literary Left, the solution is to radically defeminize the writer and literary culture itself. Gold advocates this as well; however, for Gold remasculinization also entails the promotion of a new literary genre: proletarian realism. This genre was revitalizing because it fostered the act of embracing the masses and the absorption of their vibrant untapped energy: "masses are never sterile. Masses are never far from the earth. . . . Masses are simple, sure and strong" ("Towards Proletarian Art" 66). Gold's rhetorical message appealed to the left-wing male writer of the 1930s because it offered a remedy for leisure-culture effeminacy: the promise of utopian renewal merged with the myth of phallic potency ("never sterile").

The war on the genteel tradition also extended across racial lines. Richard Wright's "Blueprint for Negro Writing" (1937) mirrors Gold's rhetoric and the hard/soft binary. Wright notes that "Negro writing" of the past was written by "prim and decorous ambassadors who went begging to white America" (1403). For Wright, the image of African American effeminacy is conveyed in sartorial terms: black writers "entered the Court of American Public Opinion dressed in the knee-pants of servility, curtsying to show the negro was not inferior, that he was not inferior" (ibid.). Wright also suggests that African American writers of the past resembled "French poodles who do clever tricks" (ibid.). Wright's colorful metaphor links the black writer to domestication and subservience. However, the metaphor is also highly gendered in that it links the sophisticated, modernist African American writer to effeminacy and leisure-culture decadence (Frenchness).

While Gold's critique of Thornton Wilder was clearly homophobic, Wright's critique of "Negro writing" should not be read as an endorsement of homophobia. Although Wright's rhetoric is directed at the writers of the Harlem Renaissance, he is careful not to mention any writers by name, nor does he seem to be terribly concerned with the issue of sexual preference. For Wright, the worst sins are conspicuous inutility and a lack of political engagement.

In "Blueprint for Negro Writing," Wright argues for politically engaged writing that contains social analysis and attempts to raise consciousness. For Wright, the "Blueprint" meant not producing sentimental literature that was designed to elicit pity and tears for the African American. Wright was particularly disturbed when his writing educed pity from an audience of white readers. In his famous essay "How 'Bigger' Was Born" (1940), he notes that his first collection of short stories, *Uncle Tom's Children,* was flawed because it evoked an emotional response from various white readers:

> When the reviews of [*Uncle Tom's Children*] ... began to appear I realized that I had made an awfully naïve mistake. I found that I had written a book which even bankers' daughters could read and weep over and feel good about. I swore to myself that if I ever wrote another book, no one would weep over it; that it would be so hard and deep that they would have to face it without the consolation of tears. (454)

Wright's objection to the cathartic response is revealing in that it conveys his gendered political views. Wright's target—the "bankers' daughters"—underscores his anti-capitalist position, but also the supposed connection between the feminine ("daughters") and affect. Wright's solution to the feminine response is Bigger Thomas of *Native Son* (1940), an unsympathetic thug whom no one would cry about. The embrace of social realism often implies a preference for the crude and unseemly and a conscious rejection of refinement and polite subject matter. Thus, for Wright, *Native Son* fulfills the ideological requirements of "Blueprint for Negro Writing" because it is sufficiently anti-affective and Marxist in that it "creates a picture which, when placed before the eyes of a writer, should unify his personality, organize his emotions, [and] buttress him with a tense and obdurate will to change the world" (1407). In gendered terms, Wright's plea for ideological discipline ("organize his emotions") is also a tacit endorsement of the hypermasculine ideal: the hard, affectless body.[11]

The existence of the hard/soft binary within Richard Wright's work indicates that racial issues in the literary culture of the 1930s were closely connected to gender myths. In "Blueprint for Negro Writing," Wright notes that some African American writers benefited from the patronage of "burned-out white bohemians with money" (1403). Wright's racially loaded phrase ("burned-out white bohemians") implies a familiar motif in the literature of the 1930s—the critique of leisure-culture effeminacy.[12] In the Depression era, whiteness—especially upper-class whiteness—is synonymous with sterility and decadence. Hence, the white patron of African American culture has a symbiotic relationship to the black writer: the "burned-out white bohemians" are attracted to the vitality of African American culture. Wright urges the "Negro" writers of the future to break this tradition by writing hard, unsentimental literature that cannot be co-opted by white patrons.

Wright's critique of leisure-culture effeminacy ("French poodles") and his preference for the remasculinization of African American writing are consistent with the gender politics of social realism in the 1930s. The tilt toward machismo and the preference for the hard body are part of a larger cultural backlash against the perceived excesses of the Prohibition years. In left-wing literary circles, homosexuality is often unconsciously wedded to the decadent excesses of capitalism. The paucity of homosexual left-wing novels in the 1930s is not an accident, but a byproduct of the cult of the virile proletariat and the ubiquitous association of homosexuality with capitalistic decadence. Hence, the gay working-class body is pushed under-

ground in the 1930s, although it will reemerge in the aftermath of
World War II and in the Beat movement of the late 1940s and early
1950s. George Chauncey's *Gay New York: Gender, Urban Culture, and
the Making of the Gay Male World 1890–1940* (1994) documents how
an "anti-gay reaction gained force in the early to mid-1930s" and how
various political leaders and police chiefs initiated a campaign to ren-
der gay men and lesbians invisible by cracking down on gay bars and
nightclubs throughout mid-Manhattan. Chauncey dubs this trend
the end of the "pansy craze" of the 1920s. Chauncey notes that, when
social anxiety and tension grew from economic concerns (e.g., mass
unemployment), nonnormative sexual arrangements became more
dangerous and threatening to mainstream society. Hence, the call
for a return to "traditional values" became popular during the 1930s.

Jennifer Terry, a historian and the author of *An American Obsession: Science, Medicine, and Homosexuality in Modern Society* (1999),
notes that within American culture there developed "a complex
dialectical tension between a tradition of Puritanism that valorized
hard work, self-improvement, sexual restraint on the one hand, and
an expanding consumerism that promoted pleasure-seeking and
self-fulfillment through hedonism on the other" (9–10). Within this
dichotomy, the homosexual was often associated with the "reckless
hedonism of the Roaring Twenties" that had "plunged the nation into
the Great Depression" (268). Hence, homosexuality, along with other
sexual perversions, gambling, and prostitution, were the "vices" that
needed to be rooted out.

The notion that homosexuality is a serious social problem is also
evidenced in Lewis Terman and Catharine Miles's *Sex and Personality* (1936), a psychological study that succinctly captures popular
attitudes about softness in men, the fear of homosexuality, and the
dubious status of the American male who has artistic and literary
inclinations.

TERMAN AND MILES: CREATING A SCIENCE OF
HARDNESS AND SOFTNESS FOR THE DEPRESSION

The theme of remasculinization, which dominated American literary
culture in the 1930s, was also a salient theme in the psychological literature during that time. Throughout the 1930s, the idea that effemi-

nacy is a debilitating condition and a social problem was echoed in the popular press, in works of fiction, and in various academic circles. The cure for effeminacy and homosexuality was even taken up by the burgeoning field of applied psychology.[13] Like Michael Gold, Terman and Miles were specifically concerned with the vocation of the male artist and his deficient masculinity.

Prior to *Sex and Personality*, Freud and other psychologists had speculated about gender differences in hypothetical terms, but Terman and Miles were the first psychologists who attempted to measure a subject's masculinity and femininity with a scientific scale.[14] Terman and Miles sought to establish, through extensive testing and interviewing, how and why men and women are different. In 1936, the creation of a masculinity-femininity test (M-F test) that could demonstrate that sex differences are empirically verifiable was considered to be a major breakthrough for applied psychology. The M-F test was also designed to measure and assess the masculinity of those in various professions: engineers, lawyers, police officers, fire fighters, clergy, and artists.

Terman, a Stanford psychologist who was known for his work with the Binet intelligence tests, maintained that intellectually gifted students should be identified and separated from their fellow students and placed in special classes that would not hinder their natural abilities and talents. In this way, a meritocracy would gradually emerge: the most "gifted" students would be empowered to excel in life and lead and instruct the less capable and the less fortunate. Terman's belief in meritocracy was based on his work in eugenic theory.[15] The intellectually inferior, the feeble-minded, and the mentally retarded needed to be supervised and controlled by medical authorities and social scientists. In some cases, sterilization and institutionalization were necessary to prevent certain individuals from procreating and thus weakening the gene pool of the white race and the nation as a whole. Like many other scientists in the 1930s, Terman believed that the supremacy of the white race could be scientifically proven by intelligence tests that demonstrated that certain races were more adept with logic and mathematical concepts.

I have mentioned Terman's interest in eugenics because it is crucial for understanding his conception of gender and the differences between the sexes. Much as he did in his intelligence tests, Terman sought to prove scientifically how and why women are different from men. While Terman conceded that women are basically equal to men in the area of "general intelligence"—many of the "gifted" children in his intelligence research were female—Terman maintained that the "sexes differed fundamentally in their instinctive and emotional equipment" (2). The latter phrase outlines the area of psychology that Terman and Miles attempted to isolate scientifically and analyze. At the beginning of *Sex and Personality,* they outline the nature of sex differences and how women are essentially different from men:

> In particular, she [the universal woman] is believed to experience in greater degree than the average man the tender emotions, including sympathy, pity, and parental love; to be more given to cherishing and protective behavior of all kinds. Compared with man she is more timid and more readily overcome by fear. She is more religious and at the same time more prone to jealousy, suspicion and injured feelings. Sexually she is by nature less promiscuous than man, is coy rather than aggressive, and her sexual feelings are less specifically localized in her body. Submissiveness, docility, inferior steadfastness of purpose, and a general lack of aggressiveness reflect her weaker conative tendencies. (ibid.)

Terman and Miles's assessment of the nature of women is obviously not a fresh view on the subject; their conception of feminine psychology reflects many of the gender stereotypes that had already accumulated in Western culture. However, what is interesting is that Terman and Miles want to transform these otherwise vague concepts into scientific truths. Women embody the feminine principle because they are closer to nature and, therefore, more emotional, instinctive, and nurturing. In contrast, men are more masculine: more gifted at reasoning, less ruled by emotions, more prone to aggression. The masculine is defined as the antithesis of docile and submissive femininity: "aggressive leadership, energetic activity, physical courage, masculine pursuits, and interest in warfare, adventure, outdoor sports, science, and things of a mechanical nature" (282). For Terman and Miles, the key component of masculine hardness is a greater capacity for aggression.

The measurement of "masculinity" and "femininity" was achieved by creating a scale that could approximate a given subject's gender identity. It was assumed that if one enjoyed masculine hobbies—boxing, football, auto mechanics—these gender-appropriate attitudes would be reflected in one's overall masculinity score. For example, football players (+92.54) and engineers (+77.32) had noticeably high masculinity scores that were supposed to indicate that the subjects had a strong masculine identity, or what was termed "mental masculinity." In contrast, priests (+18.9), musicians (+15.70), theologians (+10.62), artists (+0.26), and "inverts" (i.e., homosexuals; −19.75) had subpar and low masculinity scores that raised eyebrows because they evidenced a feminine identity. The results also suggest that the artist and the homosexual pose a special problem for Terman and Miles; moreover, the authors dedicate an entire chapter to analyzing why homosexuals have such low masculinity scores. In the M-F test, Terman and Miles are preoccupied with proving that homosexuals, more often than not, possess an "artistic temperament"; hence, a superior knowledge of literature and art often indicates that the subject is probably an "invert" (270–71).

For Terman and Miles, the test results seem to point to one overriding conclusion: the American male is not masculine enough. Thus, effeminacy in American males constitutes a grave social problem that should no longer be ignored by educators and psychologists alike. The test makers were interested in assessing the possible ill effects of effeminacy in men. However, their research was not able to establish that effeminate men were actually less successful in their professional careers. Nonetheless, at one point Terman and Miles raise the question: "it would be interesting to know whether . . . feminine scoring engineers . . . have less than average chance[s] to attain success in their professional work" (469). The solution to the problem of effeminacy is the creation of a society that nurtures and reinforces strong masculine identities. The goal of strengthening the masculinity of young boys and male adults through strong gender roles—the dominant father and the dutiful and submissive mother—would eventually become the foundation of sex role theory, the dominant paradigm for American psychology in the 1940s, 1950s, and 1960s.[16] Psychologists at the time believed that if individuals acquire strong "sex role identities" when they are growing up, they will later become mature (heterosexual) men and women and productive members of society. Thus, sex role theory was in part a remedy for the feminization of men, a trend that had deeply troubled psychologists and academics for decades.[17]

Terman and Miles believed that masculinity could be accurately probed, assessed, and eventually improved; moreover, an important part of the social reinvention of masculinity was the idea that homosexuality could be reversed by intervention and proper guidance:

> It is now known that the milder grades of mental deficiency can now be detected years earlier than was possible a generation ago. The same will in time be true of the potential homosexual. Early identification of the latter deviant is particularly to be desired, because we have so much reason to believe that defects of personality can be compensated for and to some extent corrected. (468)

For Terman and Miles, "mental deficiency" is analogous with homosexuality. The key to solving the social problem is the detection of the effeminate male as a youth. Therefore, the M-F tests were designed to identify effeminate males (potential homosexuals) and bona fide "inverts." If effeminacy could be detected when a boy was still an adolescent, the test makers believed that deviancy could still be reversed and eventually cured. Since homosexuality was considered developmental and not innate, identifying and classifying the problem was the first step toward the remasculinization of the American male, and the M-F test was designed to pave the way for innovative educational practices and bold social policy in the future.

The biases of the M-F test are revealing. The test makers closely studied low masculinity scores and, at the same time, were basically unconcerned about high masculinity scores. If a subject received a high masculinity score, he was judged to be psychologically desirable because he was assertive, confident, and courageous. The absence of concern about the potential negative effects of hypermasculinity is quite striking: it implicitly suggests that hypermasculinity was viewed as a cultural advantage and a social virtue. Given that the 1930s was a decade of high unemployment and failed breadwinners, hypermasculine males were identified as the successful go-getters who could buck the trend of economic stagnation.

The unspoken preference for exaggerated masculine traits in *Sex and Personality* is apparent in the extensive commentary about "passive homosexuals" and their disdain for hard labor. Lowell Kelly, the coauthor of the homosexuality chapter of *Sex and Personality,* claimed that "queens" and homosexuals "were far lazier than any persons of similar age with whom we have come in contact, being inclined to shun any occupation which promises even a small amount of labor" (qtd. in Minton 172). Like Gold, Kelly was quick to conflate idleness and homosexuality.

Kelly's research indicates how scientific "proof" can be effectively marshaled to legitimize certain familiar gender stereotypes. The test makers begin with an assumption that homosexuals are lazy and unproductive and then find a sample group—homosexuals serving prison sentences for prostitution in San Francisco—that confirms their views. A larger and diverse sample group probably would have yielded less extreme results. In this way, *Sex and Personality,* in many respects, affirms Michel Foucault's suggestion that the conclusions of social scientists are never wholly objective and value-free and that empirical truth, in the form of statistics, is shaped and controlled to validate the ideological assumptions of the authorities who administer the psychological studies. In many respects, *Sex and Personality* tells us more about the cultural values of the test makers than about the lived experience of the subjects they were assessing.

Terman and Miles's bias is, however, less pronounced in their view of lesbians, or "female inverts." In the M-F test for women, female college athletes (−13.7), highly educated women (−34.5), female college students (−36.2), and lesbians (−36.4) have the most masculine scores. In contrast, the most feminine groups are grade school girls (−95.4) and dressmakers and domestics (−103.9). Female masculinity does not appear to worry the test makers too much; they are far more concerned with the low masculinity scores of effeminate men and "passive homosexuals." However, it is also important to note that hypermasculinity is not held up as a gender ideal for women because "aggressive and independent females will be at a disadvantage in the marriage market" (452).

It is significant that the information about lesbians and their relatively high masculinity scores is placed in the appendix while the authors devote several full-length chapters to the analysis of effeminacy and (male) homosexuality. The work of Terman and Miles certainly validates Judith Halberstam's contention that our society is far more concerned about effeminate males and tends to treat examples of female masculinity with widespread indifference. The long-standing tradition of ignoring and marginalizing female masculinity only serves to reinforce male power by constantly reiterating that only men are capable of "real" masculinity.

If the American male needs to be more masculine, how do Terman and Miles define "masculinity"? To find the answer to this question, one needs to look carefully at Terman and Miles's questions as means of gauging a subject's masculinity. Although Terman and Miles never actually use the term "hypermasculinity," it is important to their methodology. In the M-F test, certain questions are bait for hypermasculine men in the sense that they contain an "element of aggression or will to power" (45). The Nietzschean flavor of the test makers' language is not accidental. Like many other eugenicists, Terman was influenced by Nietzsche's notion of the übermensch and the idea that modern man should aspire to a higher ideal of masculinity. In looking at the gender discussions of the 1930s, it is important to recognize that aggression was not a pejorative term; instead, aggression was thought to connote boldness, self-confidence, and masculine sure-footedness. In the eyes of Terman and Miles, these masculine virtues needed to be nurtured by social authorities during the Depression.

The M-F test contained a wide array of question types: ink blots, emotional attitudes, interests, opinions, and introspective responses. I will focus on the opinion section here because I believe that it best reveals the tacit assumptions that the authors made with regard to masculinity/femininity. This section was by no means the most successful part of the test. Terman and Miles admitted that the results were "disappointing" because only twenty-eight of the ninety-six questions "yielded sufficiently large and consistent sex differences." But I highlight this otherwise ambiguous section because it unveils the test makers' quasi-Nietzschean conceptions of gender. The questions in this section were supposed to measure a subject's religious beliefs, aggressive responses, and evidence of pity or sympathy. Here is a brief sample of true/false questions from the opinion section:

34. Lincoln is greater than Washington.
60. Wealth, power, and honor usually go to those who deserve them.
68. The soldier is more important than the musician.
85. The United States should take possession of Mexico and civilize that country.
96. An unmarried mother deserves the scorn that she gets.

The binary of aggression/sympathy is central to the test makers' gender attitudes. If a subject responds favorably to aggressive themes, he/she is labeled "masculine," and if a subject demonstrates sympathy, or evidence of a social conscience, he/she is deemed "feminine." This sample reveals the problematic nature of the M-F test's criteria for determining gender attitudes. For example, an answer of "true" to number 34 ("Lincoln is greater than Washington") is supposed to indicate a feminine identity because Lincoln, according to the test makers, "symbolizes feminine sympathy and Washington [symbolizes] masculine strength" (45). This rationale appears to posit that Lincoln is feminine because he favored the emancipation of slaves and this support for racial minorities is deemed feminine because it indicates sympathy or compassion. However, in this case, the test makers' assumptions are faulty in that Washington's public image could also be read as effeminate—his aristocratic status, powdered wig, and pale skin could signify femininity—while Lincoln's beard and common man status could be associated with masculine self-reliance. My point here is that masculine iconography is essentially mythic and the various gendered myths that are represented in the M-F test are often multivalent and arbitrary. Terman and Miles err in that they assume their test takers will have a uniform reading.

Number 60 ("Wealth, power, and honor usually go to those who deserve them") contains a similar problem. A "true" answer reaffirms the moral legitimacy of capitalism and its uneven distribution of wealth, a topical concern during the Depression. In this case, a right-wing view of the social order is supposed to indicate robust masculinity, and, by extension, hostility to those in power is deemed feminine. In this case, questions of a political nature are spuriously conflated with specific gender attitudes (the masculine and the feminine). In number 68 ("The soldier is more important than the musician"), the preference for the musician indicates a feminine response; thus, the low status of the artist is emphasized again. Similarly, in number 96 ("An unmarried mother deserves the scorn she gets"), misogyny is equated with masculine aggression while ethical objections are classified as feminine. In number 85 ("The United States should take possession of Mexico and civilize that country"), Terman and Miles use a xenophobic statement to elicit an aggressive response from the test taker.

Terman and Miles's goal of valorizing aggression is in stark contrast to the work of Sigmund Freud and Alfred Adler, who also attempt to define maleness and masculinity in the late 1920s and early 1930s. In *Civilization and Its Discontents* (1930), Freud posits a link between males and aggression and suggests that male "essence" is closely wedded to men's capacity for aggression:

> The element of truth behind all of this, which people are so ready to disavow, is that men are not gentle creatures who want to be loved, and who at the most can defend themselves if they are attacked; they are, on the contrary, creatures among whose instinctual endowments is to be reckoned a powerful share of aggressiveness. As a result, their neighbor is for them not only a potential helper or sexual object, but also someone who tempts them to satisfy their aggressiveness on him, to exploit his capacity for work without compensation, to use him sexually without his consent, to seize his possessions, to humiliate him, to cause him pain, to torture and to kill him. *Homo homini lupus.* (68–69)

Freud's references to "men" and "creatures" do not refer to women. When Freud speaks of treating one's neighbor as a "potential helper" (*möglicher Helfer*) or "sex object" (*Sexuelobjekt*), he is specifically referring to masculinity and male desire; thus, Freud ends his study with an open question: will the human species be able to master "the human instinct of aggression and self destruction"? (111).

Terman and Miles do not share Freud's trepidation. Read today, the most surprising aspect of *Sex and Personality* is their misty-eyed and often uncritical view of male aggression. It is not an overstatement to describe Terman and Miles's optimistic faith as utopian. They believe that men's propensity for aggression is not a negative, but a social resource that can be understood, controlled, and redirected for the benefit of American society. It is important to realize that eugenics-minded psychologists like Terman did not see themselves as racists (as we might), but as progressive thinkers who believed in the values of the Enlightenment, and they were convinced that they were working toward the creation of a productive and more efficient society.

For our purposes, Terman and Miles's flawed psychological study is useful in that it provides a clear impression of received cultural attitudes about gender during the Depression. Like the literary Left's attack on the genteel tradition, the low masculinity scores of the artist and the homosexual are used to confirm the problem of the feminized male and the low regard for the literary sphere in the larger culture. In contrast to the feminine spheres of literature and art, the valorization of aggression is presented as a masculine ideal. Fundamental to the cult of hardness is the notion of rooting out leisure-culture effeminacy and the soft male body. Thus, for Terman and Miles, the solution of remasculinization is enacted through the practice of social engineering (screening and early intervention). To some members of the academic community of the 1930s, the cultivation of aggression in the American male was an attractive idea because it suggested that hardness had mythic potential, a means of transcending the enervating economic climate of the time.

REMAKING THE MALE BODY:
THE NOVELS OF JAMES M. CAIN

The virtue of masculine assertion also becomes a popular theme in some literary works of the 1930s. The novels of James M. Cain are particularly relevant because Cain's fiction reflects the anxieties of Gold and of Terman and Miles. Cain's mode of fiction—the tough-guy novel—is illuminating in that it provides a literary portrait of the hard-shell ideal. Two of his most popular novels—*The Postman Always Rings Twice* (1934) and *Double Indemnity* (1936)—feature a similar storyline: a tough-guy narrator falls for a sexy married woman and becomes ensnared in a plot to kill her husband. In each case, coupling with the femme fatale brings about the hero's tragic demise. Thus, the price for surrendering to the desire for the feminine is death. The novels have been described as "hard-boiled" because they contain an unsentimental tough-guy narrator who describes the immediate

world as he sees it.[18] Frank Chambers, the antihero and narrator of
The Postman Always Rings Twice, is distinct from other literary heroes
in that he is reluctant to intellectualize human experience. While on
death row, the convicted murderer expresses his knee-jerk distrust
of intellectual concepts:

> There is a guy in No. 7 that murdered his brother, and says he didn't do it,
> his subconscious did it. I asked him what that meant, and he says you got
> two selves, one that you know about and the other that you don't know
> about because it's subconscious. It shook me up. Did I really do it, and
> not know it? God almighty, I can't believe that! I didn't do it! I loved her
> so, then, I tell you, that I would have died for her! To hell with the sub-
> conscious. I don't believe it. It's just a lot of hooey, that this guy thought
> up so he could fool the judge. (116)

The passage contains the familiar rhetorical tropes of hard masculinity: anti-intellectualism as an expression of class difference and
the rejection of psychological language ("subconscious") as a form
of sophistry. The hard-boiled narrator is fundamentally ambivalent
about the act of writing and turns to written expression only because
the priest requests it. Still, throughout the death row confession, the
narrator remains laconic, emotionally guarded, and uncomfortable
with the act of revealing intimate details about himself. The narrator's ambivalence stems from the notion that the act of confession
is unbecoming and a reflection of weakness. Despising all forms of
emotional leakage, the narrator keeps his composure and remains
emotionally buttoned up. The novel's suspense stems from the narrator's internal conflict: the human need to confess is counterbalanced
by the masculine desire to remain reticent and guarded. In the genre
of tough-guy fiction, the attraction to the feminine leads to death ("I
loved her so . . . I would have died for her"); hence, the hard-shell male
often strives to avoid all forms of feminine contamination.

The hard-boiled label that is often attached to Cain's fiction is
also revealing in that it comments on the public's perception of masculinity in the 1930s. The term suggests that Cain's male characters
possess a particular type of masculinity that is distinct from the
norm: a hard-shell variety that is impervious to emotionalism and
sentimentality. The hard-boiled, which signifies being unfeeling and
callous, is presented as the antithesis of the archetypal feminine. The

converse of the hard-boiled is flaccidness, mushiness, or anything that lacks hardness and solidity. Metaphorically speaking, the soft-boiled is undeniably the province of the so-called effeminate male. Hence, the hard/soft binary is entirely consistent with the gender theories of Terman and Miles; both advocate the preservation of hard masculine qualities (aggressiveness, emotional control) at the expense of the so-called soft and feminine qualities (emotionalism, timidity).

The phrase "hard-boiled" appears in James T. Farrell's *Studs Lonigan* (1935), a popular novel of the Depression. The phrase is associated with a man's attempt to stifle emotion. When Studs has an adolescent crush on Lucy Scanlon, he scolds himself:

> He [Studs] wanted to stand there, and think about Lucy, wondering if he would ever have days with her like that one, wondering how much he'd see of her after she went to high school. And he goddamned himself, because he was getting soft. He was Studs Lonigan, a guy who didn't have mushy feelings! He was a hard-boiled egg that they had left in the pot a couple of hours too long. (9)

Studs's "hard-boiled egg" is a curious metaphor to use when describing a person who is tough and unsentimental. One would have thought that the repression of emotion would be conveyed by a traditional masculine metaphor that connotes solidity and strength (i.e., steel or granite); instead, the phrase suggests that the male figure has repressed the ability to feel or emote and thus has become "hardened" by the experience of life. If the hard-boiled narrator has any emotions left at all, he must mask them and be extremely cautious about open displays of emotion. The phrase "hard-boiled" can also be read as a veiled reference to the feminine-marked fetus, or egg; thus, the hard-boiled male is never mushy or soft and reacts against feminizing forces by retaining phallic hardness at all times.

In most critical studies of the literature of the 1930s, the term "hard-boiled" is merely a reflection of the social milieu:

> An unusually tough era turns out the hard-boiled hero. A traumatic wrench like the depression, its evils and despair touching all facets of human society, causes a violent reaction in these men. . . . Those hardest hit become down-and-out, the disinherited, and soon develop a hard-boiled

> attitude that enables them to maintain a granite-like dignity against
> forces that chisel erratically at it. (Madden, *Tough Guy Writers* xvii)

While employing masculine metaphors ("wrench," "chisel"), David Madden stresses that the hard-boiled hero is a reaction to harsh economic circumstances, and this interpretation was popular with many literary critics in the 1950s and 1960s. However, it is interesting to note that the economic and social often have overshadowed the importance of gender and sexuality. The fact that men are tough was a given; therefore, the topic of masculinity did not need to be critically explored.[19] The blindness to gender concerns is a byproduct of the gender essentialism that dominated literary criticism in the decades before second wave feminism. However, more recent criticism of the hard-boiled hero and the detective novel focuses on the topic of masculinity and the genre's obvious relation to male fantasy. In an essay on Raymond Chandler, Joyce Carol Oates perceptively compares the genre of detective novels to the genre of romance novels: "the detective is all that men are not, the proper object of their envy, adulation, and desire. He is the wish-fulfillment fantasy of the (male) reader of the genre, as the heroine of romance is the wish fulfillment of the female genre" ("Raymond Chandler" 100). As Oates's commentary suggests, the hard-boiled genre can be viewed as an elaborate male fantasy. In masculinist crime fiction, effeminacy in males must be rooted out and destroyed. Therefore, it is fitting that Cain's third novel is explicitly concerned with the bête noire of Gold and of Terman and Miles: the artist with homosexual leanings.

SERENADE AND THE LITERARY
CURE FOR HOMOSEXUALITY

After writing two tough-guy novels back-to-back, Cain became worried about his own macho public image. Cain's exotic novel, *Serenade* (1937), represents his literary attempt to shake the hard-boiled label that he had acquired after the runaway successes of *The Postman Always Rings Twice* and *Double Indemnity*. In his preface to *Three by Cain*, the author is clearly uncomfortable with how his novels have been read:

I am probably the most misread, misreviewed, and misunderstood novelist now writing. . . . I make no conscious effort to be tough, or hard-boiled, or grim, or any of the things I am usually called. I merely try to write as the character would write, and I never forget that the average man, from the fields, the streets, the bus, the offices and even the gutters of his country, has acquired a vividness of speech that goes beyond anything I could invent, and that if I stick to this heritage, this logos of the American countryside, I shall attain the maximum of effectiveness with very little effort. In general my style is rural rather than urban; my ear seems to like the fields better than the streets. I am glad of this, for I think language loses a bit of its bounce the moment its heels touch concrete. (vii–ix)

Here, Cain rehearses a familiar aesthetic argument: his narrators are characters who reflect a certain sector of society, and they do not speak for nor represent the views of the author. However, Cain's Jeffersonian disdain for the corruption of city life is not apparent in *Serenade*. The novel's subject matter—opera and its upper-class milieu—suggest that Cain is now a man of high culture rather than the voice of the *lumpenproletariat*. However, despite Cain's attempt at literary reinvention, John Howard Sharp, the narrator of *Serenade*, is actually another tough-guy hero like Frank Chambers, or Walter Neff of *Double Indemnity*; the only discernible difference is that this particular tough guy sings opera.

Serenade is the story of Sharp, a tenor who abruptly loses his voice and thus finds himself out of work. The loss of his singing abilities occurs when he indulges in an illicit homosexual affair with Winston Hawes, a world-famous opera director. The plot revolves around Sharp's attempt to regain his operatic voice and heterosexual virility. While living hand-to-mouth in Mexico City, the narrator meets Juana, an exotic, hyperfeminine Mexican prostitute, and the two begin a tumultuous affair as they roam through the Mexican countryside. At one point, the protagonist attempts to sing for Juana, but the results are quite disappointing: "The echo of my voice was still in my ears and there was no getting around it. It had the same wooden, dull quality that a priest's voice has, without one particle of life in it, one echo that would make you like it" (47–48).

The narrator's comparison with the priest suggests that his voice is not only "dull" and lifeless, but eunuch-like as well. The novel's central premise is that a masculine artist's vocal capacity is inextricably linked to his sexual potency and sexual orientation. The hero's recovery of his potency and vocal abilities occurs when he seduces Juana in a deserted village church during a tropical rainstorm. Following the sexual consummation, Sharp and Juana slay an iguana and cook it in boiling water; the meal commemorates his attainment of potency and the élan vital. The narrator's return to primitivism echoes Wilhelm Reich's belief that the orgasm is therapeutic and essential for one's mental and physical well-being. Hence, the narrator's success as an opera singer in the latter part of the novel can be attributed to his return to heterosexuality and the healing properties of sexual potency.

The second half of the novel chronicles the narrator's rise to prominence in the opera world and his need to face his inner demons. In addition, as Sharp returns to New York, he must also face his ex-lover and nemesis, Winston Hawes. The homosexual Hawes is the son of a rich industrialist, and he is depicted as the embodiment of cultural degeneracy:

> Winston Hawes, the papers said, was one of the outstanding musicians of his time, the conductor that could really read a score, the man that had done more for modern music since Muck. He was all of that, but don't get the idea that he was one of the boys. There was something wrong about the way he thought about music, something unhealthy, like the crowds you always saw at his concerts. . . . He was rich, and there is something about rich people that's different from the rest of us. (127)

For the narrator, homosexuality is virtually synonymous with decadent leisure culture. Much like Michael Gold's attacks on Marcel Proust and Thornton Wilder, Hawes's homosexuality cannot be divorced from his artistic creations. The reference to him not being "one of the boys" implies that Hawes's queerness separates him from the company of heterosexual conductors and musicians. Moreover, the narrator's suggestion that the rich are "different from the rest of us" stems from the notion that the rich do not perform labor, and thus the abundance of leisure culture makes them queer and unnatural. In other passages, Hawes is equated with conspicuous consumption and bitchiness: "that woman was in him [Hawes], poodle dog, diamonds, limousine, conceit, cruel and all" (128).

The narrator's encounter with queerness is revealed when Sharp reluctantly confesses to his homosexual dalliance with Hawes: "That was the beginning of it, and it was quite a while before it dawned on me what he really wanted. As to what he wanted, and what he got, you'll find out soon enough, and I am not going to tell you any more than I have to. But I'd like to make this much clear now: that wasn't what I wanted" (129). Although the narrator promises to disclose the details of his homosexual affair ("you'll find out soon enough, and I am not going to tell you any more than I have to"), he never does describe the details of the encounter. The laconic Sharp disavows having same-sex passion ("that wasn't what I wanted"). However, he soon reveals his attraction to Hawes: "I would not be telling the truth if I didn't admit that what he meant to me was plenty" (ibid.). The narrator's struggle against latent homosexuality is also evidenced in his remark that "every man has got five percent of that in him, if he meets the one person that'll bring it out and I did, that's all" (144).

At the end of the novel, Sharp can only partially overcome his latent homosexuality on his own. Ultimately, he needs Juana's help. In a famous scene that is fraught with melodrama and primitivism, Juana, dressed in a matador's resplendent garb, slays the homosexual Hawes with a shiny *espada* during a mock bullfight at an elegant housewarming party. The cross-dressing and the wielding of the phallic *espada* suggest the masculinization of Juana, the feminine primitive. By stabbing Hawes, she is symbolically slaying Sharp's homosexuality and restoring the normative gender roles and the natural order.

At the housewarming drag party, Sharp is horrified by cross-dressing lesbians ("girls in men's evening clothes tailored for them, with shingle haircuts and blue make-up") and effeminate men ("young guys with lipstick on and mascara eye-lashes"); he remarks that the "whole thing made me sick to my stomach" (151). However, the very same narrator is thrilled and aroused when Juana dons the matador's bright costume. Sharp's contradictory reactions or his ambivalence indicate an unconscious attraction to cross-dressing and the cultural performance of female masculinity. Thus, in Cain's novel, homosexual panic is accompanied by a fascination with masculinized women; the narrator's repressed homosexuality is projected onto Juana, who is dressed like a man. The figure of Juana is also attractive to Sharp because she rescues him from his economic dependence on Hawes, the wealthy benefactor and impresario.

Read today, the novel's medical thesis—that one's sexual preference affects one's vocal abilities—is a clear case of literary quackery. Privately, even Cain was skeptical about his novel's questionable premise. In a letter to H. L. Mencken, Cain addresses some of Mencken's reservations about the novel and the supposed link between potency and singing:

> The point you take exception to, I suppose is the vocal restoration through female companionship. This is an illustration of the trap a novel writer gets into every time he grazes a scientific boundary. The lamentable sounds that issue from a homo's throat when he tries to sing are a matter of personal observation, and if I could have stopped there I could have been completely persuasive, and made a point of some interest. But the theme demanded the next step, the unwarranted corollary that heavy workouts with a woman would bring out the stud horse high notes. Right there is where it goes facile and I suppose silly. Several doctors of eminence assured me that they could believe it, and pleaded with me to write the book, as the idea interested them; all I can say is I have my serious doubts. (qtd. in Hoopes 283)

Cain's private letter reveals that he strenuously objects to the idea of homosexual men singing opera. Thus, his novel is an attempt to remasculinize the opera singer. The fact that "several doctors of eminence" pushed Cain to pursue his homophobic depiction of homosexuality as a debilitating weakness suggests that various writers, intellectuals, and medical authorities held similar ideas about homosexuality. Homosexuality was viewed as the product of a culture that had become too feminized and unmanly. Cain's private papers also contain letters from psychiatrists who supported Cain's theories about homosexuality and artistic ability. Dr. James Neilson, a psychiatrist, claimed that *Serenade* "is now required reading in most psychiatry courses in this country" (Hoopes 287). This claim seems unlikely, but it does indicate that Cain and some psychologists seemed to agree that homosexuality is the worst ailment that could befall a man and that impotence is a clear sign of masculine deficiency. Sharp's struggle with impotence and latent homosexuality are illustrative of modern man's struggle with effeminacy. Like the fiction of D. H. Lawrence and other modernists, Cain's novel suggests that the encroachment of industrialism, and urban life in general, has enervated the Western subject's vital connection to the cosmos. Thus, Cain's novel reflects the Lawrencean theme of recovered potency: by coupling with the exotic and primitive Juana, the narrator becomes whole again.

Like Gold, Rahv, and other writers from the 1930s, Cain is deeply concerned with the specter of leisure-culture effeminacy. However, unlike Gold, Cain has little interest in utopian Marxism; his tough-guy narrator is revitalized through the myth of phallic potency. However, it is interesting that Cain's project of remasculinization mirrors Terman and Miles's valorization of aggression and their notion of rooting out the homosexual self. Sharp's reattainment of potency and artistic prowess are achieved through an act of aggression. Sharp does not merely make love to Juana—he takes her by force and she submits—and thus, through the act of penetration, he regains his voice and, eventually, his status as a breadwinner. As Terman and Miles suggest, embracing one's masculine and aggressive nature—hypermasculinity—can be therapeutic for the individual who suffers from the ailment of homosexuality and sex role confusion. By engaging in vigorous bouts of heterosexual sex (what Terman and Miles term "sex appropriate traits"), Sharp is able to conquer idleness, poverty, and effeminacy all in one fell swoop; the internal struggle with latent homosexuality is resolved, and Sharp becomes a great opera singer and a productive and responsible member of society. Thus, Cain's *Serenade* offers a literary fantasy of sex role theory and a solution for the Goldian obsession with high culture effeteness.

THE GENDERED RHETORIC OF CLIFFORD ODETS'S SOCIAL PROTEST DRAMAS

Malcolm Cowley's famous book on the literature of the 1930s, *After the Genteel Tradition*, featured only one essay on American drama and the playwright selected was Eugene O'Neill. However, if Cowley had wanted to include another playwright from the 1930s, he might well have chosen Clifford Odets.[20] Odets's gritty immigrant dramas could be described as the antithesis of genteel theatre. Consider the reaction of Edith J. R. Isaacs, a reviewer for the prestigious *Theatre Arts Monthly,* an influential theatre publication in the 1920s and 1930s, to Odets's *Awake and Sing!* (1935):

> These people in this wretched Bronx flat are, it is easy to imagine, forever treading on each other's toes, stumbling across each other's sentences, knocking over each other's idols. . . . A director with the right restraint would have suggested much of this without actually letting it seem that two of the people on his stage were always trying to occupy the same space at the same time, and continually interrupting or doubling on each other's speech.

Wendy Smith, a theatre historian and the author of *Real Life: The Group Theatre and America, 1931–1940,* adds, "Isaacs and other reviewers seem to be faulting Harold Clurman's direction for qualities in the play itself that made them uneasy. It was so messy, so cluttered, so noisy, so . . . Jewish" (208). Walter Winchell remarked: "It [*Awake and Sing!*] was as non-Aryan as a Bronx Express and as swift" (qtd. in Smith 208).

Isaacs's response to Odets's first full-length play reveals apprehensions about Odets's willingness to people his stage with lower-middle-class Jewish characters. Isaacs, who was probably more comfortable with the proper English that was spoken in drawing-room comedies, was very critical of Odets's untidy theatrical aesthetic. However, Odets's plays, which feature staccato dialogue and the argot of urban life, were innovative precisely because they showcased a social milieu that was less familiar to the middle-class Broadway theatre audience of the early 1930s. Hence, Odets's anti-genteel brand of political drama can be linked to Gold's and Cowley's remasculinization projects of the 1930s. However, most theatre scholars who have written about Odets have been reluctant to consider the gendered aspects of Odets's political vision.[21] Much like Michael Gold's criticism, Odets's plays demonstrate a distinct preoccupation with masculinist rhetoric; nearly all of Odets's major plays from the 1930s—*Waiting for Lefty* (1935), *Awake and Sing!* (1935), *Paradise Lost* (1935), *Golden Boy* (1937), *Rocket to the Moon* (1938)—feature a political message that is anchored in the remasculinization of the male body. My reading of Odets's plays from the Depression foregrounds the gender clashes that are inherent in his particular conception of Jewish masculinity.

Like Gold, Odets frequently juxtaposes the impotence of the middle classes with the assumed virility of the working classes. Thus, Odets, as a playwright, is fascinated with the theme of the emasculated male and with the plight of the enervated Jewish male body that is in desperate need of masculine and political renewal.

Odets's *Waiting for Lefty* (1935), which is about a taxi-drivers' strike, is frequently cited as the most famous agitprop play in the history of American drama.[22] When it was first performed at a benefit for the League of Workers Theatres, it prompted audience members to rise to their feet and chant "Strike! Strike!" at the close of the play. Given these accounts, it is not surprising that most critics and theatre historians have strenuously focused on the political and social aspects of Odets's plays. On the surface, *Waiting for Lefty* is about the everyday life of taxi drivers and their struggle for better wages and decent working conditions. However, the play's thesis—the need for solidarity among workers and the efficacy of strikes—is communicated through an episode of sexual politics. One of the play's most effective scenes features a conflict between Joe, a cab driver who is struggling to support his family, and his angry wife, Edna, who accuses him of being a failed breadwinner. Edna even threatens to leave him for a richer man if he does not strike for higher wages. In perhaps one of the play's most famous speeches, she questions her husband's masculinity:

> JOE   This is what I slaved for!
> EDNA   Tell it to your boss!
> JOE   He don't give a damn for you or me!
> EDNA   That's what I say.
> JOE   Don't change the subject!
> EDNA   This is the subject, the exact subject! Your boss makes this subject. I never saw him in my life, but he's putting ideas in my head a mile a minute. He's giving your kids that fancy disease called the rickets. He's making a jelly-fish outa you and putting wrinkles in my face. This is the subject every inch of the way! He's throwing me into Bud Haas's lap. When in hell will you get wise . . . when a man knocks you down you get up and kiss his fist! You gutless piece of baloney. . . . Stand up and fight like men. (12)

In this tumultuous scene, Edna insists that the economics of the workplace directly affect the gender politics of the domestic sphere and that the two cannot be disentangled. Moreover, Edna's abusive phrases ("jelly-fish," "piece of baloney") are gendered terms that imply that Joe is not only spineless, but flaccid. Joe attains his manhood (and hardness) by making the decision to strike; thus, when he kisses Edna, he is instantly reinvigorated. *Waiting for Lefty* is ultimately a didactic tale about the embrace of the hypermasculine, which is presented as a social panacea; when welded to political action, it signifies the empowerment of the working class: "Hear it, boys, hear it? . . . WE'RE THE STORMBIRDS OF THE WORKING CLASS WORKERS OF THE WORLD. . . . OUR BONES AND BLOOD! And when we die they'll know what we did to make a new world! Christ cut us up to little pieces. We'll die for what is right!" (31). In this climactic speech, which is directed to the audience, the male body is fetishized as a sacrificial offering for the coming revolution.

The theme of the emasculated male is also at the heart of Odets's first popular full-length play, *Awake and Sing!* The play charts the struggles of the Bergers, a Jewish family in the Bronx struggling to make ends meet during the Depression. The play focuses on the generational conflict between the two children (Ralph and Hennie) and Bessie, their domineering mother, who controls their present lives and when and whom they will marry. When Hennie experiences an unwanted pregnancy, Bessie quickly finds a suitor whom they can dupe. Sam is a good "catch" because he is an honest and hardworking immigrant with a steady job, and he is also a gullible man who does not suspect that he is not the father of Hennie's child. Similarly, Bessie controls all of Ralph's hard-earned wages and intervenes in his personal affairs by forbidding him to see his girlfriend, Blanche, an orphan girl who is too poor for the respectable, lower-middle-class Bergers. Bessie Berger and her henpecked husband, Myron, represent the hollow, money-grubbing values of bourgeois society. For them, marriage is purely an act of convenience and economic self-interest. The plot of the play revolves around Ralph's moral transformation: his rejection of his parents' bourgeois values and his embrace of radical politics. Much like in *Waiting for Lefty*, Ralph's political conversion is linked to his embrace of working-class hypermasculinity.

In the Berger household, Ralph is surrounded by conflicting examples of masculinity. At one end of the spectrum are the soft men: his apron-wearing father (Myron) and Sam Feinschreiber, a cuckold and a domesticated "cluck [who] boils baby nipples." Myron's adoration of Teddy Roosevelt and his robust masculinity underscores his own masculine deficiencies and his status as an ineffectual father. Ralph's rebellion against his soft father is emphasized in the final scene of the play when Ralph rejects Myron's pathetic example: "when I look at him, I'm sad. Let me die like a dog, if I can't get more from life" (100). After rejecting his father, Ralph adopts the hard men of the Berger household—Moe Axelrod and his Marxist grandfather Jacob—as his new masculine role models. Axelrod is a tough, working-class World War I vet who lost a leg in the war and views the world with jaded cynicism (the stage directions say, "life has taught him to disbelieve in everything," and he "seldom shows his own feelings: fights against his own sensitivity"). Molded by his experiences in the trenches, Axelrod is a classic hard-boiled male figure who retains a skeptical view of power and American social institutions ("It's all a racket—from horse racing down. Marriage, politics, big business—everybody plays cops and robbers"). Moreover, both of Ralph's surrogate fathers harbor misogynist sentiments. Moe remarks in jest, "[W]hat do I think of women? Tak'em all, cut 'em in little pieces like a herring in a Greek salad. A guy in France had the right idea—dropped his wife in a bathtub fulla acid," while Jacob reminds Ralph that women can impede a man's desire to make revolution:

> Once I had [in] my heart a dream, a vision, but came marriage and then you forget. Children come and you forget. . . . Remember, a woman insults a man's soul like no other thing in the world! . . . wake up! Be something! Make your life something good. For the love of an old man who sees in your young days his new life, for such love take the world in your two hands and make it new. Go out and fight so life is not printed on dollar bills. A woman waits. (48)

In Jacob's view, women represent domesticity and passivity, and thus they make men forget about the need to fight for political changes and about their desire to remake the social order. Jacob's idealism is distinct from Moe Axelrod's hard-boiled cynicism, and Ralph's moral and political transformation at the end of the play represents a synthesis of the two masculine role models.

The narrative conflict of *Awake and Sing!* revolves around Ralph's moral redemption and his quest for masculine assertiveness; he becomes a man when he confronts his domineering mother and rejects the older generation's empty and complacent values. When Jacob commits suicide by jumping off the roof of the Bronx tenement, Ralph is utterly transformed by the experience of his death: he adopts Jacob's Marxist worldview and Moe Axelrod's masculine toughness. Thus, Ralph decides to forget his plans for marriage and settling down and pledges his life to revolution at the close of the play: "Did Jake die for us to fight about nickels? No! 'Awake and Sing!' he said. Right here he stood and said it. The night he died, I saw it like a thunderbolt! I saw he was dead and I was born! I swear to God, I'm one week old! I want the whole city to hear it—fresh blood, arms. We got 'em. We're glad we're living" (100–101). Much like Michael Gold's masculine rhetoric, the revolution of the future is analogized through the transformation of male bodies ("fresh blood, arms") and the collective ideal of masculine labor solidarity ("We got 'em").

Odets's vision of a utopian future in *Awake and Sing!* is also presented through a gendered conflict between Ralph and his mother. Though she has the family's best interests in mind, Bessie wields tyrannical power within the domestic sphere. When she smashes Jacob's opera records, she is symbolically destroying her father's utopian yearnings ("Caruso stands on the ship and looks on a Utopia. You hear? 'Oh Paradise! Oh Paradise on earth!'"). This pivotal scene prompts Jacob's suicide and suggests that women are incapable of understanding great art, and their ignorance impedes the masculine desire to remake the social order. Jacob's hostility to women ("a woman insults a man's soul like no other thing in the world!") is an extension of his contempt for his daughter's petit bourgeois philistinism and his contention that a true revolutionary cannot be enslaved to banal domestic concerns. Hence, the utopian yearnings expressed in *Awake and Sing!* are not simply the desire for a social revolution where the working class obtains power; rather, the utopian impulse is necessarily framed in gendered terms—the masculinist future is juxtaposed with the feminine passivity of the present.

Golden Boy, Odets's last successful play for the Group Theatre, also explores utopian themes through the fundamental conflict between the masculine and the feminine. The play, which was originally titled "The Manly Art," is the story of Joe Bonaparte, a working-class Italian American who is torn between two conflicting career choices: to be a boxer or to be a concert violinist. The battle between "the fist and the fiddle" is alluded to in one of Joe's scenes with Lorna, the beautiful woman and muse who brings out the less aggressive side of Joe's personality. Joe remarks:

> With music I'm never alone when I'm alone—Playing music . . . that's like saying, "I am a man. I belong here. How do you do, World—good evening!" When I play music nothing is closed to me. I'm not afraid of people and what they say. There's no war in music. It's not like the streets. . . . but when you leave your room . . . down in the streets it's war! Music can't help me there. (263–64)

Even though Joe plays the violin beautifully, he is pushed to abandon the feminine world of music and to enter the hypermasculine world of boxing. Joe's rapid success as a prizefighter emphasizes Odets's attempt to meld gender and class identity: the tough streets of New York and the economic climate of the 1930s push Joe to embrace his hypermasculine side and kill the feminine within himself. The inevitability of these social processes is tragic; Joe Bonaparte seemingly has little choice in the matter: he is forced to be aggressive because it offers him a means of escaping his poverty and achieving material rewards. However, Joe's tragic fate is sealed when he unintentionally kills another boxer in a heated fight. After the murderous bout, Joe vows to give up boxing forever and laments the fact that his hands are too damaged to play the violin again. At this crucial moment in the play, Lorna, Joe's lover, expresses the play's utopian vision of a classless society with gender harmony: "We have each other! Somewhere there must be happy boys and girls who can teach us the way of life! We'll find a city where poverty's no shame—where music is no crime—where there's no war in the streets—where a man is glad to be himself, to live and make his woman herself" (316).

Lorna's speech mirrors Odets's perpetual attempt to link political ideals with gender ideals. The speech also succinctly expresses the importance of stable gender identities for men and women in the Depression; a man possesses the social and biological right to be masculine and a woman possesses the attendant right to be feminine. The notion that "a man is glad to be himself" suggests that, in this utopian place, a man will be able to play the violin without being considered effeminate. In short, the masculine and the feminine will coexist without conflict or ambivalence. The last line of the speech ("to . . . make his woman herself") is also revealing: it suggests not only that men possess women, but that a man must establish the parameters for femininity and female subjectivity. Thus, Odets's vision of gender harmony resembles the utopian ideals of sex role theory: to create a space where a man can be a "real man," a woman a "true woman," and the world is not threatened by gender ambiguity or any form of gender slippage.

In *Golden Boy*, the explicit fear of gender slippage is expressed in the troublesome figure of Eddie Fuseli, a gangster and hard-boiled homosexual who desires Joe Bonaparte. The original Broadway production featured Elia Kazan in this role, and his performance apparently greatly impressed J. Edgar Hoover and Thomas Dewey.[23] Hoover felt that Fuseli was a revealing portrait of the criminal mind of a gangster; however, the FBI chief may also have been unconsciously fascinated by Fuseli's macho homosexuality, a form of queerness that mirrored his own. Fuseli is striking because he is such an aberration in the literature of the 1930s: a man with same-sex desire who is neither effeminate nor the product of a leisure-culture environment. Instead, his homoerotic desire is expressed in economic terms: he wants to buy a "piece" of Joe Bonaparte the boxer. At the end of the play, Fuseli owns thirty percent and wants to buy out the remaining shareholders and assume total control of Joe and his boxing career. The fact that Joe is bought and sold like a slab of meat suggests that he has become a fetishized male body in the marketplace. The latter is emphasized in the various scenes in the locker room that feature Joe in boxing shorts and that showcase his trim and muscular physique. On one level, Joe's suicidal car accident at the end of the play can be viewed as a desperate attempt to avoid the humiliation of being forced to box again after he has killed someone in the ring; however, in masculinist terms, it can be read as an expression of homosexual panic—in this case, the fear of being owned and controlled by a rich homosexual. Thus, the arc of the play suggests that the tragic hero must commit suicide to avoid the loss of male autonomy.

Many scholars have noted that *Golden Boy* can be read as a veiled confession by Odets about his own ambivalent reaction to success and his decision to abandon the Group Theatre for Hollywood. In *Golden Boy*, Odets's defection to the Hollywood studio system is allegorized in the tragic figure of Joe Bonaparte. However, Joe's corruption must not be seen only in material and economic terms. Equally important is the abandonment of Joe's masculine and political ideals. His fame in the boxing ring and his acquired wealth alienate him from his music-loving immigrant father, who has little interest in boxing, and separates him from his working-class forebears. *Golden Boy*, like all of Odets's plays, reinforces the notion that one's masculine body—or gender style—cannot be divorced from one's class identity. In this sense, Odets's dramas are paradigmatic of the 1930s Left's conception of masculinity, epitomized in the tough-talking hypermasculine proletarian figures that are products of their immediate social environments. The challenge for Odets and other leftist writers is to imagine a world where the hypermasculine response— Joe's embrace of the fist and the rejection of the fiddle—is no longer necessary or inevitable.

Although I have argued that the politics of masculinity is central to Odets's political and dramatic vision, I would also emphasize that Odets's particular conception of masculine identity is less easy to pin down. Unlike Gold, Odets does not necessarily conflate leisure-culture effeminacy with homosexuality (e.g., Fuseli in *Golden Boy*), and unlike the work of Terman and Miles, Odets's plays display ambivalence toward hypermasculine aggression. In *Awake and Sing!* the political awakening of Ralph Berger glorifies the theme of hypermasculine assertion; however, in other plays there is a distinct critique of aggressive masculinity, especially the form that is produced by hostile economic circumstances (*Paradise Lost*, *Golden Boy*). Although Odets's view of the masculine and masculine identity often shifts from play to play, the transformation of the Jewish male body is, nonetheless, central to his work. Since many of Odets's plays are familial dramas (*Awake and Sing!*, *Paradise Lost*, *Rocket to the Moon*), the emasculated Jewish male struggles against the feminizing forces within his household—a wife or mother—who represent complacent bourgeois values (Bessie Berger of *Awake and Sing!*). In each case, the Jewish male must find his manhood by confronting the forces that emasculate and repress him (his boss, his domineering mother, the system of capitalism itself). In most of the plays, the narrative of remasculinization functions as a political baptism: the male hero finds himself forever transformed and reborn as a class-conscious political subject.

The tragic suicide of Joe Bonaparte in *Golden Boy* alludes to the ambivalent status of the American male with artistic leanings in the 1930s. The battle of the fist and the fiddle is resolved when Joe breaks his fingers in the boxing ring and realizes that he will never play the violin again. Thus, the loss of the feminine (the violin) is presented as tragic because the American male is denied access to the feminine realm of artistic expression. Odets's attempt to valorize the feminine and the artistic is in stark contrast to Terman and Miles's and Cain's attempts to defeminize the male artist. However, Joe Bonaparte's suicide can also be read as a coda for the grandiose remasculinization project of the 1930s. Although the attack on the genteel tradition was certainly influential, the attempt to remasculinize the male writer and American literary culture produced mixed results. Gold's vituperative attack-dog mode of criticism and Cain's literary quackery are not persuasive because they merely call attention to their own excess and hypertrophy. In effect, the masculinist hyperbole of Gold and the other anti-genteel writers often backfires in the sense that it articulates—and confirms—the popular culture's ambivalence about literary culture and the literary endeavor itself.

2

Doughfaces, Eggheads, and Softies: Gendered Epithets and American Literary Culture in the 1940s

At a certain point in the 1940s, the concept of hardness became a recurring metaphor in American cultural life. In the area of foreign policy, it became a vivid and arresting way of discussing national identity. Therefore, it is perhaps fitting that the theme of penetration, a perennial concern of hard masculinity, became one of the most popular tropes of anti-Communist discourse during that time. The word "penetration" itself appears five times in George Kennan's famous "long telegram" to the State Department in 1946.[1] Kennan, the architect of the policy of containment, was fond of evocative and emotionally charged metaphors that boldly asserted the need to restrain the expansionist policy of the Soviet Union. In Kennan's anti-Communist scenario, the government of the Soviet Union was a masculine brute that had illegitimately assumed power by raping the feminine Russian people. In another document, Kennan describes the Russian people as "a beautiful lady being guarded by a jealous lover" (the Communist Party).[2] In this case, Kennan's gendered rhetoric evokes the narrative of chivalrous romance: the West must respond to the aggressive, hypermasculine Soviets who are threatening to violate the smaller nations that cannot properly defend themselves. In each case, Kennan views the USSR as doubly masculine, and thus the United States must not cede any ground; it must shore up its own masculine identity to measure up to the Russian bear.

Kennan also insists that the West must act because it contains "a wide variety of national associations or bodies which can be dominated or influenced by such [Communist] penetration" (qtd. in Costigliola 1333). Thus, it is not surprising that the converse of porousness—the state of imperviousness—becomes a central tenet of U.S. foreign policy. Kennan also urges policy makers to "tighten" up and act with "cohesion, firmness and vigor" (ibid.).[3] In this case, the gendered metaphors even suggest that the national body must protect itself from the frightening prospect of anal rape.[4]

This preponderance of gendered metaphors was not unique to Kennan. The hard/soft dichotomy was an extremely popular rhetorical paradigm during the Cold War, and those who were perceived as "soft" on Communism were frequently attacked and berated. The distinction between hard and soft first appears in the late 1940s in the writings of Arthur Schlesinger, a liberal historian and prominent Democrat. Schlesinger's *The Vital Center* (1949) was an influential text that served as a blueprint for liberal anti-Communism during the Cold War. Like Kennan's long telegram, Schlesinger's language and imagery are structured around gendered metaphors and, in some cases, homophobic tropes. Unlike Kennan's allusions to chivalric duty, however, Schlesinger uses macho phraseology and phallic metaphors that identify penile hardness with a tough-minded and realistic view of the world. In the coming years, Schlesinger would become an important architect for John F. Kennedy's New Frontier and its attempt to merge muscular anti-Communism with a liberal domestic agenda. In terms of gender, the most interesting part of *The Vital Center* is Schlesinger's masculinist attack on the soft and "impotent" left-wingers and fellow travelers, who are not hard-boiled and realistic enough to recognize the essential brutality of the Communist movement.[5]

In Schlesinger's attack on softness, Michael Gold's obsession with leisure-culture effeteness is revived; Schlesinger actually coined a new phrase that never became a part of the Cold War parlance: "doughface progressive." Much like the Pillsbury Doughboy, the term implies a male body that is essentially soft and pliable. The term "dough" also connotes the notion of being "uncooked" and implies a state of stunted adolescence. Schlesinger's attempt to link the dough-face to immaturity is an extension of the then popular psychological notion that homosexuality is a form of arrested development. Hence, "doughface progressive" can be read as a code word for effeteness and, in many cases, homosexuality. The doughface progressive is "soft not hard and he believes himself genuinely concerned with the welfare of individuals" (36). As in Terman and Miles's diagnosis of softness, altruism is regarded as a sign of femininity. Doughface pro-gressives, according to Schlesinger, are fellow travelers, academics, and "ivory tower types" who possess a "sentimental belief in prog-ress" and simply do not understand the grim facts of life. Like many of his supporters, Schlesinger had served in the military in World War II and had worked for the Office of Strategic Services (OSS), and his wartime service and firsthand experience with Nazism and the Soviet Union made him critical of soft left-wingers who did not fear totalitarian governments.

The homosexual valence of the term becomes more clear when Schlesinger discusses the doughface's masochistic tendencies. The doughface progressive is linked to sadomasochistic narratives which stress the theme of subservience and penetration: "America has its quota of lonely and frustrated people, craving social, intellectual and even sexual fulfillment they cannot obtain in existing society. For these people, party discipline is no obstacle; it is an attraction. The great majority wants to be disciplined" (104). Moreover, the Ameri-can Communists "enjoy the discipline" (54), and "the infiltration of contemporary progressivism by Communism [has] led to the same self-flagellation, the same refusal to take precautions against tyranny" (38). In this case, there is a distinction between the So-viet Communist, who is masculine, aggressive, and hard, and the American Communist, who is weak, feminine, and penetrable. Thus, in Kennan's antifeminine rhetoric, the soft American Communist becomes a potential security risk: "his sentimentality has softened up the progressive for Communist permeation and conquest" (ibid.). Although Schlesinger never mentions Alger Hiss—whose trial I will discuss later—Hiss's presence is clearly evoked through the doughface metaphor. *The Vital Center* was published in the same year (1949) as the Chambers-Hiss trial, and Hiss fits the profile of the typical doughface, an urbane statesman and fellow traveler who allows himself to be "penetrated" by Soviet spies.

For Schlesinger, the doughface is fundamentally different from the straight male because he is ruled by passion. The doughface rejects the exercise of power and instead seeks affective compensation: "the emotional orgasm of passing resolutions against Franco" becomes a meaningful surrogate experience. Schlesinger also notes the doughface's "feminine fascination with the rude and muscular power of the proletariat" (46). The attraction to the working class satisfies "the intellectual's desire to compensate for his own sense of alienation by immersing himself in the broad maternal expanse of the masses" (ibid.). In this passage, Schlesinger alludes to "the mother complex," a popular psychological theory that stresses the idea that overprotective mothers produce effeminacy. However, Schlesinger's rhetoric seems curiously unaware of its own contradictions: in one case, the doughfaces are fascinated by the "muscular power of the proletariat," and in another passage he cites "the broad maternal expanse of the masses." Moreover, Schlesinger uses homophobic rhetoric to describe the clandestine nature of totalitarian Communism: "it perverts politics into something secret, sweaty, and furtive, nothing so much . . . as homosexuality in a boys' school" (151).

The theme of stigmatizing the feminine, and by extension homosexuality, is not surprising; it is a typical trope in the gendered language of the 1930s and 1940s. The antifeminine bias can be found in both psychological discourses and literary culture. However, the shifting meaning of effeminacy is most confusing to the gender historian. As the previous chapter argued, in the 1930s effeminacy was inevitably associated with leisure culture and the effete male body, but it was rarely associated with left-wing literary culture. The literary author of the 1930s was typically a self-styled "man of the people," and the dominant figure of the Depression was often the down-and-out, hard-boiled proletarian hero, who appears in the novels of James T. Farrell and James M. Cain. Given this literary trend, how do we explain the fact that leisure-culture effeteness (Schlesinger's doughface) was suddenly linked to left-wing literary culture in the late 1940s? Or, more specifically, how and why does left wing become synonymous with softness and effeteness in the late 1940s?

What is most curious about this period is how the effete male body as a signifier of effeminacy is utterly transformed. The shift is most apparent in the paranoid anti-Communist rhetoric of Joe McCarthy. Much like Michael Gold, McCarthy uses homophobic tropes to attack his political opponents. One of his favorite targets is Dean Acheson, Harry Truman's secretary of state. McCarthy labels Acheson "a pompous diplomat in striped pants, with a phony British accent" who attacks Communism with "a lace handkerchief, a silk glove, and . . . a Harvard accent" (Goldman 142). In other instances, McCarthy's attack on "pinks, pansies, and punks" is so crude that journalists cannot print his words: "If you want to be against Mc-Carthy, boys [reporters], you've got to be either a Communist or a cocksucker" (Reeves 299). By the time McCarthy arrives on the scene in 1950, the homosexual is inextricably linked to leisure culture and left-wing politics. How exactly did this rhetorical shift happen, culturally and politically?

In the following discussion of the 1940s, I will trace chronologically the evolution of the hard/soft dichotomy in its various mythic guises and examine how softness becomes reconfigured in the aftermath of World War II. In short, the stigmatization of effeminacy is common to both the 1930s and the 1940s; however, what effeminacy signifies in relation to literary culture is less easy to pinpoint. I also will examine three distinct trends of the 1940s: (1) the emergence of a cultural and intellectual critique of aggressive masculinity in the aftermath of World War II; (2) a greater openness to same-sex eroticism and a more pluralistic understanding of homosexuality, a trend that has both cultural and literary dimensions; and (3) a countertrend of antifeminine and anti-homosexual discourse that is often rooted in the vehement critique of American mothers ("momism") that distinctly emerges during this time. I will examine how these opposing trends coexist and eventually collide during the late 1940s when the Kinsey Report (1948) makes the specter of homosexuality more visible in American culture. Finally, I will analyze how the Hiss-Chambers trial can be viewed as the quintessential public interrogation of soft masculinity.

Any discussion of the hard/soft dichotomy in the 1940s must begin with World War II. The masculinity of the Depression era was utterly transformed by the collective experience of the war; wartime mobilization and the drafting and enlisting of millions of American men had profound implications for the gender and social attitudes of American society. Prior to World War II, the hard-boiled ideal of the Depression—the tough-guy narrator and the macho cinematic personas of James Cagney and Humphrey Bogart—was familiar to many American males. These heroic representations of maleness were the products of literary and cinematic myths, but the experience of World War II changed this. The war experience, including hand-to-hand combat on the battlefields of Europe and the South Pacific, made hard-shell masculinity more than a state of mind: male toughness was not only an expression of braggadocio, but also a means of survival on the field of battle. Hence, the hard-boiled masculinity of the Depression era was well suited to the all-male world of the armed forces.

Much like Terman and Miles, the American military considered "courage and aggression" to be the most desirable qualities on the battlefield and important aspects of maleness. *The American Soldier,* a four-volume sociological study of the armed forces that was begun in 1943 and published in 1949–1950, documents and analyzes thousands of interviews with those who served in Europe and the South Pacific. Most important, *American Soldier* highlights the U.S. military's conception of masculinity in the 1940s and how it conveniently overlapped with combat motivation: "Conceptions of masculinity vary among different American groups, but there is a core which is common to most: courage, endurance, and toughness, lack of squeamishness when confronted with shocking or distasteful stimuli, avoidance of weakness in general, reticence about emotional or idealistic matters, and sexual competency" (Stouffer et al. 2:131). This definition of maleness closely mirrors the laconic, hard-shell masculine ideal that I discussed in the previous chapter. The authors of *American Soldier* argue that the code of masculinity ("be a man!") is "very likely to have been deeply internalized" (2:131–32). To defy the code and act with cowardice in battle could bring social censure and the "strong likelihood of being branded a 'woman,' a dangerous threat to the male personality" (2:132).

One of the most interesting parts of *American Soldier* outlines the methodology for "screening psychoneurotic soldiers." On this point, the authors posit that "a strong sex role" equals an effective soldier. Tellingly, the army also favored enlisted men who had "established satisfactory heterosexual relations" (this apparently means that the enlistee had dated women on a regular basis). The latter is regarded as evidence of virility and a healthy sex role. Like Terman and Miles, the test makers also recognize that aggression is an asset and is linked to masculine maturity. The authors note that "good [psychological] adjustment was defined as some degree of aggressiveness as indicated by getting into fights and not being afraid of fights" (Stouffer et al. 4:521). However, it is important to note that the phrase "some degree of aggressiveness" reveals that the armed forces were not as ecstatic about aggression as Terman and Miles; the authors realized that hypermasculinity could also indicate mental instability and other psychological problems.

The military's conception of masculinity also can be compared with the work of Terman and Miles in that both suggest that excessive masculinity can be useful on the field of battle. *Gung Ho* (1943), a fairly generic Hollywood film specifically made for the war effort, is concerned with the training of an elite squadron as it prepares for combat in the South Pacific.[6] During the marines' training, the film suggests that male aggression can become a virtue when it is harnessed to the spirit of camaraderie and a moral ideal—the defeat of the Japanese. Each man who volunteers for the marines' special forces discovers courage by embracing his aggressive side as a means of self-defense and a form of moral transformation. Ultimately, *Gung Ho,* which means "work together" in Chinese, attempts to represent male aggression as a healthy social ideal. Hence, a militaristic version of hypermasculinity is celebrated and revered; it becomes a common bond that allows a group of men from different ethnic and religious backgrounds to become a successful and unified group of soldiers. The act of appropriating the Chinese expression encourages the American soldiers to become one unit in battle. The military's view of aggression is similar to that of Terman and Miles in that it is viewed as a social resource that can be understood, controlled, and redirected for the betterment of all. *Gung Ho* celebrates militaristic values and a Manichaean view of the world and omits morally ambiguous situations; thus, the hypermasculine ideal is presented in a playful and positive light. *Gung Ho* does not suggest that it is at all difficult to forget acts of violence on the battlefield; one simply kills and then returns to one's former state of being without any discernible moral qualms or experience of trauma.

The theme of soft recruits being initiated into hard masculinity is also present in *Sands of Iwo Jima* (1949), an enormously popular and influential World War II film. Sergeant Stryker (John Wayne), a classic hard-nosed marine, must train a fresh group of soft and inexperienced recruits and prepare them for battle. Much like *Gung Ho,* the film documents the rigorous physical training of the marines and how their survival skills serve them well when they reach the beachheads of the South Pacific. Sergeant Stryker possesses an impenetrable hard shell, and his binge drinking and emotional reticence are consistent with his hard-boiled persona. The plot of *Sands of Iwo Jima* revolves around an Oedipal conflict between Sergeant Stryker and his adopted son, Conway. At the beginning of the film, Conway passionately rejects his father's devotion to masculine hardness and the esprit de corps of the marines. In a heated exchange, Conway, a recent father himself, tells Sergeant Stryker that he wants his newborn son to be a "considerate, intelligent, and cultured" child who reads "Shakespeare, and not the Marine Corps Training Manual." With this conflict, the film is, of course, recycling the familiar binary opposition between softness (effete leisure culture) and hardness (the working-class ruggedness of the marine corps). The conflict is finally resolved when the rebellious Conway is symbolically reconciled with Sergeant Stryker on the beach of Iwo Jima: Conroy is brought back into the fold when he finally embraces the warrior ethos and the masculine hardness of the marine corps. In contrast to Conway, Sergeant Stryker's hidden soft side is revealed only when he dies in battle. After he is shot, the remaining soldiers from his squadron read his last words, an unfinished letter to his ten-year-old son that is found in his breast pocket. The letter expresses his sensitive side and his sincere desire for moral transformation and forgiveness. After the reading of the letter, Conway emblematically adopts the voice and stern manner of the dead Sergeant Stryker as he barks out orders to the other marines. In doing so, he is finally accepting his stepfather's legacy and the hypermasculine imperative. *Sands of Iwo Jima* suggests that masculine hardness has ill effects (emotional reticence and alcoholism), but on the field of battle devotion to hardness is necessary and ultimately justified because it aids the defeat of the enemy and ensures survival.

In the years after World War II, the aggressive masculinity that was presented in Hollywood's war films was profoundly questioned and reexamined. The horrors of Auschwitz and the fifty million casualties of World War II made American psychologists and sociologists seriously reconsider their optimistic faith in male aggression as a social panacea. In fact, it would be difficult to find a postwar social scientist who did not adopt a critical view of aggression. Theodor Adorno's *The Authoritarian Mind* (1950), an influential study, examined the destructive masculinity of the Nazis and the psychology behind the German foot soldier and his blind obedience to authority. In the postwar era, excessive masculinity came to be viewed as a serious social malady. This willingness to treat aggression as a social problem represents a fundamental shift in Western cultures' understanding of maleness and the supposed link between masculinity and aggression.

The critique of male aggression was also reflected in numerous Hollywood films that examined hypermasculine behavior as a social problem. *Crossfire* (1947), based on Richard Brooks's novel *The Brick Foxhole* (1945), examines both the battle-scarred soldier's attempt to reenter civilian society and anti-Semitism within the armed forces. *Crossfire* is often compared with Elia Kazan's *Gentleman's Agreement* (1947), another message film concerned with anti-Semitism. Although *Gentleman's Agreement* won the Oscar for best picture in 1947, *Crossfire* actually presents a more sophisticated analysis of racism and of how aggressive masculinity often coincides with racism.

Crossfire follows a group of off-duty soldiers who are drinking and barhopping after the war is over. At one Washington, D.C., bar, they encounter a Jewish intellectual (Samuels), who befriends them. After much drinking, they follow Samuels home, enter his apartment uninvited, and become belligerent toward him. Montgomery (Robert Ryan), a racist ex-cop and volatile soldier, initiates a fistfight and bludgeons Samuels to death in his apartment. The film's plot revolves around a police detective's investigation of the crime and the interrogation of various soldiers who served with Montgomery during the war. At one point, Montgomery attempts to frame Mitchell, a Hollywood cartoonist turned GI, with the murder; however, the Irish American detective (Robert Young) eventually uncovers Montgomery's culpability and his virulent anti-Semitism. During the course of the police investigation, Montgomery asserts that Samuels used his money and influence to avoid military service. However, at a key moment, the truth is revealed: Samuels actually served in the South Pacific and was wounded at Okinawa. The revelation underscores Montgomery's anti-Semitism and the falsity of his suggestion that American Jews are untrustworthy and unpatriotic foreigners.

Crossfire features several speeches that dramatize the intense psychological dilemmas that soldiers face when they attempt to reenter civilian society and leave their violent battle experiences behind them. One of the film's most poignant speeches is delivered by Samuels:

> It's a funny thing isn't it? It's worse at night. I think it is maybe not having a lot of enemies to hate anymore. Maybe it's because for four years, we have been focusing our minds on winning the war peanuts [holds up a peanut from the bar]. Get it over. Eat the peanut. All at once no peanut. Now we don't know what are we supposed to do? We don't know what supposed to happen. We're too used to fighting, but we don't know what to fight. You can feel the tension in the air. A whole lot of fighting and hatred that doesn't know where to go.

In contrast to films set during World War II, *Crossfire* attempts to view the soldier's attempt to reenter civilian society. The critical gaze is directed away from the foreign enemy and placed on the American soldiers themselves and their potential for mindless aggression and racial scapegoating. The film posits that the ability to disengage from violent behavior is far more difficult than other war films would suggest, and Montgomery is a familiar postwar figure: a sociopath with a violent temperament who freely exercised his aggressive urges in war and then, when he returns home, lashes out against soft domestic "enemies"—Jews, intellectuals, and effeminate males.

Crossfire is an important film because it represents a new postwar trend in Hollywood and in mainstream American culture: the reflective war film that examines the institutions and mores that produce violent behavior and posits the notion that aggressive masculinity is a social problem. However, *Crossfire*'s critique of aggressive masculinity should not be read as an endorsement of soft masculinity. Mitchell, the Hollywood cartoonist, is the soft figure in the film; his artistic temperament and the prospect of being separated from his wife make him unfit for the armed forces. During his crisis, he seeks guidance from an older and tougher soldier, Keely (Robert Mitchum), who protects him from being framed by Montgomery and steers him to safety. Although *Crossfire* criticizes hypermasculine aggression, it affirms hardness through the presence of sturdy and reliable men who are both tough and honorable.

In contrast to the hard masculinity of Keely and the police detective, Samuels, the Jewish intellectual, is linked to leisure-culture effeminacy. In Richard Brooks's novel *The Brick Foxhole*, the theme is even more explicit: Montgomery attacks and kills a gay interior decorator who invites the off-duty soldiers to his posh apartment for drinks. Adrian Scott, the producer of *Crossfire*, knew that the brutal murder of a homosexual would be too controversial for the Motion Picture Production Code; hence, he proposed what now seems to be a curious solution: Edwards, the homosexual, becomes Samuels, the Jewish intellectual.[7] However, the notion that Jews and homosexuals are interchangeable is less bizarre when one considers the nexus of stereotypical associations linked to the Jewish intellectual—effeminacy, wealth, leisure culture, and idleness. Thus, Samuels, who wears fashionable clothes and reads books, personifies leisure-culture affluence. When Montgomery's anti-Semitic beliefs are exposed—the suggestion that Jews use their wealth and influence to avoid military service—the narrative of *Crossfire* negates the various pejorative stereotypes associated with Jews by vindicating the masculine honor of Samuels. Thus, the decision to replace a homosexual character with a Jewish one implies a tacit scale of visibility in Hollywood. After the Holocaust, some Hollywood studios (Warner Brothers, RKO) were more willing to openly criticize anti-Semitism, but certain egregious forms of softness—Edwards's overt homosexuality—were still beyond the pale.[8]

The critique of hypermasculinity in *Crossfire* was part of a larger trend of intellectual thought that emerged after World War II. In the field of sociology, Talcott Parsons's groundbreaking article "Certain Primary Sources and Patterns of Aggression in the Social Structure of the Western World" (1947) outlines a theory of "compulsory masculinity."[9] Parsons examines how many boys in Western society develop an attachment to their mothers during their childhood because they are primarily raised by their mothers. However, a problem emerges at a certain point in their development: they are socially and culturally encouraged to "be a man" and to disengage from their identification with their mother. The process of disengagement is termed "compulsory masculinity," and boys, in this phase, must adopt the cult of toughness: "they become allergic to all expressions of tender emotion" (171). Thus, "sissy" and "pussy" become two of the worst possible insults in the teenage lexicon. In each case, the epithet publicly reinforces the rejection of femininity. The soft male is particularly suspect because he is often explicitly linked to overt identification with the mother figure ("mama's boy").

Parsons also points out that a male child's rebellion against the mother figure is linked to the structure of the nuclear family. In many homes, the mother is the adult figure who "administers discipline" within the home. The mother symbolizes "good" behavior and "conformity with the expectations of the respectable adult world" (172). If "being good" is associated with the mother figure, the adolescent male often unconsciously gravitates toward the antithesis of femininity: being a "bad boy." In the milieu of teenage males, being a bad boy becomes a "positive goal" (ibid.).

The ambivalence (needing and rejecting the mother figure) that the male child experiences during this phase is an important source of anxiety that is never fully resolved in most adolescents (and men). Hence, aggression often resurfaces at various points during adolescence. Parsons notes that aggressive tendencies can be directed toward women ("all women are to blame") and toward foreigners in the form of scapegoating. Children, especially adolescents, disengage from the "feminine complex" (attachment to the mother) by adopting a scapegoat. For Parsons, the would-be scapegoat can take any number of forms—the homosexual, the foreigner, the African American, the Jew—and these groups are merely the most common examples in the 1940s. However, the ubiquitous "sissy" is the most likely person to be targeted. For the confused adolescent male, the sissy is the enemy because he is the literal embodiment of the feminine-identified male. Parsons also notes that the foreigner is particularly vulnerable because he/she exists outside the "principle [*sic*] immediate system of law and order"; hence, "aggression toward [the foreigner] does not carry the same opprobrium or immediate danger of reprisal that it does toward one's fellow-citizen" (179). Parsons's critique of aggression is also connected to nationalist discourses and patriotism; they note that military propaganda often exploits the male propensity for violence by encouraging the racial scapegoating of the foreign enemy during times of war.

Parsons's notion of racial scapegoating is evident in Arthur Laurents's Broadway play *Home of the Brave* (1945). This war drama examines the plight of a Jewish soldier, Coney (Peter Coen), who is traumatized during a dangerous mission to a Japanese-occupied island. When a fellow soldier is killed during the mission, Coney is suddenly paralyzed and must be carried to safety. The army doctor who treats Coney discovers that his paralysis is actually a psychosomatic condition that is triggered by racial scapegoating. In the play's most poignant scene, the doctor barks out anti-Semitic epithets to prompt Coney to overcome his psychological paralysis:

> DOCTOR   There's nothing wrong with your legs. They're fine, healthy legs and you can walk. You can walk. You had a shock and you didn't want to walk. But you're over the shock and now you do want to walk, don't you?
> CONEY   Yes. Yes.
> DOCTOR   Then get up and walk.
> CONEY   I—can't . . .
> DOCTOR   . . . Get up and walk you! (Pause.) You lousy Jew bastard, get up and walk! (*At that, Coney straightens up in rage. He is shaking, but he grips edge of bed and swings his feet over. He is in a white fury, and out of his anger comes this tremendous effort. Still shaking, he stands up, holds for a moment, glares at DOCTOR. Then, with his hands outstretched before him as though he is going to kill DOCTOR, he starts to walk.*) (71)

Coney's Lazarus-like recovery is directly linked to his visceral response to anti-Semitic baiting. *Home of the Brave* resembles Parsons's analysis in that racial scapegoating produces a paralyzed and bedridden body. Therapeutic restoration occurs when the patient confronts the repressed scene of trauma (the experience of racism).

In terms of the evolution of the hard/soft dichotomy, Parsons's work is important because it provides a critique of the cult of hardness and a much-needed critique of Terman and Miles's valorization of aggressive masculinity. However, Parsons's essay also reveals a psychological explanation for the hypermasculine abhorrence of the various cultural forms of soft masculinity. Compulsory masculinity—or the psychic need to attack and disavow softness—is not only a byproduct of adolescence, but also a mentality that lingers on in adulthood. However, it is important to realize that Parsons's attempt to deal with the "problem of aggression" does not imply their embrace or acceptance of soft masculinity. This distinction will become more clear when we examine the rise of soft masculinity in the 1960s. For Parsons, hardness is still an honorable ideal, and it will be the foundation for Parsons's theory of sex roles.[10]

The culture of compulsory masculinity is highly visible in the cultural life of the 1940s, and the attack on softness that surfaces in the rhetoric of the Cold War (Kennan, Schlesinger, McCarthy) can be read as a political version of the master narrative of compulsory masculinity. In the hypernationalist narrative of compulsory masculinity, sexual minorities (gays and lesbians) and political minorities (American Communists) become the scapegoats that must be excised from the body politic.[11]

The critique of hard masculinity and aggression that characterizes *Crossfire* and Parsons's theory of compulsive masculinity should be juxtaposed with the rise of homosexuality in the popular culture of the time. Although the 1940s are sometimes superficially associated with pre-Stonewall repression, the decade is actually a period of stark contrasts. For many historians of sexuality, the 1940s is a decade when homosexuality becomes more visible to the culture at large. For John D'Emilio, a gay historian and the author of *Sexual Politics, Sexual Communities: The Making of a Homosexual Minority in the United States, 1940–1970* (1983), World War II was a watershed in gay and lesbian history, "a nationwide coming out experience" for many gay members of the military (24). The war effort and mass mobilization were catalysts for a dramatic change in sexual mores, as young men from all over America were uprooted from their homes and placed in all-male environments for extended periods of time. In many cases, the sex-segregated units provided the opportunity to pursue clandestine same-sex relationships. Thus, in the larger cities where many servicemen were stationed—New York, Los Angeles, San Francisco—gay members of the military discovered the burgeoning gay enclaves, which would thrive during the postwar period of relative permissiveness.[12] Many gay servicemen from small towns and rural areas opted to remain in large cities where they could pursue same-sex relationships with greater freedom and ease.

The visibility of homosexuality in America's larger urban centers during the late 1940s was not an isolated historical trend; there were distinct repercussions in America's literary culture as well. In hindsight, the year 1948 can be seen as a watershed for gay literature. It marked the publication of the much-anticipated Kinsey Report, which documented that homosexuality was more common than anyone had expected. It witnessed the arrival of two classics of gay fiction: Truman Capote's *Other Voices, Other Rooms* and Gore Vidal's *The City and the Pillar* (both even appeared on the *New York Times* best-seller list in the spring of 1948, a totally unprecedented feat for novels that are so explicitly and unapologetically concerned with homosexuality). The same year also saw the publication of Leslie Fiedler's "Come Back to the Raft Ag'in, Huck Honey!" in the *Partisan Review*.[13]

Fiedler's essay has been recognized as a critical breakthrough that boldly addressed issues of race, gender, and sexuality at a time when many literary critics were often inclined to look the other way. Using Mark Twain's *Huckleberry Finn* as a model, Fiedler uncovers the central importance of homoeroticism and the ideal of chaste male love in the American literary tradition. In contrast to the European literary tradition's ideal of heterosexual love, Fiedler examines how many American novelists of the nineteenth century—Melville, Twain, Cooper—often nostalgically idealized same-sex relationships between two adolescent males, and he posits that chaste male love between teenagers represents a period of lost innocence and the "ultimate emotional experience." Central to Fiedler's provocative argument is the primacy of interethnic bonding that unites the hero and the racial outsider (e.g., Ishmael and Queequeg in *Moby-Dick*).

When the essay was published in the *Partisan Review*, it caused a controversy because many readers felt that Fiedler was asserting that Huck and Jim were as "queer as three dollar bills" (*Love and Death* vi). Fiedler later responded to such criticisms by pointing out that he used the term "homoerotic" because he "wanted to be quite clear" that he "was not attributing sodomy to certain literary characters or their authors" (349). However, the distinction was lost on many readers. The controversy indicates that the subject of homoeroticism in American letters in the 1940s was a fairly taboo topic that often aroused alarm and suspicion in literary circles. Like the Kinsey Report, Fiedler's essay evidences a historical moment when homosexuality is becoming more visible, more talked about, less unspeakable. In the essay, Fiedler cites the two novels mentioned above—Capote's *Other Voices, Other Rooms* and Vidal's *The City and the Pillar*—as contemporary examples of the homoerotic ideal in American literature. Fiedler has this to say about *The City and the Pillar:* "and still the dream [of homoeroticism] survives; in a recent book by Gore Vidal, an incipient homosexual, not yet aware of the implications of his feelings, indulges in the reverie of running off to sea with his dearest friend" (149). It is curious that Fiedler groups Vidal with Melville, Twain, and Cooper because the explicit homosexuality that is depicted in *The City and the Pillar* is defiantly not an example of chaste male love. Vidal's novel is striking precisely because it refuses to relegate homosexuality to the literary margins; the narrator openly engages in homosexual sex and dreams of sexually reuniting with Bob Ford, the lost love of his youth. Fiedler's misreading underscores the Freudian suggestion that homosexuality is merely an extended and somewhat delusional phase of arrested development that one eventually outgrows.

The City and the Pillar can be read as a useful historical document that provides a fairly accurate picture of gay life in the 1940s, supporting D'Emilio's contention that homosexuality was becoming increasingly visible in the aftermath of World War II. In many respects, the novel reflects on the changes in sexual mores that occurred during the war years; one character notes: "I think the war has caused a great change. Inhibitions have been broken down. All sorts of young men are trying out all sorts of new things away from home and familiar taboos" (159). The novel, a gay bildungsroman, charts Jim Willard's attempt to come to terms with his same-sex desires, his identity as a homosexual man, and his ostracism from mainstream American society. Jim represents a departure from the popular culture's conception of a homosexual because he is neither effeminate nor the product of leisure culture and affluence. In many respects, he is a fairly conventional all-American boy who plays sports, enjoys generic masculine pursuits, and is not particularly bookish or intellectual; the novel's conceit is that this rather normal specimen of American manhood happens to be sexually attracted to men. At the beginning of the novel, Jim is confused about his sexuality because he does not identify with many of the homosexuals whom he encounters: "Too many of them behaved like women. Often after he had been among them, he would study himself in a mirror to see if there was any trace of the woman in his face or manner; and he was pleased that there was not. Finally he decided that he was unique" (66).

This interior monologue contests the supposed link between homosexuality and effeminacy; at this point in the novel, Jim regards himself as "unique" because he is unable to reconcile his hard masculinity with the popular culture's insistence that homosexuals must be soft and effete. However, later in the novel, Jim encounters other homosexuals who resemble himself. Ronald Shaw, one of Jim's lovers and a famous Hollywood actor, embodies homosexual doubleness. His public identity is a Hollywood fiction: a heterosexual matinee idol who plays swashbuckling roles that emphasize his robust masculinity. Yet, privately, Shaw is a homosexual who throws opulent, clandestine parties for the gay demimonde of Hollywood. Shaw's double identity mirrors the nation's need to construct a heterosexual fantasy that suppresses same-sex passion and renders the masculine homosexual invisible. When Jim encounters Ronald Shaw, he is intrigued because Shaw's construction of a public self and a private self resembles his own dual identity. Thus, his sexual relationship with Shaw signifies the beginning of his coming out experience.

In erotic terms, Shaw expresses the novel's unequivocal preference for hard masculinity: "'I hate those others, those lousy queens,' said Shaw. 'I mean for sex. If a man likes men, he wants a man, and if he likes women, he wants a woman, so who wants a freak who's neither? It's a mystery to me'" (70). On one level, Shaw's commentary reflects the views of the larger society: his homophobic distaste for "queens" is a mirror image of the popular culture's tendency to demonize effeminacy in men. However, from another point of view, the relationship between Shaw and the narrator also functions to legitimize hard homosexuality and thereby negate the popular connection between homosexuality and effeminacy. Jim Willard's hard masculinity and his sheer ordinariness are offered as antidotes to the mythic image of the homosexual as effeminate and exotic.[14] Vidal's desire to write a novel about butch homosexuality is also visible in his stylistic choices. Wanting to avoid the so-called effete prose style that Michael Gold so abhorred, Vidal emulated the lean and masculine prose of James T. Farrell's *Studs Lonigan*.[15]

While the penchant for hardness in *The City and the Pillar* serves to demystify homosexuality and the various social myths associated with it, much of the novel's content reflects the popular psychological theories about homosexuality that are circulating in the 1940s. One of the most common ideas is the belief that homosexuality is fostered by mollycoddling mothers. This notion is alluded to in *The City and the Pillar* through the figure of Shaw, who is "abnormally" close to his mother.

The anxiety surrounding overprotective mothers is also expressed in Philip Wylie's *Generation of Vipers* (1942), a work of nonfiction that reflects many of the gender anxieties of the 1940s. Wylie's book of social criticism quickly became a best-seller during the war years, eventually sold over 180,000 copies, and remained popular well into the 1950s. The book even received the seal of respectability when the American Library Association named it one of the major nonfiction works of the first half of the twentieth century. Wylie's jeremiad is an important text in that it illuminates not only the growing fear of the feminization of men, but a psychosocial explanation for the rise of softness in American culture in the 1940s. Wylie's text elucidates many of the prejudices and myths that underpin softness and the widespread belief that the American male was becoming emasculated.

Throughout his career, Wylie remained a cantankerous and controversial figure who frequently offended people on both the left and the right. On one hand, Wylie was a traditional anti-Communist conservative who advocated a strong defense policy and nuclear weapons to ensure security for the United States. In matters of gender, Wylie is also fairly conservative, since he favored traditional gender roles for men and women and maintained that the growing feminization of men was of grave concern to the well-being of the nation. However, on social issues, Wylie considered himself to be a progressive freethinker who advocated sexual liberation, the legalization of birth control, and public instruction in sex hygiene. Today, Wylie is primarily remembered for his hyperbolic indictment of "momism" and his unvarnished expression of male anxiety. The famous critique of "mom" is contained in the "Common Women" chapter of *Generation of Vipers*. As a result of certain social and technological changes, modern women have been freed from domestic drudgery; however, this transformation is cause for alarm because women now possess an undefined role in society. For Wylie, this is a disturbing trend because both men and women are now confused about their social roles. The primary example of gender role confusion is mom. She begins as Cinderella, but after she is married she soon discovers that her Prince Charming is really just an ordinary man. After this realization, she acquires access to her husband's income and quickly transforms into the "puerile, rusting, raging creature we know as mom." At any given time, Wylie estimates, mom possesses "eighty percent of the nation's money" (213). Mom is self-righteous, sexually repressed, and tyrannical at home and in the world at large. Wylie's rhetorical thrashing of mom emphasizes her aggressive side: "she is a middle-aged puffin with an eye like a hawk that has just seen a rabbit twitch far below. She is about twenty-five pounds overweight, with no sprint, but sharp heels" (201). Wylie also highlights her capacity for economic waste: "In a thousand of her there is not sex appeal enough to budge a hermit ten paces off a rock ledge. She none the less spends several hundreds a year on permanents and transformations, pomades, cleansers, rouges, lipsticks, and the like—and fools nobody but herself" (ibid.). For Wylie, America was "a matriarchy in fact if not in declaration" in which "women raped the man" (200).

However, it is important to note that Wylie's attack on mom is not one-sided; he blames men and American society at large for participating in the cultish veneration of mom:

> Meanwhile, megaloid momworship has got completely out of hand. . . . Mom is everywhere and everything and damned near everybody, and from her depends all the rest of the U.S. disguised as good old mom, dear old mom, sweet old mom, your loving mom, and so on, she is the bride at every funeral and the corpse at every wedding. Men live for her and die for her, dote upon her and whisper her name as they pass away, and I believe she has now achieved in the hierarchy of miscellaneous articles, a spot next to the bible and the flag, being reckoned part of both in a way. . . . [N]o great man or brave . . . ever stood in our halls and pronounced the one indubitably most-needed American verity: "Gentlemen, mom is a jerk." (198)

At the root, Wylie's assault springs from the notion that the American male is in grave peril because he has been "emasculated" by mom: "the mealy look of men today is the result of momism and so is the pinched and baffled fury in the eyes of womankind" (210). Wylie and many of his followers argued that mothers everywhere were smothering male children with affection and effectively feminizing the American male (the term "mama's boy" echoes the tenets of momism).[16] In Wylie's scenario, these feminized boys become the "emasculated males" of the future.

Wylie's argument against the feminization of the American male was predicated on the notion that mom is incapable of using critical reasoning or even higher education: "[mom knows] nothing about medicine, art, science, religion, law, sanitation, civics, hygiene, psychology, morals, history, geography, poetry, literature, or any other topic except the all consuming one of momism" (203–204). On one hand, Wylie's attempt to link "poetry," "morals," and "literature" to the masculine realm flatly contradicts Terman and Miles's suggestion that the latter are irretrievably feminine. Nonetheless, Wylie's contention that women are incapable of reason is consistent with Terman and Miles's attempt to establish a scientific link between the feminine and the emotional while maintaining that rationality and logic are the "natural" province of the masculine male. However, after reading through Wylie's rhetorical outbursts, one gets the sense that he is really unnerved by the notion of female masculinity and the idea that women are capable of masculine aggression and of wielding power over men. *Generation of Vipers* contains an apparent contradiction: if mom is capable of female masculinity and aggression, why does she necessarily make her sons soft and feminine? Why don't her sons inherit her aggressive and mean-spirited side? Underneath the bombast, *Generation of Vipers* is fundamentally an expression of male anxiety: Wylie is nostalgic for an epoch when there was no gender confusion—a time when men and women knew their proper gender roles. Momism, or female masculinity, is deemed dangerous because it upsets the "rational" and "natural" gender order of society.[17]

Wylie's portrait of the emasculation of the American male is important in that it attempts to shift the blame to mom, and thus softness becomes the result of male-female relations within the domestic sphere. The distinction is crucial because Wylie's genealogy of softness does not suggest that the emasculated American male is the product of too much leisure culture or consumer abundance. *Generation of Vipers,* unlike Schlesinger's *The Vital Center,* does not imply that softness has any relation to intellectuals or left-wing culture. Although Wylie connects momism to the emasculation of the American male, he does not directly suggest that momism produces homosexuality; however, many of the social critics who followed Wylie were more than willing to make the connection.

Edward Strecker, a psychiatric consultant to the Army and Navy Surgeons and the author of *Their Mothers' Sons: The Psychiatrist Examines an American Problem* (1946), posits that mothers were ultimately responsible for the great number of psychoneurotic rejections by the Selective Service Administration. Strecker also alleges that "dear old mom" was responsible for a large number of "psychoneurotic breakdowns" during training camp and for soldiers who "cracked" under combat stress. Strecker includes alarming statistics to back up his claims: "500,000 men resorted to any device, however shameful, even to the wearing of female clothing" to avoid being drafted. Moreover, the author concludes that some 1,825,000 men were rejected as "psychoneurotic cases" and that another 600,000 had to be discharged a few weeks into their service for similar reasons. For Strecker, this social problem is easily diagnosed: American mothers impede masculine development by smothering their sons with affection. Mom derives emotional satisfaction from "keeping her children paddling about in a kind of amniotic fluid rather than letting them swim away with bold and decisive strokes of maturity" (31). Although Strecker attempts to adopt a more scientific tone than that of Wylie, his conclusions are equally hyperbolic and anxiety-ridden. Like many other psychiatrists in the 1940s, Strecker is deeply concerned about the apparent rise of homosexuality in American society. Although he is willing to concede that homosexuality can "be rooted in biological deviations," he also concludes that prudish moms often poison their sons' minds "against normal, mature, heterosexual living" (130). Thus, the male child may eventually turn to homosexuality "in his need for some sex outlet, as the lesser evil" (131). Although Strecker's concerns sound alarmist and ill-informed today, his ideas about gender were often accepted in medical and psychological circles. For psychologists and military authorities, soft masculinity was a perplexing social malady that the nation had to address in order to remain a dominant global power.[18]

The widespread obsession with proper childrearing and mollycoddling mothers reflects the growing anxiety about the various forms of soft masculinity that were emerging in the 1940s. With the publication of Kinsey's *Sexual Behavior in the Human Male* (1948), Wylie's and Strecker's worst fears were confirmed: homosexuality was more widespread in American life than anyone had hitherto imagined. Kinsey's research is significant because it challenged the traditional conception of male sexuality. It served as a corrective to the rigid sex typing of Terman and Miles and their obsessive attempt to establish unquestionable differences between males and females. While Terman and Miles attempted to envision a society that would nourish hypermasculine behavior, the Kinsey Report attempted to destigmatize male sexuality and treat it as a biological act. As a whole, Kinsey's scientific study empirically established that male sexuality—and, by extension, masculinity—is far more diverse and adventurous than conventional society had hitherto imagined. The most disturbing discoveries—the claim that 37 percent of the male population have homosexual experiences at some point in their lives and that 10 percent of the general population is actively homosex-

ual—sent shock waves through middle America, and Kinsey himself
was assailed by politicians, civic leaders, and theologians.[19]

In one sense, the findings of the Kinsey Report undermined
the puritanical sensibilities of postwar America; however, they also
indirectly represented a challenge to the hard-shell ideal of masculinity that dominated the popular culture of the 1930s and early 1940s.
Kinsey's research represented a significant breakthrough because it
demystified the hard/soft binary. Kinsey's chapter on homosexuality challenged the stereotypical images of homosexuals by pointing
out seemingly incongruous social facts: in "the most remote rural
areas there is considerable homosexual activity among lumbermen,
cattlemen, prospectors, miners, hunters and others engaged in out-
of-door occupations" (631). Kinsey noted that the homosexual activity of the outdoorsmen "rarely conflicts with their heterosexual
relations" (ibid.). *Sexual Behavior in the Human Male* also posited
an alternative view of the sexuality of the Old West: "it is the type
of homosexual experience which the explorer and pioneer may have
had in their histories" (ibid.). Kinsey's research was groundbreaking
in that it challenged society's limited understanding of working-class
sexualities and identified the existence of a new sexual paradigm:
bisexual and homosexual masculinities that had little to do with
leisure-culture effeminacy.

Like Vidal's *The City and the Pillar, Sexual Behavior in the Human Male* attempts to break the mythic link between homosexuality and effeminacy that had been posited by Terman and Miles. In
his critique of the hard/soft binary, Kinsey identifies the physical
stereotypes that social scientists generally employ in their studies:
"it is commonly believed that homosexual males are rarely robust
physically, are uncoordinated or delicate in their movements, [or that
they generally possess] fine skins, high-pitched voices, obvious hand
movements, a female carriage of the hips, and peculiarities of walking
gaits [that] are supposed accompaniments of a preference for a male
as a sexual partner" (637). Similarly, Kinsey also challenges the idea
that homosexuals universally possess shared psychological traits:
"it is commonly believed that the homosexual male is artistically
sensitive, emotionally unbalanced, temperamental to the point of

being unpredictable, difficult to get along with, and undependable in meeting specific obligations" (ibid.). However, one of Kinsey's boldest claims is to challenge the foundational assumptions of the hard/soft binary: "[m]ales do not represent two discrete populations, heterosexual and homosexual. The world is not to be divided into sheep and goats" (639). In place of the homosexual/heterosexual binary, Kinsey posits that our society's understanding of male sexuality is shrouded in mystification: "only the human mind invents categories and tries to force facts into separated pigeon-holes. The living world is a continuum in each and every one of its aspects. The sooner we learn this concerning human sexual behavior the sooner we shall reach a sound understanding of the realities of sex" (ibid.).

To counterbalance the assumption that all males necessarily fall into two categories (heterosexual/homosexual), Kinsey introduces a 0–6 rating scale that allows for bisexuality and a more pluralistic conception of male sexuality. At one end ("6") is the exclusively homosexual male and at the opposite end of the spectrum is his exclusively heterosexual equivalent ("0"). Thus, Kinsey has come up with a scientific paradigm that posits that male sexuality is not a static and fixed object, but rather a complex and mutable continuum of multiple possibilities.[20] Kinsey's 0–6 scale offers an alternative narrative of male sexuality and masculinity that attempts to deconstruct the crude and often monolithic assumptions of the hard/soft binary.

After *Sexual Behavior in the Human Male* was published, the "unspeakable" became speakable in public discourse, but, unfortunately, the conversation was not always an enlightened one. Kinsey's attempt to demystify homosexuality and free it from its association with effeminacy was only partially successful. The various attacks on Kinsey from the pulpit and in the press suggested that the culture at large was not prepared for many of Kinsey's radical discoveries about male sexuality. Thus, his pleas for greater tolerance in the legal prosecution of homosexuals and a more open-ended conception of male sexuality often fell on deaf ears. Predictably, the book helped to fuel a cultural backlash that would have repercussions during the late 1940s and throughout the following decade. In 1950, as a result of McCarthyism, ninety-one homosexual employees of the State Department were dismissed from their jobs for "moral turpitude." It is ironic that

Kinsey's findings in *Sexual Behavior in the Human Male* were used in a senatorial report documenting that homosexuality was a growing social and moral problem in American society.[21]

If 1948 was a watershed year for the visibility of homosexuality in American culture, 1949 can be read as the beginning of the backlash against soft masculinity and the "doughfaces" in government. In the genderspeak of the Cold War, the biggest doughface of them all was Alger Hiss. On the surface, the Hiss-Chambers trial of the late 1940s was concerned with Communist "penetration" of the U.S. State Department. Alger Hiss, a former official in the Franklin Roosevelt administration, was accused by Whittaker Chambers, an ex-Communist operative and spy, of passing government documents to the Soviet Union in the 1930s. Historians typically describe the trial as a referendum on New Deal liberalism and as an ideological struggle over national security at the beginning of the Cold War. Chambers appealed to the nationalist wing of the Republican Party, which was fiercely anti-Communist and anti-elitist, while Hiss, a symbol of New Deal liberalism, garnered support from progressive circles and the educated middle classes. While these political concerns were certainly important, many historians have paid insufficient attention to the gendered implications of the trial and how the trial was, in many respects, an ideological battle that was constructed through conflicting narratives of soft masculinity that ultimately implied that certain soft individuals could not be trusted with government secrets.[22]

The various details from Hiss's personal life that emerged during the trial—his Ivy League education, his pressed Irish linen suits, his fondness for cocker spaniels, and his passion for bird-watching—seemed to suggest that Hiss was a stereotypical case of the soft male who was susceptible to Communist penetration. Moreover, Chambers, according to various rumors circulating in the media, was viewed as Hiss's desperate and jilted homosexual lover who was hell-bent on destroying Hiss's reputation. In the words of one media insider at *Time* magazine, the case was a "battle between two queers" (Tanenhaus 579). These rumors surfaced again in Hiss's *Recollections of a Life* (1988), a memoir that was published nearly forty years after the trial. Hiss alleges that Chambers was a "closet homosexual" and "a psychopath" and that Chambers had never forgiven him for refus-

ing his sexual advances: "my rebuff to him wounded him in a way I did
not realize at the time. I think the rebuff, coupled with his political
paranoia, inspired his later machinations against me" (208).

Like Hiss, Chambers, a confessed ex-Communist, also had no-
table soft credentials. During the 1930s, he had been an intellectual,
a bohemian, a clandestine bisexual, a translator of *Bambi*, and the au-
thor of several proletarian short stories that were featured in the *New
Masses* in 1931. In a private pre-trial questioning session with the FBI,
Chambers confessed to homosexuality and Communist subversion.
Chambers described the testimony as "my darkest personal secret."
An account of Chambers's closed-door confession is provided in Sam
Tanenhaus's biography of the anti-Communist crusader:

> Since that time [1933–1934] and continuing up to the year 1938, I engaged
> in numerous homosexual activities both in New York and Washington,
> D.C. At first I would engage in these activities whenever by accident the
> opportunity presented itself. However, after a while the desire became
> greater and I actively sought out the opportunities for homosexual
> relationships. (344)

Tanenhaus notes that when Chambers broke with Communism, he
also "managed to break" himself of his homosexual "'tendencies'"
(345). And a decade later, Chambers said, though not "completely
immune to such stimuli . . . my self-control is complete," and "I have
lived a blameless and devoted life as a husband and father" (344–45).
Chambers felt the need to confess because he thought that the Hiss
defense might decide to raise the homosexual issue as a smear tactic. However, Hiss's defense attorneys never played the queer card
because they were afraid that the homosexual allegations might
backfire and be used against their client. Although homosexuality
was never directly mentioned during the trial, the tacit references to
"softness" were not ignored by the media nor by the general public
that watched the trial on television. To many, the private and lurid
act of homosexuality was considered similar to espionage and the
act of betraying one's country: both involved clandestine and furtive
behavior and a transgression against the shared values of the nation.
Although Chambers's homosexuality never surfaced in the actual
trial, his testimony about his years as a subversive and a Communist

spy suggested that soft types could not be trusted with government secrets.

When Chambers published his autobiography, *Witness* (1952), he omitted all references to his homosexuality and was careful to emphasize his intimate and devoted relationship to his wife and children. In the preface, Chambers describes the epiphany that led to his moral and philosophical break with atheistic Communism:

> I date my break from a very casual happening. I was sitting in our apartment on St. Paul Street in Baltimore. It was shortly before we moved to Alger Hiss's apartment in Washington. My daughter was in her high chair. I was watching her eat. She was the most miraculous thing that had ever happened in my life. I liked to watch her even when she smeared porridge on her face or dropped it meditatively on the floor. My eye came to rest on the delicate convolutions of her ear—those intricate, perfect ears. The thought passed through my mind: "No, those ears were not created by any chance coming together of atoms in nature (the Communist view). They could have been created only by immense design." (16)

On one level, Chambers's revelation is merely an example of the philosophical argument for design—that the perfection of the human form is proof of a supreme being—but the epiphany also suggests another narrative: moral transformation through the act of embracing the heterosexual ideal of procreation and fatherhood. Throughout *Witness*, Chambers continually emphasizes his loving relationship to his wife and children and how his honest work on the farm restored his moral and religious faith in God. Chambers's interest in his child's ear also perhaps alludes to the notion of listening and being listened to; his fascination evokes the world of surveillance, his past participation in covert operations, and his perpetual fear of being found out.

The airbrushing of Chambers's homosexual past is not surprising, given the moral climate of the 1950s; thus, it is logical that Chambers would stage and perform a socially acceptable form of heterosexual masculinity for the mainstream readers of his anti-Communist memoir. More important, however, is that Chambers is also tacitly demonstrating a familiar Cold War narrative: softness, and by extension Communist sympathies, can be overcome through self-discipline and perseverance. This narrative of self-improvement was the story that the right wing wanted to hear because it reinforced

the conflation of Communism and homosexuality and the perception that the Communist was a social deviant who must be exposed
and rooted out through the humiliating ritual of public confession.

In his autobiographical writings, Chambers expressed his keen
awareness that the mythology of the hard/soft binary could be used
as an effective rhetorical tool in his political writings. In his hard
phase in the early 1930s, Chambers omitted references to his middle-
class upbringing and recast himself as a masculine proletarian writer.
When Chambers was first published (in the *New Masses* in July 1931),
the following caption appeared below his author photo: "Boyhood in
eastern United States, Youth as periodically 'vagrant laborer' in deep
South, Plains, Northwest. Brief Columbia college experience, ending
with atheistic publication. Formerly member Industrial Union, 310
I.W.W. Joined revolutionary movement 1925" (also cited in Tanenhaus 73). The references to "vagrant laborer" and the I.W.W. were
proffered to butch up his image as a worker-writer and man of the
people. *Witness* includes demonizing portraits of soft Communists.
Though Chambers makes no references to his own homosexuality,
he discredits his former comrades by deliberately highlighting their
soft masculinity:

> Noel [a Communist colleague of Chambers] was a big, fair, effete, rub-
> bery man, who lolled in his chair or over his desk, collapsed in a kind of
> hereditary fatigue, or as if he had recently been boned. With me he was
> so grossly upper class that I suspected him [of] being a caricature of the
> type, and doing it rather amusingly, for he had a catlike grace and craft.
> . . . A hundred patrician Noels must have toddled out of the public baths
> in the warm dusks of dying Rome, with nothing more real on their minds
> than supper and the vomitorium. (51)

Chambers's over-the-top portrait of Noel, a supposedly typical
American Communist, is laden with all of the trappings of effete
masculinity. Much like Schlesinger's doughface or Michael Gold's
caricature of Thornton Wilder, Noel's body type is not simply soft,
but "rubbery," flaccid, and boneless. The punning reference to having
"been boned" also suggests the not-so-subtle theme of anal penetration. Furthermore, the hyper-softness that is evoked contains all the
stock clichés of leisure-culture queerness: Roman baths, decadence,
a life devoid of labor ("hereditary fatigue") and devoted to sensual

appetite ("supper and the vomitorium"). For Chambers, American Communism is a cabal of homosexuals and effete intellectuals who are, more often than not, the sons of wealth and privilege. Thus, for Chambers, the political, the sexual, and the religious are necessarily, and cleverly, intertwined. When he makes his famous break with Communism, he is a wayward sinner who is renouncing his life of debauchery and returning to the devout religious faith of his youth.

The Hiss-Chambers trial represents a crucial turning point in the American public's understanding of soft masculinity and Communism. It signifies the historical moment when the stereotype of softness becomes manifest and culturally embedded. Effeminate masculinity is no longer simply proof of one's privileged background; instead, it becomes shorthand for the nexus of softness, queerness, and the specter of Communist subversion. In the coming decade of the 1950s, it would be increasingly difficult to separate homosexuality from Communism. For many ardent anti-Communists, the Hiss-Chambers case represented a rhetorical victory because it demonstrated that sexual deviancy and political subversion went hand in hand, and it paved the way for McCarthy's attacks on homosexuals and Communists alike.

While Alger Hiss was imprisoned for perjury in the early 1950s, right-wing ideologues coined a new term for the liberal intellectual: the egghead. In political circles, it acquired a certain degree of popularity as a term of abuse. In an article for the *Freeman*, a forerunner of the *National Review*, Louis Bromfield, a conservative social critic, even offered a definition:

> Egghead: A person of spurious intellectual pretensions, often a professor or the protégé of a professor. Fundamentally superficial. Over-emotional and feminine in reactions to any problem. Supercilious and surfeited with conceit and contempt for the experience of more sound and able men. . . . A doctrinaire supporter of Middle European socialism as opposed to Greco-French-American ideas of democracy and liberalism. . . . An anemic bleeding heart. (158)

Bromfield's definition can be read as Hiss's political obituary. The New Deal intellectual is turned into an object of ridicule. Bromfield is careful to emphasize how the liberal intellectual is necessarily an effeminate male. The "over-emotional" egghead is juxtaposed with the ideal of resolute masculine hardness ("the experience of more sound and able men"). Thus, the male body of the intellectual becomes the site of softness: mushy, pliable, and porous. The intellectual's most identifiable characteristic is his "bleeding heart," a synecdoche for the affective response. In Bromfield's estimation, Germany (because of Marx) is depicted as the epicenter of soft masculinity; this is curious because for the next generation of right-wing critics, France will be the locus classicus of soft masculinity. The attack on the egghead also appears in McCarthy's anti-Communist rhetoric; in one speech, he rails against "phony egg-sucking liberals." The curious phrase resonates because it encapsulates the various themes of softness: misogyny merged with homophobia. The liberal intellectual is revealed to be a pseudo-man ("phony") because he is simultaneously linked to the feminine embryo and the homosexual act of fellatio.

The progression from the doughface to the egghead embodies not only various degrees of mushiness, but also levels of maturity. The doughface is young and naïve. When he grows up, he becomes an egghead intellectual. The cultural and political Right is empowered by attacking the Left with gender-coded epithets and by associating it with leisure-culture affluence. This attack could not be made in the 1930s when the left-wing intellectuals remained closely aligned with protest movements that were in harmony with the common man. However, in the postwar era, the right wing was successful at associating intellectuals with Communism and fellow traveling. The American Left was vulnerable to attack because many intellectuals were attracted to Soviet Communism in the 1930s and 1940s. Moreover, the Hiss-Chambers trial and the Rosenberg trial were public inquisitions that ultimately reinforced the right-wing belief that intellectuals are untrustworthy ("un-American") and prone to disloyalty.

The stigma of intellectualism and effeminacy surface again in the 1952 election when Adlai Stevenson is mocked as effeminate in the popular press; his "fruity speeches" feature "tea cup words" that are reminiscent of a "genteel spinster who can never forget that she got an A in elocution at Miss Smith's finishing school" (qtd. in Hofstadter 227).[23] The fact that Stevenson was a civilian during both wars also did not help matters. Furthermore, the Republicans' selection of Dwight Eisenhower, a former football player and four-star general, promoted the pro-masculine credentials of the GOP.

It is interesting to note that the Right's critique of intellectuals coincides with the intellectual Left's reexamination of hypermasculine aggression (Adorno, Parsons, Marcuse, etc.). In most cases, the Right of the 1950s is less concerned with the problem of hypermasculine aggression and more comfortable asserting its manliness and its open disdain for bookish masculinity. In 1952, a partisan supporter of Eisenhower offered the following assessment: "Eisenhower knows more about world conditions than any other two men in the country, and he didn't obtain his knowledge through newspapers and books either" (qtd. in Hofstadter 227). In the right-wing rhetoric of the 1950s, manly experience trumps book learning. Although this pro-Eisenhower argument echoes Schlesinger's liberal critique of the bookish doughface, the Right was far more comfortable than the Left with anti-intellectual rhetoric.[24]

With the rise of the Right in the early 1950s, soft masculinity appeared to be thoroughly discredited; however, the right-wing prophecies about the death of soft, affect-centered masculinity were certainly premature. Soft masculinity would be dramatically reclaimed and reinvented by the various youth cultures that were beginning to emerge in the 1950s.

3

Highbrows and Lowbrows: Squares, Beats, Hipsters, White Negroes, New Critics, and American Literary Culture in the 1950s

In 1945, Alfred Kinsey, the not-yet-famous sexologist, visited the respectable and staid Lincoln Hotel in midtown Manhattan. Kinsey was busy gathering sexual histories for his report *Sexual Behavior in the Human Male*, which would be published with great fanfare in 1948. During his stay in New York, he encountered the colorful Herbert Huncke, a hustler, small-time thief, and cohort of Allen Ginsberg and Jack Kerouac. Kinsey provided Huncke with cash ($2.25 per interviewee), and Huncke supplied him with subjects for his research: "thieves, pickpockets, a few stick-up men, prostitutes male and female" (Huncke qtd. in Gathorne-Hardy 239). In addition, during his six-week stay at the Lincoln, Kinsey gathered sexual histories from Ginsberg, Kerouac, Burroughs, and many others. However, after watching a seemingly endless parade of social misfits enter the lobby, the hotel manager decided enough was enough: he would not have Kinsey "undressing people's minds in his hotel" any longer (Gathorne-Hardy 239). The hotel manager formally asked Kinsey and his associate Wardell Pomeroy to conduct their research elsewhere; Kinsey and Pomeroy obliged and soon found lodging at the local Salvation Army.

The serendipitous meeting between Kinsey and the Beats marks an important cultural convergence for historians of masculinity. The Beats were literary artists who espoused an alternative form of masculinity that would ultimately pose a challenge to the reticent, hard-boiled ideal of maleness that had dominated the Depression era. In a similar fashion, Kinsey's report would challenge the existing understanding of male sexuality and serve as a corrective to the rigid sex typing of Terman and Miles and their obsessive attempt to establish absolute differences between men and women. Kinsey's study attempted to destigmatize sexuality and treat it as a biological act; thus, his work empirically established that human sexuality—and, by extension, masculinity and femininity—is far more diverse and adventurous than conventional society had hitherto imagined.

To the reserved and laconic men of Kinsey's generation, the confessional mode and openly discussing one's sexuality were both unseemly and unmanly. However, Kinsey's innovative interviewing techniques managed to overcome these moral and social obstacles. The promise of complete confidentiality and anonymity—no names were recorded with the sexual histories—and the interviewer's kind and reassuring manner encouraged interviewees to feel open and comfortable during the questioning. For some male interviewees, the pretext of scientific rigor made the confessional mode socially acceptable by detaching it from its unseemly and feminine associations. Kinsey's conclusions ultimately challenged the existing sexual mores by suggesting that alternative forms of sexuality—homosexuality, masturbation, even animal contacts—exist and are more common than mainstream society imagined or wanted to admit.

Much like the findings of the Kinsey Report, the Beat movement of the 1950s would also pose a challenge to the hard-shell varieties of masculinity that dominated the Depression and the World War II eras. However, before we can fully understand the Beats and the other alternative conceptions of masculinity that emerged in the 1950s, it is necessary to discuss the nebbish counterpart of the Beats:

the square. The square is crucial because the Beats, as a social and cultural movement, consciously position themselves in opposition to the square.

Who is the square? Why does he/she appear in the cultural landscape of the 1950s? According to the *Oxford English Dictionary*, the term "square" first appears in 1944, and it indicates, "in musician's jargon, anyone who is not cognizant of the aesthetic beauties of true jazz." Thus, the square is essentially a clueless philistine. In other definitions, the term is associated with someone, presumably an engineering student, who often carries a slide rule. The pejorative expression also denotes a person who abstains from drinking, smoking, and recreational drugs and who does not appreciate jazz (and, later, rock music). Although the square could be from any social class, he/she is usually from the middle class.

However, for Norman Mailer, the square is not merely abstemious. In *The White Negro* (which I will discuss later in this chapter), the term is also synonymous with the notion of conformity; the square is specifically linked to the growth of suburbia, tract homes, and the rise of consumer culture in the postwar years. The term's geometric definition ("a rectangle having four equal sides") suggests that a square lacks unique characteristics and is presumably at home in Levittown, the ubiquitous symbol of postwar conformity. In racial terms, the square is usually white, and in *The White Negro* Mailer suggests that the embrace of hipness—racial otherness—allows one to overcome the affliction of squareness.

The square also makes an appearance, though not by name, in several important studies of the 1950s. He is certainly lurking in David Riesman's *The Lonely Crowd* (1950), C. Wright Mills's *White Collar* (1953), and William Whyte's *The Organization Man* (1956). In *The Lonely Crowd*, a best-seller, Riesman is deeply concerned about the contemporary man's penchant for conformity and the apparent loss of autonomy in the corporate world and in society at large. *The Lonely Crowd* focuses on nineteenth-century "inner-directed" men, who are tradition-bound and who internalize a clear set of goals and moral values. They are strong-willed men who tame frontiers and build empires. The inner-directed male's fidelity to traditional mores often results in a "rigid" social character and a "hardened" personality. Thus, in masculinist terms, the inner-directed person is firm, resolute, and ultimately less dependent on peer approval. In contrast, the "other-directed" man of the younger generation of the 1940s and 1950s is considered more socially malleable and therefore more influenced by the mass media and advertising. The other-directed male is often a square (in the Maileresque sense of the word) because he depends upon peer approval and is typically afraid of standing out from the crowd. Riesman's tacit preference for the hard, inner-directed man can only be detected when one examines his Spenglerian phrasing: the other-directed male of the postwar era is linked to "incipient decline" (17). While Riesman intends his terms to be neutral, it is evident that the other-directed male is ultimately less attractive, less vital, and less manly. Both Riesman and Whyte make the a priori assumption that American individualism and the Protestant work ethic are in a general state of decline in the 1950s, and they both argue that the deterioration is a byproduct of the softening of the American male.

For Riesman, the rise of the affluent society is central to the social transformation of the American male of the twentieth century. An individual's relation to consumer goods roughly determines whether he will be inner-directed or other-directed. The hardness of the inner-directed individual is directly attributed to the psychology of scarcity of the nineteenth century, when people had limited access to consumer goods and labor-saving technologies. The transition to an other-directed society is marked by the emergence of "abundance psychology" and the "wasteful luxury consumption of leisure and of the surplus product" (19). Hence, the other-directed individual tends to be more "metropolitan," more "upper-middle class," and more attached to consumer goods. The latter generalizations about the other-directed male invoke the familiar Veblenian prejudice against leisure-culture affluence and the notion that access to the consumer culture's luxuries *softens* the rugged individual and makes him less productive and more pliable.[1]

The gendered difference between the inner-directed male and the other-directed male is even more apparent in "Ten Years Later," a follow-up essay published in 1960. Here, Riesman notes that most readers prefer the "inner-directed cowboy" to the "other-directed advertising man." This preference indicates to Riesman that many readers feel that the inner-directed man is more of a rugged individualist and an independent thinker, while the other-directed man is more soft, pliable, and molded by consumer culture. Riesman also adds, "no lover of toughness and invulnerability should forget the gains made possible by the considerateness, sensitivity, and tolerance that are among the positive qualities of other-direction" (xx). Hence, Riesman encourages readers to see the positive aspects of other-directed maleness. For our purposes, this passage is important because it reveals how Riesman's study was often read through the lens of masculinity and how conceptions of hard and soft masculinity influence his sociological analysis. The inner-directed male is, not surprisingly, associated with the "cowboy," a perennial symbol of masculine prowess, while the other-directed male is associated with the fickle and superficial "advertising man" and the soft virtues of "sensitivity" and "tolerance." Riesman's analysis is prophetic because the latter virtues are often associated with the counterculture of the 1960s. Riesman's use of masculine nouns and pronouns throughout his book ("cowboy," "advertising man") is not accidental; as Barbara Ehrenreich has pointed out, all women are assumed to be other-directed—fickle and mutable—by nature. Thus, there are no inner-directed women to speak of in Riesman's study.[2]

Although Riesman tries to encourage the reader to view the positive virtues of other-directed maleness in "Ten Years Later," his rhetoric and phraseology reveal his tacit preference for inner-directed maleness. When Riesman alludes to the other-directed "advertising man," he is offering a thinly veiled critique of the culture of the square and his slavish devotion to consumerism.

The square is also central to Mills's *White Collar*, an important sociological study of the emerging lower-middle class. Mills notes that, in the 1850s, 75 percent of the American population were farmers, but by 1950 agricultural workers only made up 10 percent of the population. For Mills, the urbanization of the American male signifies the rise of the "white-collar" worker, who is basically an emasculated figure: "the hero as victim, the small creature who is acted upon but does not act, who works along unnoticed in somebody's back office or store, never talking loud, never taking a stand" (xii). Like Whyte and Riesman, Mills is pessimistic about the rise of the white-collar class and its role in American society: "The decline of the free entrepreneur and the rise of the dependent employee on the American scene has paralleled the decline of the independent individual and the rise of the little man in the American mind" (ibid.). For Mills, a leftist critic of capitalism, the white-collar square is alienated and socially malleable: "Newly created in a harsh time of creation, white collar man has no culture to lean upon except the contents of a mass society that has shaped him and seeks to manipulate him to its own ends" (xvi). His alienation also makes him "excellent material for synthetic molding at the hands of popular culture—print, film, radio, and television" (ibid.). Although the white-collar class outnumbers the proletariat, "no one is enthusiastic about them, and like political eunuchs, they themselves are without potency and without enthusiasm for the urgent political clash" (xviii).

Like Riesman and Mills, Whyte is also concerned about the problem of conformity and the softening of the American male. In Whyte's influential study of the suburban-bound white-collar class, the faceless "organization man" certainly possesses some square-ish tendencies. Most notably, for Whyte, the rise of the corporation and the modern bureaucratic state have "stifled initiative and native ingenuity" and produced widespread social conformity (5). The collective ethos of the bureaucracy—whether capitalist or Communist—leads to "soft-minded denial" and a general loss of masculine vigor and drive (13). In broad terms, the rise of the organization indicates the decline of the Protestant work ethic that has made America a successful nation. Whyte's final appeal to the reader is presented in masculinist terms; the organization man is an emasculated figure who must ultimately stand up to the organization: "he must *fight* the organization. . . . But fight he must, for the demands for his surrender are constant and powerful, and the more he has come to like the life of the organization the more difficult does he find it to resist these demands, or even to recognize them" (404). Although Whyte's rhetoric appears radical in this passage, he is also quick to point out that his study is not simply for bohemians and social rebels: "This book is not a plea for non-conformity," for "the man who drives a Buick

Special and lives in a ranch-type house just like hundreds of other ranch-type houses can assert himself as effectively and courageously against his particular society as the bohemian against his particular society" (11). Thus, in a way, Whyte's book is meant to help the square who has quietly sold out and surrendered his individuality to the collective ethos of the organization. However, unlike Riesman and Mills, Whyte does not suggest that the organization man's fondness for consumer goods poses a particular problem. Whyte declares in his introduction, "There will be no strictures against ranch wagons, television sets, or grey flannel suits . . . [because] they are irrelevant to the main problem, and, furthermore, there's no harm in them" (10). Unlike Mailer, Whyte does not suggest that consumer goods have a feminizing effect on the square.

Just as the white-collar worker/square is certainly a popular figure in the sociological literature of the early 1950s, this much-maligned figure also has many literary precursors. Most notably, the rise of the square and the problem of social conformity are prefigured in two classic American dramas of the 1940s: Tennessee Williams's *The Glass Menagerie* (1945) and Arthur Miller's *Death of a Salesman* (1949). The plays of Williams and Miller are interesting because they present a literary diagnosis of the square. They also attempt to present alternative narratives within their plays that imply a critique of the square.

The Glass Menagerie, written some twelve years before *The White Negro,* contains a literary progenitor of the hipster/Beat poet (Tom Wingfield) and a portrait of the conformist square and the society that produces him. In the stage directions, Williams describes the Wingfield apartment as "one of those vast hive-like conglomerations of cellular living units that . . . are symptomatic of the impulse of this largest and fundamentally enslaved section of American society to avoid fluidity and differentiation and to exist and function as one interfused mass of automatism" (1). Williams suggests that modernism and industrial capitalism have made the American lower-middle classes robotic and emasculated, and he also suggests the notion that "fluidity" and individuality are concomitant with nonconformity and social rebellion. The conflict between the self and the forces of external society is embodied in the figure of Tom Wingfield, a part-time poet and full-time employee of Continental Shoemakers. The play revolves around Tom's inner conflicts: his desires to escape both his mundane existence as a warehouse clerk and his familial obligation to his mother and sister, who desperately need his economic support. The latter conflict is depicted but never fully resolved at the end of the play; we learn that Tom eventually leaves St. Louis, but we do not know how his sister and mother manage to survive without his income. While Tom is certainly plagued with moral doubts, he also wrestles with his inner need to achieve autonomy over his life; this struggle inevitably places him in conflict with the conformist society that he encounters each day.

The indictment of square-ish conformity is also conveyed through his conflict with his puritanical mother, Amanda Wingfield. In many respects, Amanda resembles Wylie's notion of momism: she is obsessive, prudish, and delusional, and she attempts to monitor and control every aspect of her children's lives. The end result of her faulty childrearing is two maladjusted children who cling to escapist fantasies and live in the feminine world of the imagination. Laura is painfully shy and incapable of functioning in the outside world, and her older brother, Tom, is a dreamer who frequently fantasizes about leaving his warehouse job and pursuing a life of passion and romantic adventure.

Tom's conflict with his mother's prudishness is dramatized when Amanda confiscates Tom's D. H. Lawrence novel and remarks, "I took that horrible novel back to the library—that awful book by that insane Mr. Lawrence. I cannot control the output of a diseased mind or people who cater to them, but I won't allow such filth in my house" (22). In many respects, Amanda embodies the genteel tradition of American letters; her attempts to censor Tom's reading material imply the desire to civilize him and make him adhere to her authority and her prim and proper code of morality. In other instances, Amanda implies that Tom's table manners are uncouth: "Honey, . . . You must chew your food. Animals have secretions in their stomachs which enable them to digest their food without mastication, but humans must chew their food before they swallow it down" (12). In defiance of his mother's genteel attitudes, Tom responds by quoting Lawrencean maxims:

TOM   Man is by instinct a lover, a hunter, a fighter, and none of these
instincts are given much play at the warehouse!
AMANDA   Man is by instinct! Don't quote instinct to me! Instinct is
something that people have got away from! It belongs to animals! Christian adults don't want it! (30)

Tom's embrace of Nietzschean primitivism implies a critique
of modernity and suggests that industrial capitalism produces au-
tomatized workers who exist in a world without feeling, sensation, or
excitement. Similarly, in other speeches, Tom claims that American
popular culture and modernity encourage voyeurism and repression:
"People go to the movies instead of moving. Hollywood characters
are supposed to have all the adventures for everybody in America,
while everybody in America sits in a dark room and watches them
having it! Yes, until there's a war. That's when adventure becomes
available to the masses" (48). Tom's proposed solution—joining the
merchant marines in order to travel the world and have adventures—
suggests that he has inherited his mother's rich fantasy life. However,
Tom's determination and willingness to act upon his fantasies set him
apart from his mother and his timid sister.

   In contrast to Tom, the figure of Jim O'Connor, the much-
awaited gentleman caller who appears in the second act of *The Glass
Menagerie*, embodies the notion of squareness. Jim is everything that
Tom is not—optimistic, frugal, and career-minded. He embraces
the American doctrine of self-improvement and is proud to be an
organization man who is working his way up the corporate ladder. In
many respects, he epitomizes the mode of conformist thinking that
Whyte rails against. His personality—a mixture of positive thinking
clichés and Dale Carnegie aphorisms—is largely other-directed: he
has been molded by the success ethos of American capitalism and the
will of the corporation. Jim O'Connor also functions as a representa-
tive of the social world that exists outside of the Wingfield household
("an emissary from a world we [the Wingfields] are set apart from").
Tom's rejection of Jim's strategy for self-improvement symbolizes his
need to define himself by rejecting the values of mainstream society.

   Tom's quest for liberation is dramatized in the final scene of the
play, when he leaves the Wingfield home for the final time: "I left Saint
Louis. I descended these steps of this fire-escape for the last time and

followed, from then on, in my father's footsteps" (68). Thus, Tom's desire for autonomy becomes a masculinist struggle to escape from his mother's stifling control of the domestic sphere and to emulate his deadbeat dad ("I am like my father. The bastard son of a bastard. See how he grins? He's been absent going on sixteen years"). In this speech, Tom's preference for the independent, inner-directed male hearkens back to an earlier model of masculinity. Furthermore, Tom's garb at the end of the play—a merchant sailor's jacket—is a visual reminder that Tom has ultimately escaped his mother's attempt to civilize him and domestic him.

Tom's rebellion against Amanda's puritanism also alludes to his sexuality and the play's veiled discussion of homosexuality. In various scenes, Tom's taboo sexuality is suggested. During one heated argument, Amanda remarks, "I think you're doing things that you are ashamed of. . . . I don't believe that you go every night to the movies. Nobody goes to the movies night after night" (23). And in a later scene with Amanda, Tom alludes to the possibility of his homosexuality:

> TOM   You say there's so much in your heart that you can't describe
> to me. That's true of me, too. There's so much in my heart that I can't
> describe to you! So let's respect each other's—
> AMANDA   But why—why, Tom are you so restless? Where do you go to,
> nights?
> TOM   I—go to the movies. (30)

In this exchange, two of the uses of the dash are revealing because they indicate omission. In the first ("each other's—"), Tom appears to omit the word "privacy," or "secrets." In the latter use ("I—go to the movies"), the dash seems to indicate a moment of hesitation. Tom is on the verge of speaking the "unspeakable," but he pulls back and instead invokes his familiar subterfuge ("I—go to the movies"). In the second act, Tom remarks to Jim that he wants to "move instead of going to the movies." This expression suggests the notion of acting upon his fantasies and making them a reality as opposed to a repressed life of voyeurism ("the movies"). The veiled references to Tom's subversive sexuality ultimately reinforce the play's theme of nonconformity, the need to resist social forces that repress "differentiation," and the fluidity of the unrepressed self.

The Glass Menagerie is a prophetic play in that it offers a perceptive diagnosis of mass conformity as a social problem. Like Riesman, Williams associates soft masculinity with social conformity (Jim O'Connor). The critique of softness is thus implied through Tom's flight from social conformity and his attainment of a life of "lived experience." Tom's rebellion is twofold: he rejects the mythic promise of American consumerism, and he rebels against his mother's attempt to domesticate him. Williams's imaginary solution to the problem of social homogeneity and softness is a nostalgic return to the inner-directed maleness of past centuries. Thus, Williams's play offers an alternative representation of homosexuality and effeminacy in the 1940s: the homosexual narrator is presented as robust and vigorous while the square is soft and pliable.[3] In this sense, Williams's play can be read alongside other groundbreaking works of the 1940s: Vidal's *The City and the Pillar* (1948) and Kinsey's *Sexual Behavior in the Human Male* (1948). Each of these works attempts to challenge the assumptions of the hard/soft binary and mainstream culture's mythic construction of leisure-culture effeminacy.

Like Williams's *The Glass Menagerie*, Miller's *Death of a Salesman* also explores the problem of conformity and the softening of the American male in postwar American culture. Using the Loman family as an example of American masculinity, *Death of a Salesman* presents three distinct versions of manhood, each in its own way illuminating the problems of soft, other-directed maleness at midcentury. Willy Loman, the patriarch, is a dutiful "organization man" who has paid his dues (thirty-four years) for the company, yet suddenly finds himself unappreciated, out of work, and unable to accept his own failure. In effect, Willy is emasculated: he has little autonomy in his career, and his position in the business world is subject to the vicissitudes of the market. Willy is also pathetically other-directed; his personality is a collection of optimistic slogans and business-culture platitudes ("the man who makes an appearance in the business world, the man who creates personal interest, is the man who gets ahead"; 33). Like Jim O'Connor, he believes that being "well-liked" ensures success in one's career. Unable to accept his marginalized status and irrelevance in the world of business, Willy idolizes his older brother, Ben, a model of nineteenth-century inner-directed maleness—strong, authoritative, and hugely successful in the world of commerce. As Willy's career and mental stability become more tenuous, he clings to his fantasy of Ben, the patron saint of American rugged individualism. At the end of his life, Willy becomes obsessed with earning Ben's approval, and even his desperate act of suicide becomes a symbolic last-ditch attempt to atone for his moral shortcomings and his status as a failed breadwinner. When Biff begs Willy "to take that phony dream and burn it before something happens," Willy's response is to cling to the dream of financial success more desperately. He imagines that his insurance policy will pay huge dividends when he dies, and before he commits suicide he remarks to Ben, "Can you imagine that magnificence with twenty thousand dollars in his [Biff's] pocket? Imagine? When the mail comes he'll be ahead of Bernard again!" (135). Through his own death, Willy hopes to redeem not only himself, but the hope and promise of material plenitude and wealth. Thus, Willy's death can be viewed in religious terms; he willingly sacrifices himself at the altar of his secular faith: the American dream.

Similarly, Biff also attempts to recover the self-assurance of inner-directed maleness. Much like Tom Wingfield of *The Glass Menagerie,* he embodies the flight from consumer capitalism and the soft conformity of American business life: "To devote your whole life to keeping stock, or making phone calls, or selling or buying. To suffer fifty weeks of the year for the sake of a two-week vacation, when all you really desire is to be outdoors with your shirt off" (22). However, the myths of eternal flight and romantic escapism that sustain Tom Wingfield cannot satisfy Biff. After years of odd jobs and herding cattle in the western states, he remarks, "Whenever the spring comes to where I am, I suddenly get the feeling, my God, I am not getting anywhere! What the hell am I doing, playing around with horses, twenty-eight dollars a week! I'm thirty-four years old, I oughta be makin' my future" (ibid.). Both his rejection of the commercial values of his father's generation (other-directed maleness) and his communing with nature prove to be unrewarding. His attempt to be an inner-directed cowboy is ultimately futile because he discovers that this once-stable myth of maleness is no longer viable.

Biff's quest for his masculine identity and for moral certainty lead him to one final attempt to reconcile with his father. However, during their final meeting, he proceeds to shatter all of Willy's most

cherished illusions: "I am not a leader of men, Willy, and neither are
you. You were never anything but a hard-working drummer who
landed in the ash can like all the rest of them. I'm one dollar an hour"
(132). Unlike Willy, Biff opts to strip away all the forms of self-decep-
tion. However, Biff wrongly assumes that Willy can survive without
delusions. Biff's tragedy is that he is caught between two opposing
social roles: the inner-directed cowboy/frontiersman of the nineteenth century and the vacuous and soft organization man of the
mid-twentieth century. He is incapable of finding fulfillment in either
social role. However, he seals his fate when he steals the fountain
pen from Bill Oliver's desk (*"Biff . . . holding up the fountain pen . . .* [to
Willy]: 'so I'm washed up with Oliver, you understand?'"). His theft is
symbolic in that he is sabotaging his career in business and ensuring
that he can never return to office work again. Thus, Biff ends the play
with an understanding of Willy's alienation; at Willy's funeral, he
declares, "You know something Charley, there's more of him [Willy]
in that front stoop than in all the sales he ever made. He had all the
wrong dreams. All, all, wrong" (138). Biff implies that Willy was only
himself when he enjoyed the fruits of his own unalienated labor. In
Biff's assessment, Willy's identity as a salesman was a harmful and
pathetic fiction. Thus, Biff's struggle is ultimately Oedipal: he is able
to define his own identity only through the destruction of Willy's
delusional selves and through the honoring of the "authentic" self.

In contrast, Happy is the vacuous and affable polar opposite of
Biff. He has accepted his social role with the organization, but remains thoroughly dissatisfied with his middle-ranking white-collar
position. To compensate for his emasculated status in the office, he
seduces the fiancées of several of his bosses ("That girl Charlotte I was
with tonight is engaged to be married in five weeks . . . but I went and
ruined her, . . . and he's the third executive I've done that to"; 25). His
neurotic hypersexual behavior is a desperate attempt to strike back
at his superiors. In the last scene, his willingness to follow Willy's
dreams of economic success ("I'm going to show you and everybody
else that Willy Loman did not die in vain. He had a good dream. It's
the only dream you can have—to come out number one man") demonstrates his tragic inability to learn from Willy's failure.

Miller's play prefigures the sociological concerns of Riesman.
Like the social critics, Miller highlights the shortcomings of the

newly emerging white-collar class of the postwar era. Miller juxtaposes Willy with robust, inner-directed males from the previous
generation. The most impressive figure is Willy's father, a self-made
man and an inventor/artist who embodies the Emersonian promise
of nineteenth-century American individualism. Willy's pathetic delusions of grandeur suggest that postwar commercialism has stifled
American individuality and softened the American male by render-
ing him socially impotent. Thus, in masculinist terms, the tragedy
of Willy Loman is the extent to which his male identity is malleable.
Miller's *Death of a Salesman* is similar to Williams's *The Glass Menagerie* in that softness is a condition of one's psychosocial identity
and not conveyed through the locus of the male body. Unlike many
other literary works of the 1940s, *Death of a Salesman* is not overly
concerned with the problem of leisure-culture abundance and how it
physiologically alters the American male (Cain's *Serenade*). Instead,
Miller's play depicts softness as a masculine response to economic
and cultural forces; the play is ultimately concerned with the social
forces in American life that produced Willy's emasculated condition.

THE RISE OF SEX ROLE THEORY AND THE
PROBLEM OF THE SOFT MALE IN THE 1950S

While Riesman, Mills, and Whyte were critics of conformity and
squareness, there were also leading intellectuals and academics in the
1950s who saw utopian possibilities in social conformity. The promotion of conformity as the desired mode of socialization was a crucial
tenet of sex role theory, the dominant paradigm for discussing masculinity in American psychology from 1940 to 1970. The heyday of sex
role theory was the 1950s, and its foremost theoretician was Talcott
Parsons, the Harvard sociologist and coauthor (with Robert F. Bales)
of *Family, Socialization and Interaction Process* (1955). Sex role theory
posits that the parents in the nuclear family are "socializing agents"
who model behavior for their children, and this learned behavior is
the foundation for all social structures that extend beyond the family. One's sex role is both a biological imperative and a social norm;
by embracing one's sex role, one ensures social homogeneity. Thus,
the symbolic act of conforming is considered rational, healthy, and
desirable.

Sex role theory, which is loosely based on Freudian precepts, posits that the father must retain authority within the family structure. For example, the father acts as the "instrumental" role model who must demonstrate "technical" and "executive expertise" to the "inferiors"—the children (Parsons and Bales 51). In symbolic terms, the father is the "sturdy oak" for the rest of the family. The mother, by contrast, performs the "expressive" role: she is the "charismatic" leader who provides encouragement and moral support and acts as a "cultural expert" who determines the family's sense of taste and decorum (ibid.). Finally, the mother acts as a nurturer and caregiver for the children. Any deviation from the established patriarchal patterns can result in sex role dysfunction. Therefore, a mother who "wears the pants" in the family is considered undesirable because she upsets paternal authority and ultimately undermines the successful social integration of her children.

The influence of sex role theory can also be found in many instructional films that were made in the 1950s. In these social guidance films, which were made for children and teenagers, an omniscient male narrator with an authoritative voice specifically delineates the socially prescribed role for each member of the family.[4] Whether the topic is drug prevention or teenage dating, these films typically spell out the social and familial boundaries that must be maintained (i.e., no underage drinking or heavy petting).

Many of the social guidance films that were typically shown in educational settings suggest the utopianism of sex role theory. If parents successfully model their sex roles and if children understand and internalize their prescribed sex roles, familial bliss and social harmony will result. In Parsons and Bales's chapter "Family Structure and the Socialization of the Child," the male child becomes an "adequate technical performer" and "cooperator" and the daughter a "willing and accommodating person" who will presumably one day make a dutiful wife (Parsons and Bales 51).

The ultimate goal of sex role theory is successful integration into the larger social networks of American life. What now appears as the transparent patriarchal bias of sex role theory was largely ignored by male psychologists and social engineers at the time because they often assumed that social conformity was the highest good. To contemporary scholars of gender, the obvious patriarchal bias of sex role theory represents a conservative departure from Parsons's earlier work (e.g., his critique of masculine aggression and racial scapegoating) in the 1940s.[5] However, Parsons saw himself as a liberal and not a social conservative. He firmly believed that sex role theory was a progressive approach to psychology that would create stable families and a better and more harmonious society.

Given that sex role theory prizes social conformity as an important social imperative, it is no surprise that heterosexuality is considered essential and that homosexuality is considered a taboo practice and is severely discouraged. Parsons and Bales note that "homosexuality is a mode of structuring of human relationships which is radically in conflict with the place of the nuclear family in the social structure and in the socialization of the child" (104). They maintain that homosexuality must be discouraged because it threatens social stability. Therefore, sex role theory specifically legitimizes intervention from psychologists and counselors to ensure that "inverts" will be "straightened out" and normalized.

Another cause for alarm in sex role theory is the social problem of the overprotective mother. It was widely believed in psychiatric circles that a son who becomes too "mother-identified" has a greater chance of becoming effeminate and, in some cases, homosexual. Parsons believed that a son often develops a "feminine identification" because children tend to spend more time at home with the mother. However, at a certain age, most boys begin to adapt by refusing to have anything to do with girls and femininity ("the compulsive masculinity stage"). For sex role theorists, the doting and overprotective mother presents a serious problem because she can potentially block the compulsive masculinity stage. Parsons also had similar fears about the extremely authoritarian father who pushes a son toward the mother, who is often kinder and more charitable toward the son.

The belief that homosexuality is caused by overprotective mothers who smother their boys with affection was a fairly popular theory in the 1950s and 1960s. Even some early feminists adopted the argument to criticize the widely accepted belief that a woman's proper role in society was being a housewife. In *The Feminine Mystique* (1963), Betty Friedan argued that the full-time housewife of the 1950s had too strong an influence over her sons and that the mother's overprotective behavior might be responsible for "the homosexuality that is spreading like a murky smog over the American scene" (265). In this case, Friedan appears to be using the spread of homosexuality as a rhetorical ploy to make American men assume more responsibility in childrearing.

SEX ROLE THEORY AND *REBEL WITHOUT A CAUSE*

These egregious examples of bad sex role modeling—the overprotective mother and the indecisive and effeminate father figure—become familiar characters in the gender landscape of the 1950s. Some Hollywood films contain narratives that revolve around these stock figures and the potential damage that they can cause to the nuclear family and to society at large. Nicholas Ray's *Rebel Without a Cause* (1955), for example, reflects the tenets of sex role theory and suggests that proper masculine and feminine behavior must be learned in the home. The film focuses on three affluent adolescents who have strained relations with their parents: Jim Stark (James Dean) gets drunk in public and frequently gets into fistfights at school; Judy (Natalie Wood) frequently quarrels with her father, and Plato (Sal Mineo) has the most desperate family situation: his inattentive parents have virtually abandoned him, usually leaving him at home with their African American housekeeper. In each case, the parents have presented flawed and damaging sex roles to their children, and their poor modeling has in turn produced their children's antisocial behavior. Perhaps the most obvious case of bad sex role modeling is Jim's pathetic, apron-wearing father, who is incapable of standing up to his domineering wife. While talking with the juvenile corrections officer, Jim describes his father's emasculated position in the Stark household:

> She [Mrs. Stark] eats him alive and he takes it. It is a zoo. If he had the guts to knock Mom cold once—then maybe she'd be happy and then she'd stop picking on him because they [the mother and grandmother] make mush out of him! You know mush! . . . Now I tell you one thing: I don't ever want to be like him. . . . How can a guy grow up in a circus like that?

Jim's proposed solution echoes the tenets of sex role theory. Although Parsons obviously does not advocate violence in the home, the father must be the "executive" and "authoritative" figure in the nuclear family. The mother who "wears the pants" must be dethroned because her domineering example is subverting the crucial process of sex role modeling. *Rebel Without a Cause* is also suggesting that when a father does not adequately perform his prescribed paternal role in front of the children, social dysfunction and alienation will result. It is also significant that the juvenile corrections officer is the only strong and authoritative male figure in the film. When Jim attempts to slug the officer, he physically subdues Jim and firmly establishes his authority. His actions are effective and highly symbolic: he is presenting the correct masculine sex role and becomes the only parental figure whom Jim truly respects.

Mr. Stark's ineffectual parenting is also evoked when Jim asks for advice about how to be a man ("If you had to do something very dangerous, but it was a question of honor. What would you do?"). Mr. Stark's repeated inability to provide a firm and direct answer or to stand up to Mrs. Stark both contribute to Jim's dysfunctional behavior. In a Parsonian world of effective parenting, Mr. Stark would have asserted his unambiguous authority over Jim, and his action would have preempted Jim's rebellion.

The wish-fulfillment scenario at the end of *Rebel Without a Cause* also reinforces the themes of sex role theory. When the three disaffected adolescents are hiding out at the abandoned mansion in the hills, Jim and Judy pretend to be parents who are looking to buy the house. Later, Judy and Jim pretend to tuck Plato into bed when they drape his coat over him while he is sleeping, and then they slip away, like parents, to the master bedroom of the mansion. Symbolically, the scene evokes the fantasy of perfect parenting: tender and caring parents who understand their appropriate roles within the nuclear family and their obligation to provide unambiguous love and support. Plato responds to their love by being a well-behaved and dutiful son. At one point in the film, Plato even remarks to Jim: "If only you could have been my father."

The figure of Plato also alludes to another key concern in sex role theory: the problem of the soft male. Plato's homosexuality is suggested through his nickname, but never explicitly stated. However, Plato's soft features (his youthful and unshaven face) also suggest that he is a "sissy." His behavior throughout much of the film evokes a familiar theme of sex role theory: the effeminate male/potential homosexual who is produced by poor parenting. Hence, Plato's childishness is conflated with (potential) gayness. Plato is an affection-starved youth, and his desperate need for a strong father figure is evoked when he adopts Jim as his surrogate father. Jim is firm and compassionate with Plato, and when he offers him his jacket in the planetarium he is acting like a sincere and caring father figure. Within the analysis of sex role theory, Jim's decision to remove the bullets from Plato's gun is not an act of betrayal because he clearly has Plato's best interest in mind. However, the tragic ending of the film can be read as a critique of sex role theory: Jim's intervention in the planetarium fails, and he cannot stop Plato from acting out his self-destructive behavior.

It is also significant that Mr. Stark finally reclaims his role as a father figure in the final scene. When Jim is crying and shivering after Plato's death, Mr. Stark offers Jim his coat, and when Mrs. Stark starts to raise her voice again—a reaction to Jim's new girlfriend—Mr. Stark silences her with a stern look. The action is significant because it is the first time in the entire film that she respects his authority. Thus, the reconciliation of the Stark family at the end of the film evokes the return to patriarchy and the Parsonian fantasy of clearly defined and appropriate sex roles within the family unit.

On one level, *Rebel Without a Cause* seems to be a deeply conservative film that attempts to reinforce sex role norms and discourage familial dysfunction and teenage rebellion. However, the film's efficacy in modeling these norms is certainly questionable, as the antisocial behavior that is officially discouraged in the film ("the chicken run") is both thrilling and alluring to the viewer. Moreover, the film's social deviants (James Dean and Natalie Wood) are extremely attractive figures whose mythic actions legitimize defying parental authority and other forms of teenage rebellion. Jim Stark is appealing because he embodies the entire spectrum of hard and soft masculinity. He is hard when he defends his masculine honor with a switchblade and soft when he openly expresses his emotional vulnerability with his parents and when he displays unselfish acts of kindness (offering his coat to Plato in the police station). The ability to act out hard and soft behavior is appealing precisely because it defies the rigid social codes of the 1950s and suggests that maleness can embody both masculine and feminine qualities. In the end, the excessive emphasis on conformity in *Rebel Without a Cause* ironically makes social rebellion more attractive. Thus, in the cultural landscape of the 1950s, the rebellion against hyperconformity and restrictive sex role norms becomes an extremely popular theme for the emerging youth culture.

A GENDERED GENEALOGY OF THE HIPSTER

One is hip or one is square (the alternative which each new generation coming into American life is beginning to feel), one is a rebel or one conforms, one is a frontiersman in the wild west of American night life, or else one is a square cell trapped in the totalitarian tissues of American society, doomed willy-nilly to conform if one is to succeed.

NORMAN MAILER, *THE WHITE NEGRO*

The conflict between the adults and the adolescents which is highlighted in *Rebel Without a Cause* is also acted out in American literary culture when the figure of the hipster arrives in the mid-1950s. The hipster, who is synonymous with low culture and adolescent rebellion, is a divisive figure for highbrow intellectuals and literary critics in the 1950s. In *The White Negro* (1957), Norman Mailer provocatively makes the hipster a topic of extensive sociopsychological analysis. Published originally in *Dissent,* this groundbreaking essay is concerned with the emergence of two cultural types—the hipster and the square—and how these diametrically opposed figures embody alternate styles of masculinity. Mailer's essay devotes considerable attention to the hipster and basically ignores the square. For Mailer, the banal square primarily exists as an object of ridicule.

In objective terms, the author's examination of the hipster is nonpartisan in that Mailer does not claim to be a "hipster" or a "white Negro." However, it is readily apparent that Mailer is attracted to the hipster, who is far more colorful than the quotidian square, who merits little attention or critical analysis. Though Mailer never actually uses the word "masculine," the orgasm-seeking hipster is clearly a male figure. Mailer's reference to the "frontiersman" emphasizes the hipster's masculine pursuit and conquest of the sensorial realms of human experience. In masculinist terms, the hipster possesses the "courage" and "stubbornness" to rebel against the overbearing demands of the repressive culture. The implied polar opposite of the hipster is presumably the feminized square, who is conformist, sub-urbia-bound, and linked to the feminine consumer culture which has emerged in the 1950s; in contrast, the masculine hipster is a solitary urban figure who rejects the suburban ideal of marital bliss and con-sumer abundance—station wagons, television sets, and grey flannel suits. Unlike the free and spontaneous hipster, the soft square is a "cell trapped in the totalitarian tissues of American society," and his inability to resist conformity is a form of impotence. The term "to-talitarian" is significant because the word, in the parlance of the Cold War, is usually reserved for the Soviet Union and the Eastern Euro-pean satellite countries. Mailer, always the provocateur, is drawing attention to the repressive nature of mainstream American culture.

Although the hipster, for Mailer, is a decidedly masculine figure, the hipster should not be read as a direct descendant of the hard-boiled tradition. Mailer's hipster clearly moves beyond the hard-shell model of masculinity that dominated the 1930s and 1940s. The key rupture is Mailer's radical embrace of Wilhelm Reich's notion of "or-gastic potency" and "genital character."[6] Reich's valorization of the orgasm as the central feature of "un-neurotic character" signifies a break with the Freudian belief that sublimation is the foundation of civilization.

In the hard-boiled tradition, sexual potency is certainly a defin-ing characteristic of masculine identity; the male narrator remains the penetrator who must conquer women, but not be contaminated by the allure of the feminine. However, the obsession with sexual po-tency does not necessarily imply the negation of a rational self. A key component of the hard-boiled tradition is the desire to retain rational control over the worst of circumstances. In contrast, Mailer's rejec-tion of the rational ideal in *The White Negro* can be best understood as the expression of a preference for the irrational and the desire to live in accord with the desires of the unconscious. For Mailer, the id-centered state of being provides an experiential view of human existence and implies the existential imperative of living for and in the moment. In Mailer's essay, the preference for the id as opposed to the superego is emphasized in his understanding of the terms "psychopath" and "psychotic":

> Now, for reasons which may be more curious than the similarity of the words, even many people with a psychoanalytical orientation often confuse the psychopath with the psychotic. Yet the terms are polar. The psychotic is legally insane, the psychopath is not; the psychotic is almost always incapable of discharging in physical acts the rage of his frustration, while the psychopath at his extreme is virtually as incapable of restraining his violence. The psychotic lives in so misty a world that what is happening at each moment of his life is not very real whereas the psychopath seldom knows any reality greater than the face, the voice, the being of the particular people among which he may find himself at any moment. (305–306)

After attempting to disentangle the "psychotic" and the "psychopath," Mailer presents a sympathetic portrait of the "psychopath" and "part-psychopath"; he posits that they "are trying to create a new nervous system for themselves" (307). While not condoning the violence of the psychopath, Mailer is intellectually attracted to him and his unique ability to live in close relation to his unconscious desires and wishes. In short, Mailer is fascinated by those who lead an id-centered existence that privileges immediacy and breaks free from the sexual repression of traditional moral codes. Much like his use of the term "totalitarian," Mailer is challenging the reader's received understanding of the word and its implied pejorative connotations; the repeated use of "psychopath" in a favorable light is intended to create a rupture in the reader's understanding of Freudian thought. Less persuasive is the suggestion that African Americans naturally gravitate toward an id-centered view of human existence ("It is therefore no accident that psychopathology is most prevalent with the Negro"). Here, Mailer is attempting to valorize the streetwise masculinity of the urban African American male, who has not been feminized by consumerism and the square values of mainstream American culture.[7]

Mailer's divergence from the hard-shell formulation of masculinity is also implied in Reich's theory of "character armor." For Reich, character armor is negative because it results in "deadness" or "rigidity of the body" and a "lack of emotional contact." The physiological stage of character armor is "musculature armor," when an "individual develops a block against the breakthrough of emotions and organ sensation" (Reich, *Function of the Orgasm* 360).

Thus, Reich's concepts can be contrasted with the masculine psychology of the hard-boiled tradition of the 1930s. The male narrators of *The Postman Always Rings Twice* and *Double Indemnity* have a built-in hostility toward emotionalism and any form of feminine sentimentality; emotions must be mastered and controlled, and this is exemplified in the hard-shell ideal of emotional reticence. In Reichian psychology, the opposite is true: "character armor" and "rigidity of the body" are crucial indications of neurosis. The whole goal of Reichian therapy is the ultimate destruction of one's character armor through the creation of orgastic potency and the establishment of what Reich terms "genital character." The latter implies the act of vacating rationality; the Reichian shift from the cerebral cortex to the loins is what interests Mailer and separates *The White Negro* from the masculine rational tradition. Although many novelists (e.g., D. H. Lawrence) and the surrealists embrace the negation of the rationalist tradition, Mailer is one of the first to recognize the youth culture's growing attraction to irrationalism and how the next generation— what would later be called the counterculture—would gravitate toward this ideal in the so-called sexual revolution of the 1960s.

Despite the hipster's phallic tendencies, he should not simply be placed in the camp of hard masculinity. The hipster's ambiguous sexuality stems from his embrace of the irrational and his affective response to culture and life. Mailer also notes that the hipster is frequently bisexual. Hence, for Mailer, the hipster can be heterosexual, bisexual, or homosexual. Mailer's casual reference to a non-effeminate form of same-sex passion is significant because the possibility of being masculine and bisexual was largely inconceivable in the hard-boiled literary culture of the 1930s. In the 1930s, most references to same-sex passion were inevitably linked to the notion of leisure-culture affluence. However, the postwar era marks the arrival of the bisexual hipster, who becomes a part of the cultural fabric of the 1950s and early 1960s. The arrival of the bisexual literary figure also suggests that this particular version of ambiguous male sexuality was somewhat less stigmatized in the literary culture of the 1950s.

However, this trend should not be overstated; it did not extend to the mainstream culture that, by and large, remained fairly hostile to the various forms of same-sex passion.

When Mailer's essay first appeared in the 1950s, his supposed exaltation of the hipster was viewed with scorn and considerable skepticism. Many members of the left-wing cultural establishment felt that the hipster was essentially an apolitical figure who lacked intelligence. In an interview with Mailer, Richard Stern argued that "hipsterism" was "all action, it's all erectile, isn't it?" (Mailer, *Advertisements for Myself* 382). In a similar fashion, Jean Malaquais, a left-wing French intellectual, felt that Mailer needlessly romanticizes the apolitical hipster, who is simply another version of the *lumpenproletariat*. The various Old Left critiques of the hipster that were published in *Dissent* reveal a certain degree of paternalism, namely, the notions that the hipster is not articulate or well-read and that he does not deserve the attention he receives from the mainstream media. Norman Podhoretz and Leslie Fiedler, two *Partisan Review* writers, were also equally unimpressed with the hipster's close cousin, the "Beat." In "The Know-Nothing Bohemians," a review of Jack Kerouac's *On the Road* (1957), Podhoretz criticizes the Beats' worship of "primitivism, instinct, energy, and Blood" and cites an argument from Mailer's *The White Negro*:

> Not long ago, Norman Mailer suggested that the rise of the hipster may represent "the first wind of a second revolution in this century, moving not forward toward action and more rational equitable distribution, but toward being and the secrets of human energy." To tell the truth, whenever I hear anyone talking about instinct and being and the secrets of human energy, I get nervous; next thing you know he'll being saying that violence is just fine, and then I begin wondering whether he really thinks that kicking someone in the teeth or sticking a knife between his ribs are deeds to be admired. (316)

Podhoretz distrusts the Beats' "neo-Dadist" anti-intellectualism and their apparent "contempt for coherent rational discourse"; his greatest fear is that hipsterism will lead to mindless and gratuitous violence. Mindful of Nazi aggression in World War II, Podhoretz objects to the freeing and unleashing of the id, which he considers ethically irresponsible; in the worst case, the movement away from repression can be used to legitimize aggression and acts of violence. For Podhoretz, the Beats are merely an example of literary machismo. Although Podhoretz is right to point out the various ethical blind spots in Mailer's *The White Negro*, he unfairly implies that Kerouac's literary vision—which has little to do with violence and mayhem— will promote thuggish and brutal acts.

Leslie Fiedler takes Podhoretz's critique a step further in his remarkable essay "The New Mutants," which was published in the *Partisan Review* in 1965. Fiedler, like many other Old Left thinkers, appears to be disturbed by the actions and beliefs of the hipsters and the Beats.[8] To a large extent, Fiedler's critique of the "new mutants" echoes the familiar anxieties of the Old Left and displays an inability to understand the mores and political tactics of the younger generation. However, unlike Podhoretz, Fiedler views these changes in relation to masculinity and the Western rational tradition. In this passage, Fiedler perceptively assesses the significance of the rise of the counterculture and the impending collapse of traditional male gender roles:

> What interests me more particularly right now is a parallel assimilation-ist attempt, which may, indeed, be more parochial and is certainly most marked at the moment in the Anglo-Saxon world, i.e., in those communities most totally committed to bourgeois-Protestant values and surest that they are unequivocally "white." I am thinking of the effort of young men in England and the United States to assimilate into themselves . . . that sum total of rejected psychic elements which the middle-class heirs of the Renaissance have identified with "woman." To become new men, these children of the future seem to feel, they must become not only more Black than White but more female than male. (516)

In stark contrast to Podhoretz's macho and thuggish hipster, Fiedler argues that the "new irrationalists" are attempting to feminize Western culture and literature. And finally, Fiedler points out that the transformation of the male is the creation of "a new relationship not only with women but with [men's] own masculinity." Although the essay was written in the mid-1960s, Fiedler is suggesting that the gender transformation—the feminization of the American male— actually began with the Beats in the 1950s.

Podhoretz's "The Know-Nothing Bohemians" (1958) and Fiedler's "The New Mutants" (1965) are separated by seven years. How did Podhoretz's thuggish hipster become the androgynous and feminized hipster of Fiedler's essay? There is no simple answer to this complex question. In historical and cultural terms, the mapping of masculinity and gender difference becomes increasingly difficult to pin down and define during this epoch. The fact that Podhoretz and Fiedler occupy opposing positions is a testament to the fact that gender roles and the traditional notions of masculine and feminine were being challenged, contested, and dissolved in both high culture and popular culture. The fixed middle-class gender roles of the 1950s, that of the male "breadwinner" and the dutiful female "homemaker," were certainly less popular with the next generation. However, the gender confusion that Fiedler explicitly describes in "The New Mutants" did not begin in 1965; it was clearly prefigured in the Beat literature of the late 1950s. Allen Ginsberg's *Howl* (1956) and Jack Kerouac's *On the Road* (1957) are multivalent texts that contest and reconfigure gender demarcations and traditional notions of the masculine and the feminine. In many cases, the Beats simultaneously occupy both gender positions in an ambivalent and contradictory fashion.

In the Western humanist tradition that Fiedler outlines in "The New Mutants," the masculine is traditionally associated with rationality, logic, and science while the feminine is linked to irrationality, nature, and so-called instinctive behavior. Given this tradition, the Beats, in aesthetic terms, often adopt a "feminine" position. For example, in *On the Road,* Sal Paradise's quest for the "real" and the "authentic" expresses the desire to abandon the burden of consciousness—rationality—and thereby discover the immediate and vital feminine side of the self: the primitive, the spontaneous, the irrational. However, the feminizing of the male in Beat literature is contradictory because it is still coupled with the traditional macho reverence for sexual potency and the relegation of women to the role of beautiful and compliant muses. In terms of gender roles, this literature is innovative precisely because the male authors of the Beat tradition bend and modify the rigid male gender roles of previous generations and redefine the homosocial bonds that exist between men; however, it is important not to overstate the implications of this trend: this shift does not signify a new social relationship to women nor the alteration of their prescribed gender roles. What is often described as the nonnormative masculinity of the Beats is actually the ability to occupy more than one gender position at the same time.

The Beats' innovation in matters of gender stems from their ability to role-play and oscillate between the masculine and the feminine positions, a privilege that is, generally speaking, not available to the women of this epoch.[9]

The Beats' attempt to redefine maleness also extended to sexuality. The transgressive sexuality of the Beats—Ginsberg and Burroughs were primarily homosexual; Kerouac and Neal Cassady (the model for Keroauc's character Dean Moriarty) were bisexual—can be understood as an attempt to contest the traditional notions of masculinity and redefine the rigid male gender roles of the 1950s.[10] The bifurcated male subject of Beat literature is ultimately an amalgamation of masculine and feminine approaches to writing, myth making, and literary production.

In a larger cultural sense, the experimentation of the Beats can be viewed as a rebellion against the values and mores of what Elaine May has called the "domestic revival." During the 1950s, mainstream American culture exuberantly embraced the values of domesticity and familial stability. In *Homeward Bound*, May notes that "those who came of age during and after World War II were the most marrying generation on record: 96.1% of the women and 94.1% of the men." In this socially conservative epoch, "Americans behaved in striking conformity to each other during these years. . . . not only did the average age at marriage drop, almost everyone was married by his or her twenties" (20). The average family had between two and four children, and they "were born sooner after marriage and spaced closer together than in previous years" (ibid.). In the sociological literature of the "domestic revival," the heterosexual male was the father and the undeniable breadwinner of the family and the mother was the docile and ever-dutiful homemaker. It should be noted that this family model was essentially a middle-class ideal, and the majority of working-class mothers could not afford to be full-time housewives. However, the 1950s was also a decade of great social mobility and a time when many working-class families were entering the ranks of the middle class for the first time.

The Beat writers position themselves in opposition to the domestic revival and mainstream cultural values. Kerouac's *On the Road*, a novel in the picaresque tradition, contains many parallels with Mailer's *The White Negro;* Dean Moriarty is the literary embodiment of Mailer's masculine ideal of juvenile rebellion, petty criminality, and nascent intellectualism ("he had spent a third of his time in the pool hall, a third in jail and a third in the public library"; 7). Sal Paradise's idolization of Dean Moriarty is nothing short of hero worship, for Moriarty embodies energy, spontaneity, and the notion of an id-centered existence that ignores the domestic demands of mainstream culture. Dean's manic restlessness and multiple wives signify an attempt to avoid domestic responsibility. For the most part, the Beats' innovative redefinition of gender roles did not extend to women and their respective gender roles. Despite their sexually unconventional pairings, the women of Kerouac's novel still remain homemakers who personify domesticity and, in many respects, the antithesis of freedom and the solitary life on the road.[11]

Kerouac and the Beats also frequently position themselves in opposition to the grey-flannel masculinity of the square. The break with squareness is embodied in the Beats' devotion to the theories of Wilhelm Reich. *On the Road* is an example of Reichian maleness: a conception of masculinity that embodies movement, flow, and the act of cracking the rigid body of the square. Reich maintained that the orgasm was central to one's mental well-being; the inability to experience orgasm could lead to social conformism and psychological dysfunction. For the Beats, Reich's message was an article of faith: to be sexually active was to be liberated, enlightened, and psychologically healthy. For Kerouac, the consummate Reichian, the writing process was analogous to the act of having an orgasm: both activities are quasi-mystical experiences. In his description of the proper "mental state" of the writer in "Essentials of Spontaneous Prose," he compares writing to the act of experiencing orgasm: "write excitedly, swiftly, with writing-or-typing-cramps, in accordance (as from center to periphery) with laws of orgasm, Reich's 'beclouding of consciousness.' *Come* from within, out—to be relaxed and said" (*The Portable Jack Kerouac* 485). Much like Reich's theory of the therapeutic orgasm, spontaneous writing is a way of achieving relaxation and clarity of thought. In a letter to Gary Snyder in 1957, Kerouac notes, "I want ecstasy of mind all the time. . . . if I cant [sic] have that, shit and I only have it when I write or when I'm hi [sic] or when I'm drunk or when I'm coming" (qtd. in Johnson, *Door Wide Open* xx). The Beats' Reichian approach to literary production also leads the Beat artist to fetishize the original literary text. Kerouac's famous teletype version of *On the Road* and Ginsberg's original text of *Howl* are more than cult objects for literary collectors; for the Beats, the original texts become sacred objects because they document the immediate and spontaneous act of creation and the lived experience of the author.

Kerouac even extended his orgasm metaphor to the editing process: the writer was the masculine possessor of the sacred orgasm/ literary text, and the editor, who insisted on revision, was the emasculating agent of repression. In one of his letters to Joyce Johnson, Kerouac complains about those at Grove Press who want to edit *The Subterraneans*, "I will not stand for anymore of this castration of my careful large work by liverish pale fag editors" (qtd. in *Door Wide Open* 12). Kerouac is generally fond of employing gendered metaphors, and he positions himself as the masculine artist/rebel who is struggling against the effeminate cultural authorities, who are trying to repress his work.[12] Kerouac's epithet also reflects the Beats' bifurcated view of the homosexual in the 1950s. In an interview, Ginsberg notes that, for the Beats, there were two kinds of homosexual: the "populist, humanist, quasi-heterosexual, Whitmanic, bohemian, free-love, homosexual" and the "privileged, exaggerated, effeminate, gossipy, moneyed, money-style-clothing-conscious, near hysterical queen" (*Gay Sunshine Interviews* 108–109). As David Savran points out, "the differences are marked by gender and class. The former is a masculine, universalized proletarian, while the latter remains a feminized, minoritized, campy bourgeois."[13] The Beat literature of the 1950s tends to celebrate the former group and scorn the latter.

Kerouac's obsession with orgasms also prompted him to document painstakingly his sexual history. The Kerouac Archive in Lowell, Massachusetts, has revealed that Kerouac kept a "sex list" that documented all of his former lovers—wives included—and how many times he had sex with each woman. Kerouac, however, did not attempt to document the sex that he had with men. The sex list was strictly a private document, and there is no evidence to suggest that Kerouac wanted the list to be made public. Ellis Amburn, author of

Subterranean Kerouac, suggests that the sex list was not merely a case of "sexual braggadocio" but that the Beat novelist had a "meticulous archival passion" (216). The sex list also illustrates the narcissistic extremes of Kerouac's masculinity: a fanatical devotion to Reichian precepts coupled with an old-fashioned macho obsession with sexual potency.

In *On the Road,* the masculine pursuit of "the real" and "the authentic" is also embodied in the act of achieving orgasm. What has become Kerouac's most quoted passage can be read as a veiled reference to the pursuit of the orgasm:

> I shambled after as I've been doing all my life after people who interest me, because the only people for me are the mad ones, the ones who are mad to live, mad to talk, mad to be saved, desirous of everything at the same time, the ones who never yawn or say a commonplace thing, but burn, burn, burn like fabulous yellow roman candles exploding like spiders across the stars and in the middle you see the blue centerlight pop and everybody goes "Aww!" (8)

The image of fireworks exploding across the sky acts as a synecdoche for the ephemeral experience of orgasm. In Kerouac's passage, orgasm is no longer a solipsistic act; instead, it becomes a public performance or shared experience ("you see the blue centerlight pop and everybody goes 'Aww!'").[14] In a similar fashion, Ginsberg's *Howl* also attempts to make the orgasm a public event:

> who blew and were blown by those human seraphim,
> the sailors, caresses of Atlantic and Caribbean love,
> who balled in the morning in the evening in
> rose gardens and the grass of public parks and
> cemeteries scattering their semen freely to
> whomever come who may (13)

Much like the Kinsey Report, the Beats' use of explicit language and "public" imagery signifies an attempt to push the orgasm out of the dark bedroom and into the realm of public space; it also indirectly suggests that the public orgasm is somehow preferable to the private and solitary act of masturbation. The theatricalizing of the orgasm in Kerouac's and Ginsberg's work reflects the cult of the unseemly and the Beats' fondness for the confessional mode. However, in the

Beats' version of the latter, the experience of orgasm—both coital
and masturbatory—is not coded or veiled in any way, and it is not
addressed to a lover.

Kerouac's second novel, *The Subterraneans* (1958), is also concerned
with gender relations and the Beats' fascination with African American culture. The novel could be read as a literary companion to Norman Mailer's *The White Negro* since it contains many of the familiar
motifs of hipsterism—bisexuality, jazz, interracial coupling, and,
most significantly, the Reichian glorification of the orgasm, which
implies a surrender to the unconscious. This experimental novel
perhaps best exemplifies Kerouac's attempt to emulate the loose
and fluid style of jazz improvisation. The Beat novelist described his
technique as "spontaneous or ad lib, artistic writing . . . [prose that]
imitates as best it can the flow of the mind as it moves in its space-
time continuum" (*The Portable Jack Kerouac* 487). *The Subterraneans*,
which was reputedly written in one intense seventy-two-hour sit-
ting, is concerned with a brief affair between Leo Percepied, a North
Beach Beat novelist, and Mardou Fox, a half–African American, half–
Native American member of the Subterraneans (an avant-garde
clique in the San Francisco underground). Percepied (a familiar Kerouac narrator/doppelgänger) steals the Subterraneans' "hip chick"
and engages in a tumultuous and erotic *affaire fou*. Their brief encounter ends abruptly when Mardou abandons the narrator and falls for
Percepied's poetic nemesis, Yuri Gligoric.

In gender terms, *The Subterraneans* is a literary depiction of the
Old Left's worst fear: the feminization of the Western male subject.
The narrator of the novel clearly fits the profile of the Fiedlerian "new
mutant"—"a child of the future who seems to feel [that he] must not
only become more black than white, but more female than male"
(Fiedler, "The New Mutants" 516). The novel dramatizes the rejection of white Protestant culture and the attraction to blackness, irrationalism, and homosexuality. Throughout the novel, the narrator's
bisexuality, or gender doubleness, is conveyed in his descriptions of

various characters ("a Truman Capote haired dark Marlon Brando with a beautiful birl [*sic*] or girl in boy slack[s] with stars in her eyes and hips that seemed so soft"; 5). Moreover, Percepied's relationship with Mardou Fox is severely ruptured when he abandons her to spend the night with the famous literary lion Arial Lavalina (a character based on Gore Vidal). By oscillating between homosexuality and heterosexuality and by embracing irrationalism, the narrator is flirting with porous masculinity as exemplified in Kerouac's dictum for "modern prose": be "submissive to everything, open, listening." With this precept for writing and living, the narrator—as an artist and as a male—is abandoning the hard-boiled fear of penetration and feminine allure. However, it is important to realize that the narrator's flirtation with taboo masculinities is ephemeral and should not be interpreted as an exclusive "gay" identity; rather, his is a homosexuality that is always being disavowed at the same time. Despite his attraction to homoeroticism, the narrator also confesses to being a former "nannybeater": "Red Kelly . . . pushed a violinist a queer into a doorway and I pushed another one in, he slugged his, I glared at mine, I was 18, I was a nannybeater and fresh as a daisy too" (7–8).

Given the novel's gender ambiguity, Percepied's improvised narrative can be read as an extended psychoanalytic confession. On one level, the narrator is revealing his desire for the racial "other" and his guilt about having this taboo desire. The narrator's name (Leo Percepied) can be roughly translated as "perceptive," or as a lion with a pierced foot. The allegorical name could also signify an Achilles' heel. From a Fiedlerian point of view, the Achilles' heel in this case is the narrator's weakness for the racial "other" and the allure of the irrational. In short, the narrator rejects the masculine Western rational tradition and is attracted to the unconscious or feminine side of his self. The character of Mardou Fox evokes primitivism and the allure of the irrational; in the novel, she is mentally unstable and periodically suffers from bouts of insanity. At the beginning of her encounter with the narrator, she "flips out," strips naked, and begins walking down a back alley. As she is walking in a trance-like state, she has a vision that she is an "innocent child" again. Percepied is fascinated by the event, and it can be viewed as a representation of the narrator's repressed desire to disrobe psychically and embrace his naked, unconscious self. The ideal of nakedness can be linked to Kerouac's theory of "spontaneous prose," his contention that "shame seems to be the key to repression in writing as in psychological malady" (*The Portable Jack Kerouac* 486). In writerly terms, Mardou Fox's naked, trance-like state is inspiring to Percepied because it exemplifies his own vulnerability and his desire to vacate rational consciousness and expose his inner self—via the literary text—to the external world.

The *Subterraneans* also mirrors the primitivist concerns of Mailer's *The White Negro*, published the year before; the exotic and racial "other" provides the narrator with the vital energy that the Western rational self seems to lack: "as I pass Mexicans I feel the great hepness I'd been having all summer my old dream of wanting to be vital, alive like the Negro or an Indian or a Denver Jap or a New York Puerto Rican come true, with her by my side so young, sexy, slender, strange, hip" (Kerouac, *The Subterraneans* 70). Percepied's nostalgic attraction to vital African American culture is buttressed by a rejection of the practice of psychoanalysis. Much like the editor, the psychoanalyst can function as a censor or as a repressive agent that destroys the unconscious self. On different occasions in the novel, the narrator disapproves of the methods of psychoanalysis: "It's a big world and psychoanalysis is a small way to explain it since it scratches the surface, which is analysis, cause and effect why instead of what" (71). The narrator's skepticism about psychoanalysis mirrors the Reichian belief that rational discourse is often inimical to the authentic self because it threatens to extinguish the irrational and vital side of one's nature.

However, the ending of *The Subterraneans* suggests that the abandonment of rational culture can never be permanent. When Mardou confesses that she "made it" with Yuri Gligoric, a rival Beat poet, Percepied is emotionally destroyed. After this happens, he feels empathy for a bull that is being gored in a film that he is watching: "I cried to see even the bull that I knew would die and I knew bulls do die in their trap called the bullring" (108). In a Fiedlerian reading of the ending, the narrator identifies with the bull because he possesses masochistic tendencies. The narrator is the artist who suffers for his art and is crucified in the public realm ("the bullring"). In this case, the bull mirrors the narrator's gender doubleness: the bull, which is traditionally a symbol of male virility, becomes a feminized object that is pierced and penetrated by the matador's phallic sword. Thus, in symbolic terms, the narrator identifies with being punished for his attraction to the irrational and the feminine. The novel's masochistic undercurrent mirrors Fiedler's contention that the Western humanist tradition is in peril because it is being feminized by the younger generation's dangerous attraction to irrationality and primitivism.

"ACT[S] OF A SICK MIND": THE BEATS AND THE NEW CRITICS' MASCULINIST CRUSADE

The conflict between the hipster and the square also surfaces in the academic culture of the 1950s. The clash between the youth culture and the highbrow culture is especially evident in the work of Allen Ginsberg, a key figure in the era's cultural landscape. To fully understand the significance of Ginsberg's role, it is necessary to examine closely the literary and cultural terrain of American letters in the 1950s and the rise of the New Critics, a movement that dominated the academic literary scene during that decade.[15] New Criticism's popularity was concurrent with the growth of higher education after the passing of the GI Bill. The New Critics offered a more rigorous approach to literary criticism and, most significantly, practical skills that could be applied in the classroom immediately.

In masculinist terms, the New Critics symbolize the union of horn-rimmed square-ishness and highbrow intellectualism. The New Critics' emphatic devotion to rationality is evident in their frequent references to science and the virtues of scientific language.[16] A popular anthology of the New Critics, *Understanding Poetry* by Cleanth Brooks and Robert Penn Warren (1950), considers science and the scientific method as worthy paradigms for the practice of literary criticism:

> The primary advantage of the scientific statement [H_2O] is that of absolute precision. . . . [T]he scientist carefully cuts away from his technical terms all associations, emotional colorings, and implications of attitude and judgment. . . . The language of science represents an extreme degree of specialization of language in the direction of a certain kind of precision. It is unnecessary, of course, to point out that in this specialization tremendous advantages inhere, and that the man of the twentieth century is rightly proud of this achievement. (4–5)

In the aftermath of World War II, science increasingly became the intellectual paradigm for most academic departments.[17] Hence, if the study of literature could become more rational and more practical, then it would be taken more seriously. In theory, the English professor could become a "value-free technician" who, like the scientist, could play a key role in implementing the technocratic agenda of Cold War higher education. Thus, the New Critics are very successful squares: they are organization men who are devoted to their institution (the university). They extol rationality and science and scorn poets who gravitate toward the confessional mode, and especially those who are apt to write poems that fetishize emotional experiences ("emotional colorings") and celebrate the "inner life."

The exaltation of science can be attributed to the era's popular belief that literature did not have a clearly defined role in a society that was increasingly dominated by science and positivism. In the post–World War II era, the New Critics felt that the highly personal and private nature of poetry—its traditional association with sentiment and the arousal of emotions—made it suspicious and vulnerable to charges of irrelevance and obsolescence. The New Critics responded to the dilemma by attempting to defeminize the study of literature by aligning literary criticism with the masculine tradition of Cartesian rationalism and by attacking literature's feminine roots: the affective tradition. Much like Schlesinger's attack on "romantic utopians" and soft fellow travelers, the New Critics attempted to steer literature away from the Romantic tradition that privileged emotion and subjectivity. In the late 1940s, emotionalism was frequently intellectually dismissed because it could be linked to fascism and demagoguery.[18]

Though the rhetoric of most of the New Critics did not always contain gender-specific terms like "masculine" and "feminine," their mission was to root out the affective and to challenge the popular belief that literature relied on emotion and the arousal of sentiment. In *A Glossary of the New Criticism* (1949), William Elton argues that the "affective" in literature is "emotive and related to pleasure and pain, as distinguished from the volitional and ideational aspects of consciousness" (10). With this definition, Elton aligns the affective with neurosis and the body while stressing the virtues of masculine

Cartesian rationalism. In many New Critical works, the binary of the exalted masculine and the hated feminine is a strong subtext that underpins the New Critics' attempt to negate the affective tradition in literature.

The familiar fear of feminine contamination and softness is also a theme in the work of John Crowe Ransom, an influential theorist of New Criticism.[19] Ransom's *The World's Body* (1938), an important foundational text of New Criticism, is explicitly concerned with masculinizing literature by connecting it to the rational disciplines of the academy. Ransom argues, "Criticism must become more scientific, or precise and systematic, and this means that it must be developed by the collective and sustained effort of learned persons—which means that its proper seat is in the universities" (329). Ransom's attack on Romanticism is couched in hyperbolic, gender-specific rhetoric. In his preface, the author remarks, "The kind of poetry which interests us is not the act of a child, or of that eternal youth which is in some women, but the act of an adult mind. . . . the poetry I am disparaging is a heart's-desire poetry" (viii–ix). In Ransom, maturity and adulthood are achieved by fully embracing rationality. He offers the following assessment of Edna St. Vincent Millay, a poet who possesses a mixture of masculine and feminine qualities:

> She can nearly always be cited for the virtues of clarity, firmness of outline, consistency of tone within the unit poem, and melodiousness. Her career has been one of dignity and poetic sincerity. She is an artist. She is also a woman. No poet ever registered herself more deliberately in that light. She therefore fascinates the male reviewer but at the same time horrifies him a little too. He will probably swing between attachment and antipathy, which may be the very attitudes provoked in him by generic woman in the flesh. (76–77)

Millay's display of technical control gives Ransom anxiety because she has mastered certain aspects of masculine poetics ("clarity, firmness of outline, consistency of tone"). Ransom then attempts to qualify his "antipathy" by adding that "a woman lives for love, if we will but project that term to cover all her tender fixations upon natural objects of sense, some of them more innocent and far less reciprocal than men" (77). While Ransom concedes that Millay possesses masculine virtues, her talent is ultimately restricted by the biological limitations of her sex. Finally, Ransom closes his discussion of Millay by suggesting that the universal woman "is indifferent to intellectuality. I mean, of course, comparatively indifferent; more so than man. Miss Millay is rarely and barely very intellectual, and I think everybody knows it" (78).

Ransom's gender essentialism, like that of Terman and Miles, is ultimately rooted in the supposed binary opposition of masculine rationality and feminine emotionality. For Ransom, the tacit criterion for aesthetic excellence is the masculine poet's ability to be intellectually rigorous within the confines of the poetic form. However, Ransom's theory of poetics is not merely a blueprint for attacking female poets; it is also used to police affective male poets. Ransom is quick to point out that a feminine poet need not be a woman: "There is in every poet an evil spirit persuading him to elaborate, prettify, ritualize everything that he approaches in love" (81). For Ransom, the feminine is synonymous with overwriting and an excess of emotion while the masculine is associated with logic, order, restraint, and a return to meter. In Ransom's conservative and antimodernist theory of poetry, meter is desirable because it provides the poet with a means of controlling his feminine excesses.

Allen Tate, a leading New Critic and a colleague of Ransom, also used similar arguments in his discussions of poetry. When speaking to Robert Lowell, he remarked that a "poem had nothing to do with the exalted feelings of being moved by the spirit. It was simply a piece of craftsmanship, an intelligible and *cognitive* object."[20] The New Critics also masculinized literature by encouraging young poets to stay away from current events and to write dense, well-made poems that were filled with allusion, paradox, and ambiguity; thus, the complexity of a well-crafted poem was offered as proof of the poem's inherent rationality. The goal of the New Critics was the so-called autotelic poem: a self-contained and autonomous verbal artifact. However, in gender terms, the veneration of the autotelic poem also conveys the male fantasy of literature as a hermetic space that is impervious to feminine contamination.

The New Critics who came after Ransom (W. K. Wimsatt, Monroe Beardsley, Cleanth Brooks) do not employ over-the-top gender rhetoric and are less explicitly concerned with the feminine contamination of literature. However, it is evident that the thrust of Wimsatt and Beardsley's "The Affective Fallacy" reflects Ransom's antifeminine theories of literature.

New Criticism's fascination with rationality and the need to negate affect and emotional excess was borrowed in part from T. S. Eliot's "Tradition and the Individual Talent" (1917), a foundational text for the New Critics. An important and visible cultural figure in the 1950s, Eliot won the Nobel Prize for literature in 1948, was the darling of highbrow literary culture, and was sympathetic to many of the tenets of New Criticism. Eliot, like Brooks and Warren, displays a reverence for science and its devotion to the ideal of disinterested empirical truth.[21] Eliot famously compares poetic inspiration to a scientific experiment with filiated platinum, oxygen, and sulfur dioxide. Eliot notes that when the gases are mixed in a chamber, they produce sulfurous acid, and the platinum is "apparently unaffected" for it has remained "inert, neutral, and unchanged" throughout the transformation. Thus, for Eliot, "the mind of the poet is analogous with the platinum"; the rational poet remains a perfect artist because "he can completely separate the man who suffers and the mind which creates" (54). Hence, the ideal rational and disinterested poet is able "to digest and transmute the passions which are . . . [the mind's] material" (ibid.). Eliot's scientific analogy (the poet as "transformative catalyst") provides a justification for his theory of the "depersonalization of art" and a concomitant disavowal of the Romantic attachment to affect, spontaneity, and lived emotion.

On one hand, Eliot's theory of the depersonalization of art can be read as a classic in masculinist poetics: the metaphor of the poet as scientist becomes a strategy for masculinizing the poetic tradition, which is frequently disparaged in the popular culture because of its tainted association with leisure culture and bookish effeminacy. Eliot broaches the subject indirectly when he discusses his "program for the métier of poetry." Recommending that the poet immerse himself in poetic tradition, he, however, concedes that this "requires a ridiculous amount of erudition (pedantry)" and that "much learning deadens or perverts poetic sensibility" (52). In the same paragraph, Eliot refers to the poet's milieu ("drawing rooms") and the problem of "laziness," and he notes that the task of absorbing knowledge does involve "sweat." The perspiration, however, is ultimately not the equivalent of physical activity. These references evoke the familiar Anglo-American prejudice against leisure culture and the belief that an inordinate amount of bookish learning often produces "paleface" effeminacy.

However, it would be a mistake to read Eliot's "Tradition and the Individual Talent" as an unambiguously masculine text. Eliot's essay is also fraught with feminine imagery and associations. The femininity of the poet is conveyed in Eliot's use of sexualized language. Eliot notes that poetry requires "necessary receptivity" and that the poet must endure "the continual surrender of himself as he is at the moment to something which is more valuable." Eliot's choice of the phrase "at the moment" evokes the notion of poetic inspiration as fleeting, but it also connotes that writing poetry is akin to an erotic experience. But the latter situation is a source of anxiety for Eliot because the poet is essentially feminine in the act of composition and, for Eliot, submission is deemed necessary for great art. Eliot's insistence that the poet, in the moment of poetic inspiration, is a penetrated feminized body is striking because it directly contradicts the familiar motif of the masculine writer being visited by a feminine muse. To counteract this problem, Eliot presents an imaginary solution, a masculinist fantasy: the hard-bodied poet who remains "inert, neutral, and unchanged" during the act of composition. Eliot's emphasis on the affect-less poet and Eliot's bizarre fascination with metallic hardness ("the mind of the poet is the shred of platinum") act as a concomitant disavowal of the soft, penetrated male body and a theoretical defense against the charge of feminine contamination. Throughout the essay, Eliot alternates between the two gender positions but, significantly, ends as a hard, affect-less body.

Eliot's literary references in "Tradition and the Individual Talent" also contain other allusions to the sexual nature of poetic composition; for example, he cites an excerpt from Thomas Middleton and Cyril Tourneur's *The Revenger's Tragedy*. Vindice, while meditating on the skull of his beloved, notes: "Are lordships sold to maintain ladyships / For the benefit of a bewildering minute?" Some eighteen years later, Eliot uses the phrase "bewildering minute" again in a letter to Stephen Spender: "you don't really criticize any author to whom you have never surrendered yourself. . . . Even just the bewildering minute counts; you have to give yourself up and then recover yourself. . . . Of course, the self recovered is never the same as the self before it was given" (qtd. in Kermode). In the former passage, the ephemeral experience of orgasm is described as a "bewildering minute," and in the latter passage, the same phrase evokes the unsettling experience of momentarily surrendering to the poet's alluring language and imagery.[22]

For Eliot, the coital metaphor is appropriate because the act of reading poetry becomes an arresting and transformative experience that is so intense that it requires time for recovery. Eliot's analysis of Dante in "Tradition and the Individual Talent" contains similar themes:

> Canto XV of the Inferno (Brunetto Latini) is a working up of the emotion evident in the situation; but the effect, though single as that of any work of art, is obtained by considerable complexity of detail. The last quatrain gives an image, a feeling attaching to an image, which "came," which did not develop simply out of what precedes, but which was probably in suspension in the poet's mind until the proper combination arrived for it to add itself to. (54–55)[23]

On the immediate level, Eliot is, of course, referring to the craft of writing and how particular images *come* to the writer during the moment of composition. However, Eliot's coital imagery ("working up of the emotion," "came") also suggests that the act of composition is similar to the experience of orgasm. But Eliot is quick to distance himself from the "emotional" aspects of poetic inspiration by describing the act of composition in clinical terms ("the poet's mind is in fact a receptacle for seizing and storing up numberless feelings, phrases, images, which remain there until all the particles which can unite to form a new compound are present together"; ibid.). Eliot deploys the language of science ("particles," "a new compound") to provide masculine window dressing that conceals the intensely feminine and receptive experience of composition.

Eliot's attempt to sexualize poetic composition suggests parallels with Kerouac's Reichian attempt to link the craft of writing to the moment of orgasm. However, unsurprisingly, Eliot's view of poetic composition is markedly different. Whereas Kerouac suggests that

the orgasm is analogous with spontaneous and uncensored literary
creation, Eliot, with the eye of a puritan, is skeptical about literary
works that are spawned from ecstasy and reverie.

Eliot's "Tradition and the Individual Talent" also attempts to
remasculinize the poet by chastising the one who composes poetry
that stems from emotional experiences. Eliot offers this account of
poetic inspiration:

> The experience, you will notice, the elements which enter the presence
> of the transforming catalyst, are two kinds: emotions and feelings. . . .
> [Poetry] may be formed out of one emotion, or may be a combination of
> several; and various feelings, inhering for the writer in particular words
> or phrases or images, may be added to compose the final result. Or great
> poetry may be made without the direct use of any emotion whatever:
> composed out of feelings solely. (54)

By setting up a distinction between "emotion" and "feeling," Eliot
suggests that feelings (mere physiological reactions) are somehow
more acceptable because they are undifferentiated and directly connected to the world of physical sensations, whereas emotions are less
attractive because they imply that the poet is attempting to give subjectivity to feelings and because they suggest that the poet is injecting
"personality"—another taboo in Eliot's poetics—into the poetry.
Thus, Eliot posits two approaches to writing poetry. The first involves
a combination of emotions and feelings while the second eliminates
the need for emotions and draws solely from feelings. The phrase
"great poetry" implies that Eliot prefers the avoidance of emotion in
poetry. The low opinion of "personality" is the familiar hard-bodied
disdain for the confessional mode, while Eliot's preference for feeling reflects his reverence for science and its objective understanding
of the physical universe. The proposed distinction between emotions and feelings, which sounds curious to the contemporary reader,
remains a salient concern for Eliot because he is attempting to uncover a new method of poetic composition that mitigates the role of
subjectivity.[24]

Eliot's fantasy of the scientist/poet is especially interesting given
the fact that he was once attacked for having a "hyper-aesthetic" temperament, often a code word for effeminacy and queerness. Conrad
Aiken, a contemporary of Eliot and friend of Ezra Pound, published

a review of "Prufrock and Other Observations" in the *Dial* in 1917; the brief review ("Divers Realists"), which contains both praise and pointed criticism, is laden with gendered comments that invite the reader to speculate about Eliot's sexual orientation. In the review, Aiken is concerned about the implications of Eliot's overly autobiographical style:

> Mr. Eliot gives us, in the first person, the reactions of an individual to a situation for which his own character is responsible. Such work is more purely autobiographic than the other—the field is narrowed, and the terms are idiosyncratic (sometimes almost blindly so). The dangers of such work are obvious: one must be certain that one's mental character and idiom are sufficiently close to the norm to be comprehensible or significant. In this respect, Mr. Eliot is near the borderline. His temperament is peculiar, it is sometimes, as remarked heretofore, almost bafflingly peculiar, but on the whole is the average hyper-aesthetic one with a good deal of introspective curiosity; it will puzzle many, it will delight a few.[25]

While Aiken's review does contain praise, it presents a rather unflattering portrait of Eliot's temperament. His descriptions of Eliot ("hyper-aesthetic," "borderline") suggest, to be sure, a feminine temperament while "bafflingly peculiar" evokes a host of possibilities—queerness, effeminacy, general abnormality. Unlike Michael Gold, who was given to outing the homosexual writer he was attacking, Aiken chooses to leave the matter ambiguous.

Both Aiken's review and Eliot's "Tradition and the Individual Talent" were published in 1917. However, there is no evidence as yet that suggests that Eliot was directly influenced by Aiken's criticisms.[26] Nonetheless, one curious aspect of Eliot's essay is how it seems to respond specifically to many of the issues that Aiken raises. First, Eliot addresses the claim that his work is autobiographical by distancing himself from poets who inject "personality" into their poetic works: "The poet has, not a personality to express, but a particular medium, which is only a medium and not a personality, in which impressions and experiences combine in peculiar and unexpected ways" (786). Eliot also responds to Aiken's suggestion that his "mental character and idiom" are not "sufficiently close to the norm"; he asserts his normality by criticizing "eccentricity in poetry": "one error, in fact, is to seek for new emotions to express; and in the search for novelty in the wrong place it discovers the perverse" (57–58). By identifying and policing the "perverse," Eliot is, in a sense, insulating himself from the charge that his poetry might be considered homosexual in inclination and the suggestion that his work could be linked to Wildean aestheticism. By singling out "eccentricity," he appears to be declaring his own normality and foreclosing any future speculation about his sexuality.[27]

On one hand, Eliot's desire to masculinize the American poetic tradition is a curious failure because poetry remains associated with leisure culture and effeminacy. On the other hand, Eliot's macho fantasy of the scientist/poet is popular with the next generation of literary critics. Eliot's impersonal theory of poetry becomes the foundation for the New Criticism's critique of literary criticism that posits that the literary text is merely an extension of the writer's biography (e.g., Wimsatt and Beardsley's "The Intentional Fallacy"). Thus, with Eliot's prompting, the literary text becomes analogous to the hard and impenetrable male body: a theoretical shield against biographical literary critics who attempt to pry open and violate the literary corpus of the male poet.

However, Eliot's feminine imagery and attachment to feeling did not go unnoticed. For Ransom, it was a source of considerable anxiety. In *The New Criticism* (1941), Ransom devotes a chapter to Eliot's "unmanageable" theory of poetics and attempts to "salvage" certain parts of it. Ransom argues that emotion must be purged from Eliot's discussions of poetics: "it [is] impossible to talk clearly about these matters until we drop the vocabulary of emotions and talk about the respective cognitive objects, or the cognitive situations" (155). Then, in homage to Eliot, Ransom also chooses to sexualize the act of poetic composition: "the original emotion was the sort of affective glow that attaches to an act of practical consummation. Perhaps we might call it practical emotion" (ibid.). Thus, with the masculine trope of practicality, Ransom eliminates Eliot's peculiar and feminine suggestion that the male poet must "surrender" and become a receptacle for poetic images and impressions. In Ransom's rewriting of Eliot, the male poet plays the masculine role in the coital enterprise of composing poetry. Ransom also opts to "salvage" Eliot's dubious separation of emotions and feelings: "But probably the most important thing in Eliot's statement is his recognition of *big* emotions as set off against *little* feelings" (ibid.). Again, Ransom masculinizes the genre of poetry by eliding emotion from poetic composition: emotion becomes "our reception of the main situation" and "little feelings" become merely the "heterogeneous detail of the situation" (i.e., the poetic event). Moreover, for Ransom, "when this situation exists . . . we are freed from the . . . [emotional] domination [of the imagination] and we can attend to its texture" (156). The purging of affect implies a new sensibility: "The aesthetic consequence is easy to see. The original emotion blinded us to the texture of the object, but now there is leisure for the texture" (158). Ransom's masculinizing crusade is now complete: poetry is finally a leisure activity that is practical, rational, and manly.

I have focused on Eliot and the New Critics because I think that they provide an appropriate segue to Ginsberg's poetry and his explicit and radical attempt to refeminize American literature in the 1950s. There is no written record of Ransom's response to *Howl*. However, consider Ransom's critique of romantic and feminine poets in *The World's Body:*

> If another distinction is needed, it is poetry written by romantics, in a common sense of that term. It denies the real world by idealizing it: the act of a sick mind. . . . It indicates in the subject a poor adaptation to reality; sub-normal equipment in animal courage; flight and escapism; furtive libido. It is only reasonable that such acts, even if they are performed in the name of poetry, should be treated under the pathological category. (ix)

Written in 1938, Ransom's catalog of romantic vices is striking because it so vividly anticipates the poetic milieu of Ginsberg's *Howl:*

> I saw the best minds of my generation destroyed by
> 		madness, starving, hysterical naked,
> dragging themselves through the negro streets at dawn
> 		looking for an angry fix (9)

So many of the vices that Ransom identifies—unseemly confessions, "obscene" sexual encounters, the reverence for "flight and escapism" as modes of poetic inspiration, the glorification of the poet as a neurotic madman—are referenced in Ginsberg's famous poem. If the New Critics and their academic followers are obsessed with the idea of poetry as an extremely rational activity (the poem as "an intel-

ligible and *cognitive* object"), Ginsberg's fame rests on his ability to
challenge this perception through a radical revival of the affective
tradition of poetry. Ginsberg's innovation is his understanding that
the acts of writing and myth making—at least for the Beats—often
require the act of embracing the feminine (or what Ransom calls
"heart's-desire poetry"). In an early poem, "After All, What Else Is
There to Say," Ginsberg remarks:

> When I sit here before a paper
> Writing my mind turns
> In a kind of feminine
> Madness of Chatter

In Ginsberg's confessional poetry, much like in Kerouac's spontaneous prose, the very act of writing involves rejecting rational discourse and legitimizing the right to be feminine—in the words of
Kerouac, "submissive to everything, open, listening." For the Beats,
the feminine is a return to the uninhibited and unrepressed expression of art and to the model of Whitman-like openness. Ginsberg's
Howl is striking in that it presents a softer and more open form of
masculinity that is a stark contrast to the reticent, hard-shell model
of the 1930s. Unlike the previous male generation, the Beats are not
obsessively concerned with the threat of feminine contamination,
and in their lives and literary works they seem to revel in feminine
role-playing and other gender-blurring activities.

The notion of masculine doubleness—male subjects who adopt
simultaneously masculine and feminine personas—is crucial to
Howl. The Beats' willingness to occupy both gender positions is often linked to a masochistic sensibility that allows for a more elastic
conception of masculine identity. Much like Kerouac's *The Subterraneans*, *Howl* contains masochistic imagery that reinforces the aura of
the male body in pain. Part 1 of *Howl* presents the reader with a seemingly endless list of male victims, who "cut their wrists," "chained
themselves to subways," "ate fire," "drank turpentine," "burned ciga-
rette holes in their arms," and were "pierced by swords." In many of
these scenes of torture and suffering, the male bodies assume the
feminine position and allow themselves to be penetrated by various
drugs, needles, "swords," and "saintly motorcyclists."[28] In a bizarre
way, Ginsberg reclaims Eliot's fascination with the male poet as a

feminized body suffering for art; however, in Ginsberg's embodied
version, the act of surrendering is no longer hidden behind the guise
of poetic metaphor. At the same time, *Howl* also contains hypermasculine fantasies of virility and superhuman potency ("who sweet-
ened the snatches of a million girls"). Although the male subjects of
Howl flirt with various forms of femininity and feminine positions,
Ginsberg stops well short of presenting the subjectivity of women
and the image of the female body in pain; in Ginsberg's homoerotic
vision, only male figures are capable of enacting and participating in
gender-blurring activities. The elision of feminine subjectivity is a familiar aspect of Beat literature, which tends to romanticize homosocial bonds between men and which is often grounded in homoerotic
activities. Women exist as erotic bodies, and their primary function
is often to reaffirm masculine myths of potency.

While part 1 of *Howl* focuses on feminized male bodies in pain,
part 2 emphasizes the cause of suffering: Moloch—Ginsberg's quasi-
Blakean term for a soulless society that produces alienated subjects.
Much of the imagery in the Moloch section could be described as
masculine in that the objects are man-made and antithetical to nature ("skyscrapers," "electricity," "banks," "hydrogen [bombs]," "demonic industries," "monstrous bombs," "granite cocks"). Moloch is
also masculine in that it is entirely rational, mechanistic, and devoid
of human sensitivity. However, part 2 of *Howl* ends symbolically with
the return of the poetic feminine:

> Visions! omens! hallucinations! miracles! ecstasies!
>   gone down the American river!
> Dreams! adorations! illuminations! religions! the whole
>   boatload of sensitive bullshit!
> Real holy laughter in the river! They saw it all! the
>   wild eyes! the holy yells! They bade farewell!
>   They jumped off the roof! to solitude! waving!
>   carrying flowers! Down to the river! into the
>   street! (23)

Ginsberg's conscious use of macho phrasing ("sensitive bullshit")
emphasizes the idea of the male poet reclaiming the feminine. The
various suicidal images also emphasize the martyrdom of the male
poet/artist who is possessed by the feminine. Part 3 of the poem,
with its liturgical repetition of "I am with you in Rockland" invokes

spiritual solidarity with the tortured souls who have been driven insane by Moloch.

The "Footnote to *Howl*," which was written after the original draft, offers a Whitman-like affirmation of the sacredness of human life and various erotic male body parts ("tongue," "cock," "hand," "asshole"). However, unlike Whitman's poetry of manly attachment, the speaker of *Howl* makes no attempt to mask or disguise the various references to homosexuality and homoerotic desire. In "Footnote to *Howl*," the reclaiming of the feminine entails a return to moral didacticism; the gesture is significant because, in the eyes of the New Critics, didacticism in poetry is another form of feminine heresy.

GENDER AND THE PUBLIC RECEPTION
OF GINSBERG AND *HOWL*

It is telling that various cultural critics described Ginsberg and his reading of *Howl* at the Six Gallery in both masculine and feminine terms. In an otherwise favorable review of Ginsberg's poetry, M. L. Rosenthal of the *Nation* described Ginsberg's poetry as a "particular variety of anguished anathema-hurling in which the poet's revulsion is expressed with the single minded frenzy of a raving madwoman" (29). In contrast, Michael McClure, a San Francisco poet who read alongside Ginsberg in 1955, noted that "Allen standing up there reading—putting himself on the line—was one of the bravest things I've ever seen" (qtd. in Manso 261). Moreover, in *An Ode to Allen Ginsberg*, Norman Mailer wrote: "That queer ugly kike / Is the bravest man / In America" (qtd. in Miles). Mailer's backhanded compliment challenges the familiar Cold War belief that queerness signifies cowardice and femininity. The gender ambiguity of Ginsberg's poetic persona suggests that the Beats were able to challenge and upset traditional gender norms. On one hand, Ginsberg is associated with masculine courage; on the other hand, the notion of performance is often considered feminizing because the performer becomes a visual spectacle and, in some cases, the object of desire. Ginsberg's willingness to bare his soul and the most intimate aspects of his life during his poetic performances presents an apparent reversal of gender roles. The most humorous example of this occurred at a poetry reading in Venice, California, in 1955. When he was heckled by an intoxicated male spectator, Ginsberg, who had been drinking a considerable amount of wine himself, decided to respond to the verbal taunts:

> The drunk interrupted. "What are you guys trying to prove?" he demanded. Allen immediately yelled out, "Nakedness!" "What do you mean, nakedness?" asked the drunk. "I mean spiritual nakedness," Ginsberg explained later, "poetic nakedness—candor . . ." "All right," Allen challenged the drunk. "You want to do something big, don't you? Something brave? Well, go on, do something *really* brave. *Take off your clothes!*" The man was speechless. Allen advanced on him, tearing off his shirt. "Come and stand here, stand here naked before the people. I dare you! The poet always stands naked before the world." Allen threw his shirt and undershirt at the man's feet, and he began to back away. "You're scared, aren't you?" asked Allen. "You're afraid." Allen kicked off his shoes and socks and pulled down his pants. Doing a little hopping dance, he kicked them off and followed them with his shorts. He was now completely naked. The drunk had retreated to the back of the room. The audience sat in stunned silence. (Miles 216)

In one sense, Ginsberg's resoluteness is an example of the Beats' bravado and their unwillingness to back down from a heated confrontation. The Beat poet manages to disarm the spectator with a provocative enactment of the feminine striptease; Ginsberg's willingness to break social and gender taboos takes the audience and the drunk by surprise and reduces them to silence. However, Ginsberg's version of the striptease is hardly feminine and alluring; it begs the question: what does it mean to have a striptease without a woman? In Ginsberg's case, the masculine, matter-of-fact enactment of the striptease conveys an aggressive, albeit momentary, restaging of traditional gender markers. Ginsberg's performance is illustrative of the Beats' willingness to act out feminine behavior in public without fear of chastisement. Ginsberg's rushed and non-titillating style of disrobing ("pulled down his pants," "Doing a little hopping dance") clashes with the traditional striptease routine, which favors the gradual and erotic unveiling of the flesh. Thus, Ginsberg's incorporation of the feminine—becoming the object of the male gaze—disrupts the narrative of the striptease and does violence to the traditional gender categories of masculine and feminine by creating an ephemeral moment of gender blurriness. In a larger cultural sense, Ginsberg's anti-striptease symbolizes the Beats' ability to adopt masculine and feminine roles and thereby pose a challenge to the fairly rigid gender norms of the 1950s. In a literary context, Ginsberg's revival of the affective is neither timid nor coy—as the New Critics would have it—but comes across as a bold example of masculine assertion. Ginsberg's performance of masculinity in the 1950s is also interesting in that his homosexuality is not linked to effeminacy. Ginsberg openly performs his queerness, ignores the conventions of the literary closet, and aggressively repudiates the notion that queerness should be linked to leisure culture.

Thus far, I have been arguing that Ginsberg's poetry represents an attempt to demasculinize and derationalize American poetry; however, Ginsberg's poetic project also has an aggressively masculine side as well. In other poems, Ginsberg's brash and confrontational style often resembles the punk rock aesthetic of the late 1970s: self-styled pronouncements that are designed to provoke and antagonize the general public. "America," a poem that was published in the *Howl* collection, illustrates the in-your-face style that becomes Ginsberg's poetic signature in the late 1950s:

> America I've given you all and now I'm nothing.
> America two dollars and twenty seven cents January 17, 1956
> I can't stand my own mind.
> America when will we end the human war?
> Go Fuck yourself with your atom bomb.
> I don't feel good don't bother me. (39)

In many respects, Ginsberg's declamatory style begs for a public reaction. Therefore, it is no surprise that the publication of *Howl* caused a furor in 1956; U.S. Customs and the San Francisco police decided to seize copies of the poem. *Howl* also became the subject of a protracted legal battle in which the court eventually ruled that the poem was "not obscene." In many respects, the Beats' explicit and bombastic style signifies an attempt to masculinize literature by making poetry a confrontational and public activity.

The oscillation between masculine and feminine roles was crucial to the Beats and to Ginsberg's poetic oeuvre and public persona. Ginsberg's genius for breaking social and literary taboos enlarged the scope of what men could do and say in literature and in public life, and his success at reviving the affective and confessional mode posed a significant problem for the New Critics' postwar project of defeminizing American literature.

Ginsberg and the Beats, as Fiedler suggested, are indirectly responsible for the feminization of American literature in the 1950s. The Beats introduced a male figure who is less interested in maintaining the borders between the masculine and the feminine and who represents a movement away from the restrictive, hard-boiled masculinity of the pre–World War II generation. The Beats' willingness to contest the rigid male gender roles of the 1950s and their self-styled sexual experimentation indirectly contributed to an enlargement of the social parameters of masculinity. By simultaneously adopting masculine and feminine positions in their lives and in their works, the Beats helped to redefine these demarcations. The works of Kerouac, Ginsberg, and others revealed that the categories of masculine and feminine are constantly shifting and evolving. Thus, the Beats, through their literary myth making, were able to redefine masculine and feminine—not in relation to women but in the context of male homosociality. Many young women were attracted to the Beats' gender rebellion because it appeared to present an alternative to the traditional domestic myths that were presented to them. However, it is important to not overstate the Beats' role in the feminization of American literature and culture. The latter was less a conscious political decision and more a byproduct of the Beats' rejection of the domestic revival that dominated the cultural landscape of the 1950s.

During the 1950s, the Beats and Kinsey were cultural allies who made an important discovery: the act of self-disclosure becomes a way of escaping rigidity and the cultural inheritance of the hard body. Kinsey, a trained scientist and a bow-tied square, discovered that the act of self-disclosure can have a transformative effect on the repressed male speaker. Through confession, the square can overcome the condition of squareness: the absence of an inner life. In the 1950s, the act of self-disclosure was a crucial trope because it was a way of culturally separating the soft body from the hard body, the Beat from the square. The clash between the affective tradition (the Beats) and the hyperrational New Critics also set the stage for the literary politics of the 1960s, the decade when the Old Left and the New Critics would encounter the long-haired offspring of Ginsberg.

1. Whitman's famous frontispiece for the first edition of *Leaves of Grass* (1855). The poet's open collar and workingman's clothes embody the redskin ideal of Philip Rahv's essay. Whitman epitomizes the outdoor approach to literature; his robust masculinity is the antithesis of paleface effeminacy. *Photo courtesy of Library of Congress*

2. Henry James posing for a writer-at-work photo in 1915. James's debonair clothing and feathered pen link him to the leisure-culture tradition. For Philip Rahv,
James epitomized the paleface tradition of American literature. The epithet
tacitly implies that an abundance of leisure culture produces an unhealthy and
impotent body. *Photo courtesy of Art Resource, New York*

3. Ernest Hemingway posing for the dust jacket of *For Whom the Bell Tolls* at the Sun Valley Lodge in Idaho. The staged photo of the novelist at work was taken the same year (1939) that Philip Rahv published "Paleface and Redskin." The frontier location and Hemingway's healthy appearance—his rolled-up sleeves, open collar, hairy forearms, and tanned body—align him with the redskin school of writers. Hemingway's reputation as an outdoorsman also distances him from the effete drawing rooms of the paleface tradition. *Photo by Lloyd Arnold, courtesy of Library of Congress*

4. (*facing*) Mike Gold on Hemingway's boat in Miami, Florida, during the winter of 1929–1930. Gold and Hemingway became friends in the late 1920s. The photos were taken roughly a year before the Gold-Wilder scandal of 1930. Short and slight of build, Gold appears eager to display his masculine prowess at fishing. *Photos courtesy of Gold-Folsom Papers, Labadie Collection, University of Michigan*

Foster on Ernest Hemingway's boat, Miami, Fla.—winter of 1929–30

5. Marcel Proust perched delicately on a small antique divan in 1896. In left-wing literary circles of the 1930s, the French novelist became synonymous with leisure-culture effeminacy and capitalist decadence. *Photo courtesy of Art Resource, New York*

6. (*facing*) T. S. Eliot poses for a poet-at-work photo in 1926. The image-conscious modernist poet carefully guarded his public persona. The indoor setting and Eliot's dapper appearance link him to the leisure-culture tradition of American literature. *Photo from Lady Ottoline Morrell Album Collection (album 7, 1925–1926), courtesy of National Portrait Gallery (London)*

7. The bearded Allen Ginsberg personifies the open and porous masculinity of the Whitmanic tradition. His celebration of the affective dimension of literature and the primacy of feeling is crucial to his popularity in the 1950s and 1960s. The author of *Howl* (1956) is also the link between the Beats and the hippies. *Photo courtesy of Library of Congress*

8. Julian Beck's set for the Living Theatre's production of Kenneth Brown's *The Brig*. The chain-link fence separates the performers from the audience. After *The Brig*, the Living Theatre became fascinated with the notion of removing the barriers that traditionally separate the performers and the audience. *Photo by Gianfranco Mantegna; used by permission of John Giorno; courtesy of UC Davis Special Collections*

9. Audience members symbolically take over the stage and form body piles during the Rite of Universal Intercourse section of *Paradise Now*. The Living Theatre's revolutionary production embodied the emergence of Dionysian masculinity in the late 1960s. During the height of the sexual revolution, Dionysian masculinity emphasized the primacy of affect and the attempt to transform the culturally inherited hard body. *Photo by Gianfranco Mantegna; used by permission of John Giorno; courtesy of UC Davis Special Collections*

10. Transformed male audience members greet one another in the theatre foyer after a performance of *Paradise Now* in 1968. The post-performance photo emphasizes Dionysian masculinity's utopian appeal and desire to create soft (non-aggressive) bodies. *Photo by Gianfranco Mantegna; used by permission of John Giorno; courtesy of UC Davis Special Collections*

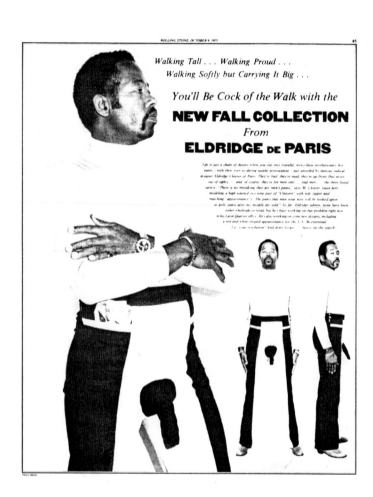

11. Eldridge Cleaver models the infamous codpiece trousers that he designed in the 1970s. Cleaver's mock advertisement appeared in *Rolling Stone* magazine in 1975. *Photo from* Rolling Stone, *Oct. 9, 1975, Rolling Stone, LLC, ©1975. All rights reserved. Reprinted by permission*

4

Reforming the Hard Body: The Old Left, the Counterculture, and the Masculine Kulturkampf of the 1960s

During the 1960s, cultural critics often viewed social and cultural changes as products of a generational conflict. Lewis Feuer's *The Conflict of Generations* (1969), for example, posited that the student protests of that time were essentially a collective Oedipal rebellion against the values of the older generation. Feuer, a philosophy professor at Berkeley who witnessed firsthand the emergence of the free speech movement of 1964 and the rise of the student-led antiwar movement, argued that the students were intent on defining themselves as "uncorrupted" (unlike their parents) and "determined to change the world the elders [would] transmit to them" (416).[1] Feuer's Freudian analysis of the student movement is critical of the counterculture and the New Left: "Large numbers of vigorous youth, often enjoying the securities of bourgeois existence, with all their free-floating aggressive energies seeking an outlet, a cause, congregate in the universities" (523). At the same time, the popular adage "don't trust anyone over thirty" suggested that many younger people were also apt to view the social conflict in generational terms. Timothy Leary, a guru of the counterculture, often used ageist rhetoric that pitted the older generation ("white, menopausal, mendacious males";

Politics of Ecstasy 363) against the youth culture of the 1960s ("the gentle, the peace-loving, the young"; ibid.). The fact that Leary was technically a member of the over-forty generation was conveniently ignored by the advocate of LSD and his youthful supporters.

Much like Feuer and Leary, Leslie Fiedler in "The New Mutants" (1965) also attempts to examine the tumultuous 1960s as a generational conflict. However, Fiedler's analysis of the counterculture is complicated by a literary and cultural understanding of the "new sensibility" that spawned both the New Left and the counterculture.[2] Feuer's portrait of the younger generation, *The Conflict of Generations,* clearly expresses the older generation's point of view, but fails to acknowledge the actual political issues at stake. Moreover, his monocausal thesis—that the New Left and the counterculture were fundamentally motivated by repressed resentment and aggression— prevents him from appreciating the disparate intellectual and cultural influences that fostered the various youth movements of the time. Although Fiedler often patronizes the younger generation, his essay presents a more well-rounded view of the younger generation and their gender attitudes, a topic that Feuer only marginally discusses. Fiedler's provocative essay is of interest to today's scholars of gender because it outlines the parameters of macho criticism in relation to the counterculture and the New Left.[3] When approaching literary texts and artifacts of popular culture, Fiedler polices painstakingly the boundaries between the masculine and the feminine and castigates the male authors who have been seduced by feminine tropes. Fiedler is particularly adept at uncovering homoerotic narratives and motifs. Whereas Feuer focuses on the Oedipal conflict between the fathers of the Old Left and the rebellious sons of the New Left and the counterculture, Fiedler emphasizes a gendered view of America's evolving literary culture and stresses how various cultural texts of the 1960s are saturated with a gendered subtext and how the American male is gradually becoming more soft and more effeminate.

In *Gates of Eden,* Morris Dickstein argues that Fiedler is the first literary critic who sets out to prove that he is "more macho" than the author he is discussing. While Fiedler's hyperbolic style certainly encourages this view, it would be a mistake to read Fiedler's work in a purely hypermasculinist vein. Fiedler's apparent anxiety about the feminization of American letters is often a rhetorical device that is deployed to shock and amuse the reader. Fiedler's later work in the 1960s and early 1970s, especially *Being Busted* (1969) and *Cross the Border—Close the Gap* (1972), suggests that he is often sympathetic to the counterculture and the student protest movement. Fiedler relishes playing the role of the conservative éminence grise who pretends to be appalled by the antics of the younger generation. Fiedler was particularly good at playing this role in his critical essays, and this is partly why his work was so popular in the 1960s. Younger readers responded to Fiedler's work because they took pleasure in the fact that Fiedler was so shocked and appalled.

Among Old Left critics, Fiedler is unique because he is explicitly concerned with gendered themes and the cultural evolution of masculinity.[4] Fiedler's essays from the 1950s and 1960s demonstrate his anxiety about the cultural outbreak of soft masculinity, the rise of homosexual authors, and the feminizing of the Western male humanist tradition. In "The New Mutants," Fiedler offers this view of the emerging youth movements in the aftermath of the free speech movement of 1964–1965:

> But what the students were protesting in large part, I have come to believe, was the very notion of man which the universities sought to impose upon them: that bourgeois-Protestant version of Humanism, with its view of man as justified by rationality, work, duty, vocation, maturity, success; and its concomitant understanding of childhood and adolescence as a temporarily privileged time of preparation for assuming those burdens. The new irrationalists are prepared to advocate prolonging adolescence to the grave, and are ready to dispense with school as an outlived excuse for leisure. To them work is as obsolete as reason, a vestige (already dispensable for large numbers) of an economically marginal, pre-automated world; and the obsolescence of the two adds up to the obsolescence of everything our society understands by maturity. (511)

For Fiedler, two key components of masculinity are rationality and maturity. Immaturity is thus linked to the feminine: the youth of the 1960s are effeminate because they lack the courage to assume the sober responsibilities of adulthood. Moreover, the males of the younger generation are also experiencing what Fiedler terms "the technical obsolescence of [traditional] masculinity." The excess of leisure culture in Western society produces a new male who is less concerned about his "sex role" and less interested in "the conquest of . . . women." Fiedler also asserts that the masculine, bourgeois, Protestant tradition is being hopelessly tainted by a feminine sensibility. However, for Fiedler, the feminization of American culture is not merely a literary concern. Fiedler even links drug use to femininity:

> The widespread use of such hallucinogens as peyote, marijuana, the Mexican mushroom, LSD, etc., as well as pep pills, goof balls, airplane glue, certain kinds of cough syrups and even, though in many fewer cases, heroin, is not merely a matter of a changing taste in stimulants but of the programmatic espousal of an anti-puritanical mode of existence—hedonistic and detached—one more strategy in the war on time and work. But it is also . . . an attempt to arrogate to the male certain traditional privileges of the female. What could be more womanly, as Elémire Zolla was already pointing out some years ago, than permitting the penetration of the body by a foreign object which not only stirs delight but even (possibly) creates new life? (522)

In one sense, Fiedler is no different from the other Old Left critics who objected to the counterculture's enthusiasm for recreational drugs. However, Fiedler's anxiety about the notion of penetration is revealing on several levels. On one hand, Fiedler contends that the surrender of consciousness to a mind-altering substance is a feminine act because it necessitates the act of vacating rationality. However, Fiedler is also suggesting that masculinity should entail fixed and stable boundaries that should remain clearly defined. Fiedler's concern about gender impurity and the feminizing of the sacred Western male humanist tradition is in many respects the literary equivalent of Terman and Miles's belief that the masculine must remain solid and impervious while only the feminine can be passive and mutable. This obsession with feminine contamination is significant because it suggests the dissolution of the hard-shell ideal and the attraction to the mythic cultural feminine. In the 1960s, many male subjects, including those in mainstream society, become increasingly interested in greater sexual and cultural openness. Receptiveness and the pursuit of the irrational are leitmotifs of the new decade. In his implicit argument for clear boundaries between the masculine and the feminine, Fiedler, a self-confessed "oldster," is aware that he is, culturally speaking, swimming against the current of the 1960s.

Fiedler's anxiety about the displacement of traditional masculine ideals and the feminization of literary culture also extends to the notion of heterosexual male authorship. Fiedler posits that heterosexual male writers are losing their cultural influence and are being outflanked by homosexual writers: "Even heterosexual writers, however, have been slow to catch up, the revolution in sensibility is running ahead of that in expression; and they have perforce permitted homosexuals to speak for them (Burroughs, and Genet and Baldwin and Ginsberg and Albee and a score of others)" (521). The influence of homosexual writers extends beyond the parameters of literary culture: "the Beatle hairdo is part of a syndrome, of which high heels, jeans tight over buttocks, etc., are other aspects, symptomatic of a larger retreat from masculine aggressiveness to female allure—in literature and the arts to the style called 'camp'" (520). For Fiedler, "camp" is responsible for a wave of softness that remains largely undetected by the masculine cultural establishment: "Fewer still have realized how that style [camp], though the invention of homosexuals, is now the possession of basically heterosexual males as well, a strategy in their campaign to establish a new relationship not only to women but with their own masculinity" (521). However, Fiedler's greatest fear is the abandonment of phallic male identity; whereas most critics view the students' advocacy of nonviolence as a new political tactic, Fiedler sees feminine passivity and the negation of the phallic male identity; he is concerned about "[n]on-violence or passive resistance, so oddly come back to the land of its inventor, that icy Thoreau who dreamed a love 'which . . . has not much human blood in it, but consists with a certain disregard for men and their erections'" (ibid.). For Fiedler, the phallus is the most elementary way of defining one's maleness; hence, the "rejection of conventional male potency" signifies a heretical act for Fiedler and the Old Left critics.

As a work of cultural criticism, "The New Mutants" succeeds in that it demonstrates that traditional masculinist values are in peril. However, Fiedler's macho criticism is not terribly persuasive because he never mounts a serious defense of the Old Left's version of masculinity. Rhetorically speaking, the masculinity of the Old Left— rational, sober, productive, mature—is easily upstaged by the exotic description of the new sensibility and its utopian promise of sexual liberation and drug-induced ecstasy. For this reason, Fiedler's essay upset critics on both sides of the ideological divide.[5] Today, Fiedler's essay can be read as a lucid representation of the Old Left's anxiety about the supposed feminization of the American male; at the same time, his vivid and effusive descriptions of drug taking and of the soft and feminized male convey an unmistakable sense of warmth and endearment, which is why Irving Howe and other Old Left critics felt that Fiedler was, politically and culturally speaking, in bed with the New Left and the counterculture.

I have begun this chapter with Fiedler's essay because it provides a new way of understanding the cultural and political conflicts between the Old Left and the younger generation. In *The New Left and Labor in the 1960s* (1994), probably the best book on the schisms between the Old Left and the New Left and between the New Left and the counterculture, Peter B. Levy argues that "the counter culture probably antagonized workers more than the New Left's politics. Its symbols—long hair, drugs, promiscuous sexual mores, informal and unkempt clothing . . . antagonized older Americans" (86). Levy also adds, "Labor leaders and the working class came to share a common view of the New Left that identified radical politics with deviant cultural behavior" (ibid.). Levy's analysis of the cultural divisions between the Old Left and the counterculture points out that the older generation often made no distinction between the New Left and the counterculture. Levy's view of the schism between the Old Left and the counterculture and New Left is, in many respects, the widely accepted historical view of the cultural conflict. In this discussion of the 1960s, I move beyond the traditional interpretation by foregrounding gender concerns and specifically focusing on how generational attitudes about maleness dramatically collide and how the so-called lifestyle differences are a reflection of opposing masculine sensibilities. Using Fiedler's approach in "The New Mutants" as a starting point, I argue that the conflict over lifestyle differences should not be considered a minor concern for literary critics and cultural historians of the 1960s. The conflict over lifestyle differences is not simply an Oedipal struggle, as Feuer would have it, but a profound clash over gender sensibility and, ultimately, masculine identity.[6] The masculine subtext is, in many cases, a veiled debate about the feminization of the American male and the question of which masculine style (hardness or softness) is appropriate social behavior. In this discussion of the 1960s, the affective soft-bodied masculinity of Ginsberg and the Beats morphs into a Dionysian sensibility. The phrase, as its Nietzschean valence suggests, implies the cultural embrace of the irrational and the willful act of vacating rationality. The act, to a certain extent, implies a disdain for the Apollonian intellect and a quasi-mythic return to instinct, passion, and the will of the body. The Dionysian sensibility is, of course, fueled by the availability of psychedelic drugs and the ubiquitous interest in sexual liberation in the 1960s. By invoking the Dionysian, I am speaking less of hard and soft, but instead of a transformative potential, a liminal space that exists between the poles of masculine vigor and feminine porousness, and a mode of behavior where the male figure can, in some cases, occupy opposing subject positions at the same time.[7] Culturally speaking, the Dionysian sensibility is also significant in that it initiates a turning away from the literary text and, in many cases, literary culture itself. In place of the text, the male body becomes a site of metamorphosis and wonderment. To contextualize the rise of the Dionysian mode of masculinity in the 1960s, I will situate this cultural trend within an intellectual debate between Irving Howe and Susan Sontag over the rise of the "new sensibility," and I will examine how various artists in the 1960s (William S. Burroughs, Timothy Leary, the Living Theatre) experiment with the pliability of the male body. For Leary and for Julian Beck and Judith Malina of the Living Theatre, the salient theme is the attempt to make the hard body more porous, more affective, and less aggressive. Lastly, I will examine how the different modes of transformative masculinity pose a serious cultural and intellectual threat to the ideals of hard-shell masculinity and how the mythical return to instinct and passion has specific ethical limitations.

THE 1960S AND THE INTELLECTUAL ROOTS
OF THE DIONYSIAN SENSIBILITY

It has been said that the politics of the Left during the 1930s rested on different interpretations of Marx (e.g., Stalin versus Trotsky); it can further be argued that the fissures between the Old Left and the

counterculture begin with different readings of Freud. The counterculture's reading of Freud was heavily influenced by Norman O.
Brown, a classics scholar at Wesleyan University who became a cult
hero when his radical reinterpretation of Freud, *Life against Death*
(1959), found an eager audience in the early 1960s. Brown's work offers a reevaluation of Freud's notion of sublimation. Whereas Freud
believes that sublimation is the only viable means of displacing
instinctual forces (the libido), Brown proposes the embrace of the
life force (eros) as a means of overcoming repression and frustration. Freud's notion of *thanatos* (the death instinct) is also crucial to
Brown's revisionist reading. In *Civilization and Its Discontents* (1930),
Freud argues that Western civilization is unconsciously attracted to
self-annihilation. The rise of Hitler and the Nazi party in the 1930s
only seemed to confirm Freud's worst fears. Thus, Brown, a Freudian reader of history, sees *thanatos* in the bombing of Hiroshima and
in the proliferation of nuclear weapons during the Cold War, and he
argues that the growing presence of *thanatos* creates the concomitant
need to embrace the life force more vigorously. The radical embrace
of eros implies that the world need not be ruled by aggression and
anxiety. The negation of aggression also suggests a rejection of hard-
shell masculinity and a utopian return to polymorphous perversity
(infantile sexuality). For Brown, the latter is desirable because it presents a way of overcoming repression and establishing a higher state
of physical awareness and an erotic relation to life.

In some respects, Brown's reading of Freud could also be described as Nietzschean for it emphasizes the reclaiming of Dionysian
consciousness. For Brown, the embrace of the Dionysian implies the
revival of the mythic cultural feminine—the irrational, the intui-
tive, and the affective. However, unlike Nietzsche, who advocates a
synthesis of the Apollonian and the Dionysian, Brown proposes "the
construction of the Dionysian ego" (*Life against Death* 176). It is also
significant that Brown turns to Isadora Duncan, and not Nietzsche,
for his final image of Dionysian consciousness:

> Since we are dealing with bodily realities, not abstract intellectual prin-
> ciples, it is well to listen to one who knew not only the life of the mind,
> but also the life of the body and the art of the body as we do not—Isadora
> Duncan, who tells how she experienced the Dionysian ecstasy as "the

defeat of the intelligence," "the final convulsion and sinking down into nothingness that often leads to the gravest disasters—for the intelligence and the spirit." But her Dionysian ecstasy is the orgasm—that one moment, she says, worth more than all else in the universe. (ibid.)

Brown's glorification of Isadora Duncan, a woman, is symbolically appropriate because he is advocating a rejection of the masculine tradition of rationalism ("abstract intellectual principles") and stating a preference for radical embodied praxis. Unlike Freud and Nietzsche, Duncan is a dancer and a practitioner who understands "the life of the body." Moreover, Brown's embrace of anti-intellectualism ("the defeat of the intelligence") is a popular trend in the literature of the counterculture. However, in the context of the early 1960s, Brown's radical embrace of eros is utopian in that it ignores the potentially aggressive aspects of the attempt to return to polymorphous perversity.

Like Brown, Irving Howe also charts the counterculture's Freudian inheritance, in "The New York Intellectuals" (1968), a famous essay that documents the cultural and political fissures that divided the Old Left from the New Left and the counterculture. Howe argues that the politics of the counterculture often stem from the rise of a "new sensibility" that champions "the psychology of unobstructed need." Howe asserts that this theory suggests that "men should satisfy those needs which are theirs, organic to their bodies and psyches, and to do this they must learn to discard or destroy all those obstructions, mostly the result of cultural neurosis, which keep them from satisfying their needs" (271). Howe points out that "the psychology of unobstructed need" also has an assumed moral dimension: "once everybody is allowed to do his own thing, a prospect of easing harmony unfolds. Sexuality is the ground of being, and vital sexuality the assurance of moral life" (ibid.). Here, Howe is skeptical about the counterculture's utopian reinterpretation of Freud, especially the fanciful idea that "easing harmony" will result when repression is lifted.[8]

Like Howe, Lionel Trilling also views the counterculture's enthusiasm for sexual liberation with skepticism and moral disapproval. In his essay "Freud and Literature," Trilling establishes the primary importance of Freud's notion of sublimation and the crucial need to privilege reason over emotion and instinct ("irrational, non-logical, pleasure-seeking dark forces" should be replaced by the ego, which represents the triumph of "intelligence and control"; 41). Though Trilling was writing in the late 1940s, his essay remains an important text for cultural historians because it represents the Old Left's inter-pretation of Freud and foreshadows the Old Left's skepticism about the counterculture's attempt to venerate the irrational and the notion that sexual liberation is a moral ideal.[9]

The intellectuals associated with the Old Left—Howe, Trilling, Fiedler, Podhoretz—are eager to stress the importance of reason and the danger of Dionysian readings of Freud that appear to condone violence and embrace a surrender to irrational forces.[10] The most-feared heresy is the doctrine of polymorphous perversity. For the traditional Freudians of the Old Left, it represents a naïve attempt to return to a guiltless state of infantile sexuality.

In "New Styles of Leftism" (1965), Howe, unlike Fiedler, at-tempts to mount a defense of the Old Left's version of maleness and what could be termed the old gender sensibility. In the essay, Howe laments the rise of art that is designed to shock the middle-class pa-trons, who seem to enjoy "the titillating assaults":

> So when a new sensation (be it literary violence, sexual fashion, intel-lectual outrage, high-toned pornography, or sadistic denunciation) is provided by the shock troops of culture, the sophisticated middle class responds with outrage, resistance, and anger—*for upon these initial responses its pleasure depends*. But then, a little later it rolls over like a happy puppy dog on its back, moaning, "Oh, baby *épatez* me again, harder this time, tell me what a sterile impotent louse I am and how you are so tough and virile, how you are planning to murder me, *épatez* me again." (206; emphasis in original)

Howe's critique of the middle-class patron of counterculture art is prescient in that it anticipates Tom Wolfe's notion of "radical chic." However, it is interesting that Howe's satire is conveyed through an explicitly gendered metaphor. Howe's use of masculinist language ("sterile impotent louse") implies the spectacle of a feminized man who assumes the passive role in homosexual sex. The hyperbolic as-pects of Howe's mockery convey two of the Old Left's recurring gen-der phobias: the fear of feminization (in this case, the counterculture is "tough and virile") and the familiar horror of anal penetration.

Howe's anxiety about the Old Left becoming feminized is also evident in his defense of the cultural values of high modernism. In "The New York Intellectuals," Howe points out that the new sensibility of the 1960s represents a direct challenge to high modernism. However, Howe's discussion of literary taste is not merely a reiteration of the modernism-versus-popular-culture debate of the 1940s.[11] Consider Howe's polemical attack on the new sensibility:

> The new sensibility is impatient with ideas. It is impatient with literary structures of complexity and coherence, only yesterday the catchwords of our criticism. It wants works of literature—though literature may be the wrong word—that will be as absolute as the sun, as unarguable as the orgasm, and as delicious as a lollipop. It schemes to throw off the weight of nuance and ambiguity, legacies of high consciousness and tired blood. It is weary of the habit of reflection, the making of distinctions, the squareness of dialectic, the tarnished gold of inherited wisdom. . . . It [the new sensibility] breathes contempt for rationality, impatience with mind, and hostility to the artifices and decorums of high culture. (273)

Howe's passionate defense of the Old Left and high modernism is anchored in gendered binary oppositions. The rational—read: masculine—tradition of high modernism is pitted against the indulgent sensibility of "lollipops" and "orgasms": the frivolous devotion to camp (e.g., Warhol's pop art) and Dionysian fantasies of easy ecstasy (e.g., the Living Theatre's *Paradise Now*). Furthermore, Howe's rhetoric elevates high-minded reflection and stresses that great literature is wedded to the Cartesian rationalistic tradition. Howe's aesthetic taste is informed by the idea that art that is easy to consume must be bad. Hence, the Old Left's scorn for the market and the feminine neatly come together. The "nuance and ambiguity" of literary high modernism also ensure that it will never be too popular in the marketplace. Howe's invocation of "tired blood" implies not only the generation gap, but the suggestion that the Old Left is losing its intellectual and phallic potency. Although it can be argued that ideas also have emotional power, the unstated gendered subtext of Howe's literary and cultural aesthetic is similar to the New Critics' scorn for the feminine: both conceive of literature as a properly hermetic space for rational reflection. Thus, at this particular moment, the Old Left, culturally speaking, is closer to the sensibility of the Old Right (John

Crowe Ransom, John Simon); both are equally alarmed by the counterculture's hedonistic ideals and drug usage. Howe's objections to
the counterculture also stem from his moral prudery. In "New Styles
of Leftism," Howe is appalled by the younger generation's cultural
habits and sexual mores:

> If he [the young male radical] cannot change it [society], then at least
> he can outrage it. He searches in the limited repertoire of sensation
> and shock: for sick comics who will say "fuck" in nightclubs; for drugs
> that will vault him beyond the perimeters of the suburbs; for varieties,
> perversities, and publicities of sex so as perhaps to create an inner,
> private revolution that will accompany—or replace?—the outer, public
> revolution. (204)

Howe views the sexual revolution as harmful, self-indulgent, and,
worst of all, a surrogate experience that replaces real and meaningful
political engagement.

When examining the cultural values of the Old Left, Howe's
views should not be considered an aberration. In general, the Old
Left critics (Rahv, Podhoretz, Trilling) remain quite hostile to the
counterculture's lifestyle choices. The Old Left's conception of masculinity is wedded to puritan values and the virtues of diligence and
sobriety; the Old Left did not welcome the sexual revolution and was
especially skeptical about mind-expanding drugs. For Howe, sexual
liberation is merely an extension of a narcissism that is, in most cases,
antithetical to political change. The desire to keep the sexual and
the political separate is therefore a defining characteristic of the Old
Left's cultural values.

However, Howe, unlike Fiedler, does not view the younger generation as soft and effeminate. For Howe, the males of the New Left
and the counterculture are "tough" and "virile." He objects to the
New Left's and the counterculture's brash and outspoken rhetoric,
and he admits to having doubts about his own traditional aesthetic
values and devotion to puritanism: "There are moments when it must
seem as if the best course is to be promiscuously 'receptive,' swinging
along with a grin of resignation" (277). This confession, which comes
at the end of "The New York Intellectuals," captures the gender attitudes of the Old Left. Much like Howe's "*épatez* me again, harder this
time" passage in "New Styles of Leftism," sexual experimentation is
not associated with pleasure or enjoyment, but with the loss of mas

culine control and hardness; thus, the surrender to Dionysian consciousness is associated with feminine submission or with the passive role in homosexual sex. For Howe, "being receptive" is framed as an act of resignation that necessarily implies the loss of dignity and self-respect. Howe's denigration of the mythic cultural feminine ("being receptive") reveals his anxiety about the waning status of the Old Left in relation to the next generation of intellectuals (the New Left and the counterculture).

If Howe represents the old gender sensibility and the rearguard of the Old Left's cultural values, Susan Sontag is the intellectual champion of the "new sensibility" and a fellow traveler of the New Left and the counterculture.[12] Although Howe has many targets (Norman O. Brown, Herbert Marcuse, Leslie Fiedler, Marshall McLuhan, and the hipsters and hippies of the New Left and counterculture), in "The New York Intellectuals," he singles out Sontag as a defector who "has gone over to the other camp" (the New Left/counterculture). Howe remarks that Sontag "employs the dialectical skills and accumulated knowledge of intellectual life in order to bless the new sensibility as a dispensation of pleasure, beyond the grubby reach of interpretation" (276).[13] Although Sontag's two critical works—*Against Interpretation* (1966) and *Styles of Radical Will* (1969)—are largely concerned with aesthetic issues, they also can be read as foundational texts for Dionysian masculinity and the new gender sensibility that is emerging in the mid-1960s. Sontag's attack on the New Critics and the Old Left's allegiance to high modernism also contains a veiled critique of the Old Left's masculinity. In Sontag's view, high modernism is predicated on the venerated act of interpretation:

> Thus, interpretation is not (as most people assume) an absolute value,
> a gesture of the mind situated in some timeless realm of capabilities.
> Interpretation must itself be evaluated, within a historical view of
> human consciousness. . . . Today is such a time when the project of
> interpretation is largely reactionary, stifling. In a culture whose classical
> dilemma is the hypertrophy of the intellect at the expense of energy and
> sensual capability, interpretation is the revenge of the intellect upon art.
> (*Against Interpretation* 7)

Sontag's critique of interpretation, as a critical activity, is buttressed by her attempt to revive Nietzsche's notion of the Dionysian; thus, in Sontag's estimation, Western culture has become excessively rationalistic at "the expense of energy and sensual capability." Sontag's revival of the Dionysian feminine also contains an implicit critique of the egghead masculinity ("hypertrophy of the intellect").[14] Much like Howe, Sontag's argument is also predicated on gendered metaphors. In this case, the Old Left and the New Critics are associated with impotence and unsexiness (they lack "energy and sensual capability"). Much like Nietzsche's distaste for excessive rationality (the Apollonian) in *The Birth of Tragedy* (1872), Sontag is indirectly attacking the cultural politics of the New Critics and the high modernists of the Old Left who, like Matthew Arnold, maintain that the experience of literature should be an occasion for high seriousness and focused rational reflection.[15]

Sontag's "Against Interpretation" also dares to question another verity of the Old Left: the primacy of literature in the sphere of culture. In her critique of egghead rationality, Sontag singles out fiction and drama as the two genres that are plagued by interpretation:

> Interpretation runs rampant here in those arts with a feeble and negligible avant-garde: fiction and drama. Most American novelists and playwrights are really either journalists or gentlemen sociologists and psychologists. They are writing the equivalent of program music. And so rudimentary, uninspired, and stagnant. . . . To the extent that novels and plays (in America), unlike poetry and painting and music, don't reflect any interesting concern with changes in their form, these arts remain prone to assault by interpretation. (10–11)

For the Old Left (Rahv, Howe, Trilling, Dwight Macdonald) and the New Critics, literature is the highest form of cultural expression. Hence, Sontag's attempt to elevate soft and feminine forms of expression—painting and music—over the written word is perfectly scandalous to the Old Left.[16] In the gender politics of culture, literary culture is the arena where the masculine "New York intellectuals" wage their wars. For Sontag to suggest that the mainstays of literary culture—fiction, drama, criticism—are obsolete is perceived as an attack on the virility of the Old Left critics.

Sontag's critique of the Old Left's hyperrationality in "Against Interpretation" was followed by her influential essay "Notes on 'Camp'" in the *Partisan Review*. Some critics viewed the essay with disfavor because it indirectly challenged the New York intellectuals' reverence for highbrow culture. Sontag's informal essay was perceived as an attempt to promote effete masculinity; to some on the Old Left, the mere act of discussing camp in print would lend it intellectual legitimacy.

John Simon, a conservative critic who has made a career out of being outraged, voiced his displeasure with Sontag's "Notes on 'Camp.'" Though not a member of the Old Left, Simon mounted a defense of traditional cultural values. It is interesting to note that, at this point in the 1960s, Simon and the Old Left, culturally speaking, were not very far apart.[17] Simon attacks Sontag and her tribute to camp in the "Correspondence" section of the *Partisan Review* (1965). Simon's strategy is to emphasize camp's connection to homosexuality and leisure-culture effeminacy (points that Sontag openly acknowledges); the tacit assumption in Simon's attack is that camp culture is bad because it is homosexual. Simon begins his discussion of camp with a quotation from Eric Partridge's *Dictionary of Slang* that states that camp signifies "effeminate, esp. homosexual mannerisms of speech and gesture" (156). Simon then proceeds to demonstrate camp's cultural mission of "inversion" and what he terms "esthetic transvestitism": "All this camping serves the purpose of confusing esthetic as well as moral issues, by ultimately making the bad indistinguishable from the good" (ibid.). Clearly alarmed, Simon maintains that, if camp culture continues to flourish, our established aesthetic hierarchy will no longer exist: "The outré and the inverted become the quotidian, [and] the aberrant become[s] the order of the day" (ibid.). Simon's phraseology ("effeminate," "inversion," "transvestitism") trumpets camp's homosexual affiliation. Simon's guilt-by-association argument then suggests that camp is slowly contaminating our aesthetic sensibilities: "'camp' spreads: the heterosexual Smiths will be induced, through the mediation of the androgynous 'fashion world,' to keep up with the homosexual Joneses" (ibid.). Simon's metaphor of contamination evokes not only homophobia, but the spectacle of queer culture dominating the cultural scene.

Simon's anxiety about camp reflects the conservative fear that a softening of cultural and aesthetic standards would undermine the status of the critic and the need for rigorous criticism. The debate about the rise of camp culture in the 1960s demonstrates how aesthetic and cultural debates often revolve around masculinist appeals for high seriousness; it also underscores the Old Left's attempt to prize intellectual rigor as the highest good in aesthetic discussions. Simon is also uneasy about Sontag's attempt to collapse genre distinctions ("Miss Sontag can juxtapose as seemingly equivalent Beardsley, Bellini, *Swan Lake* with Scopitone, the Cuban pop singer La Lupe (whoever she may be), and 'stag movies without lust'"; 156). The act of genre blurring represents an attack on order and rationality and the a priori preeminence of high culture. In the 1960s, Simon and the Old Left critics are especially touchy about the rise of popular culture and the apparent cultural decline of the written word.

Nonetheless, the Old Left's prejudice against camp culture should not be simply read as a case of garden-variety homophobia. The Old Left's distaste for the excessive stylization of camp was a byproduct of their Marxist contempt for the "conspicuous consumption" of the upper classes. In the austere social environment of the 1930s, an individual who openly embraced "the spirit of extravagance" and the fruits of leisure culture was often considered a class enemy. However, the Old Left's discomfort with camp does not end there: the notion of men possessing feminine allure—what Laura Mulvey would later call feminine "to-be-looked-at-ness"—was also a fairly frightening concept to many of the males of the Old Left, who were simply not at ease with the spectacle of dandyism and the notion of the male body on display. As a rule, the Old Left avoided ostentatious display and preferred not to draw attention to their persons. While the rhetoric of the Old Left was often loud, acerbic, and witty, their attire and appearance, in most cases, remained fairly traditional and devoid of the sartorial exuberance that characterized the peacock males of psychedelic culture.[18] Moreover, camp's open veneration of frivolity—its fondness for the fake, the superficial, and various self-adoring poses—did not sit well with the Old Left's cultural sensibility of restraint, sobriety, and circumspection. Camp's attempt to dethrone the serious was in many respects antithetical to the New York intellectuals' preference for modernism and their Arnoldian belief that literature should be an occasion for solemnity and high seriousness. Moreover, the mockery of seriousness threatened the cultural hegemony of the Old Left because the egghead critics of the Old Left would no longer be able to assert their masculine dominance through the display of rigor. Finally, Sontag's attempt to theorize camp was ultimately disturbing to Old Left males because it threatened and exposed the Old Left's rigid notions of high culture and low culture and its obsessive desire to erect interpretive fences (highbrow, middlebrow, lowbrow, etc.) around all forms of culture. The New York intellectuals' desire to maintain fixed boundaries is analogous to their attempt to defend and hold on to static notions of heterosexual maleness.

Sontag's critique of the Old Left's "old gender sensibility" is also evident in her essay "What's Happening in America" (1966). The essay features Sontag's responses to several questions about various political issues and the "activities of young people" in America. Sontag's answers foreground the importance of the gender issues in politics, and her essay even includes a rebuttal to Fiedler's "The New Mutants." At one point, Sontag alludes to the lifestyle differences between the Old Left and the counterculture and posits that the present understanding of politics and political behavior needs to be enlarged:

> From my own experience, I can testify that there is a profound concordance between sexual revolution, redefined, and the political revolution, redefined. That being a socialist and taking certain drugs (in fully serious spirit: as a technique for exploring one's consciousness, not as an anodyne or a crutch) are not incompatible, that there is no incompatibility between the exploration of inner space and the rectification of social space. (*Styles of Radical Will* 202)

With this controversial argument, Sontag takes aim at several Old Left pieties. The central issue is that the Old Left's conception of politics as the bread-and-butter issues—full employment, access to education, the right to unionize, etc.—needs to be redefined; for Sontag, politics must also attempt to address the issues of pleasure and the individual's right to attain personal fulfillment.[19] In the passage above, the cultural battle lines over lifestyle differences are being drawn; Sontag is making the case for what Howe disparagingly terms "the psychology of unobstructed need." To the older generation, to speak of personal issues is to engage in an individualistic agenda and in a form of narcissism that is morally contrary to the collective ethos of sacrifice and commitment, which forged the Old Left's political and social identity during the Depression. Thus, Howe's critique of the new sensibility reveals a distinct set of traditional masculinist attitudes that favor the separation of sexual matters and political matters and display a conservative disdain for the Dionysian impulse. Hence, Sontag's promotion of the politics of self-liberation ("being a socialist and taking certain drugs . . . are not incompatible") is an attempt to identify the cultural blind spot in the Old Left's conception of politics and to align herself with the New Left and the counterculture.

The gendered nature of the cultural debate between Sontag and Howe is also evident in Sontag's definition of the "new sensibility." For Sontag, "a great work of art is never simply (or mainly) a vehicle of ideas or of moral sentiments. It is, first of all, an object for modifying our consciousness and sensibility, changing the composition, however slightly, of the humus that nourishes all specific ideas and sentiments" (300). Sontag is also eager to emphasize the experiential aspects of the new sensibility: "[f]or we are what we are able to see (hear, taste, smell, feel) even more powerfully and profoundly than we are what furniture of ideas we have stocked in our heads" (ibid.). Sontag's definition privileges the sensorial aspects of the experience of culture, an approach that revives the Dionysian feminine while denigrating the cerebral dimension by associating it with cumbersome weight ("furniture of ideas we have stocked in our heads"). Thus, by implication, Sontag's rhetoric links the Old Left to moral didacticism and sterility of the intellect. It is not difficult to see why the Old Left often took issue with Sontag's new sensibility. Her radical attempt to divorce art from didacticism suggests that nontraditional "objects" (i.e., psychedelic drugs or pornography) could have enormous aesthetic potential. In fact, it could be argued that certain psychedelic drugs are superior to traditional aesthetic forms (i.e., literature and the pictorial arts), which have a limited ability to modify "consciousness and sensibility."

As the new sensibility debate suggests, in the 1960s there is a distinct movement away from the primacy of the literary text in American intellectual culture in favor of disparate cultural forms that provide means of modifying consciousness and subverting rationality. For the elders of the Old Left, the arrival of mind-expanding drugs is viewed as an outgrowth of frivolous, consumer-culture narcissism.

However, the Old Left's alarm also stems partly from fear of the visible male body and of the notion that the male body, as flesh, could act as a conduit for self-transformation. This trend is particularly disturbing to the Old Left because the male body itself and the so-called psychedelic experience often upstage the literary text and challenge its elevated status in American literary culture. In certain sectors of the New Left and counterculture, psychedelic drug taking fosters an emphasis on lived experience and praxis and a general disdain for the printed word and what Howe terms "the artifices and decorums of high culture."

WILLIAM S. BURROUGHS AND THE RISE OF SOFT-BODIED DIONYSIAN MASCULINITY

The debate about the new sensibility and the feminization of American literary culture takes place in the mid- and late 1960s. However, many of the issues that Howe and Sontag debate can be detected in the late 1950s. As a novelist and cultural icon, William Burroughs is a harbinger of the psychedelic revolution and the wave of transformative masculinity that comes to the forefront in the late 1960s. It is therefore no accident that Fiedler considers Burroughs a central figure in the revolution of masculine attitudes that he describes in "The New Mutants."

Literary critics have had a hard time classifying Burroughs's fiction and his form of literary masculinity. For many, Burroughs remains an ambiguous and contradictory figure; his elusive version of masculinity seems to defy the traditional approach to marking and classifying masculine identity in literary culture. Burroughs complicates matters by frequently presenting and juxtaposing opposing masculine styles in his fiction and public life. In some respects, he resembles the dandified man of leisure that Michael Gold often attacked in the 1930s, and Burroughs's preference for dapper clothes and hats also reinforces the effete man-of-letters image. Moreover, the subject matter of Burroughs's fiction—graphic drug addiction, homosexual sex, chronic displays of idleness—would only seem to confirm Gold's belief that an abundance of wealth and leisure time is sure to produce moral degeneracy. However, the image of the effete

gentleman is offset by Burroughs's hard-boiled alter ego: the tough-
talking, self-described "gun nut" who frequently delights in target
shooting and other hypermasculine pastimes. The most notorious
aspect of Burroughs's macho side is undoubtedly the tragic shooting
death of his wife, Joan Vollmer, during a game of William Tell that
went awry in Mexico City in 1951. Although the incident happened
long before Burroughs was a published writer, the event has clearly
become a crucial part of his literary persona.

Although the literary/mythic image of Burroughs has both hard
and soft characteristics, Fiedler and other Old Left critics tend to
focus on Burroughs's soft attributes. In "The New Mutants," Fiedler
singles out Burroughs, argues that he is "the chief prophet of the post-
male post-heroic world," and implies that Burroughs's *Naked Lunch*
(1959) "is no mere essay in heroin-hallucinated homosexual pornography—but a nightmare anticipation (in Science Fiction form)
of post-humanist sexuality" (517).[20] For Fiedler, Burroughs is not
merely a homosexual author, he represents a new form of masculine
identity ("more seduced than seductive and more passive than active"), which signifies a gender paradigm shift, including the demise
of the traditional Protestant masculinity of sobriety and diligence
that characterizes Fiedler's generation and much of the Old Left.

In *Waiting for the End* (1964), Fiedler attempts to psychoanalyze
the youth culture's attraction to Burroughs, and his analysis is quite
similar to Michael Gold's gendered critique of Hemingway's readers
in the 1920s and 1930s.[21] Like Gold, Fiedler speculates about Burroughs's literary audience and why certain readers gravitate toward
the Beat novelist:

> Reading him [Burroughs], the disaffiliated bourgeois young (bohemians
> we used to say, "beats" we call them now) can believe that their own
> affectless lives, their endless flirtation with failure, their repulsion from
> their failed selves, and their pride in repulsion, are neither specific and
> particular disasters, nor mere by-products of the life of a leisure class in a
> high-standard-of-living society, but symptoms of a more general cosmic
> catastrophe. (186)

The "cosmic catastrophe" is presumably the social and political divide
that is emerging in the United States in the 1960s and the youth culture's rebellion against the values of the previous generation. Fiedler's

analysis of the counterculture's fascination with Burroughs is interesting in that he is suggesting that the younger generation receives psychic and cultural validation from Burroughs's fiction and mythic image. In a way, Fiedler has turned Lewis Feuer's notion of a generational divide on its head: Burroughs becomes a father figure for the counterculture, a simultaneously hard and soft figure who rejects "whiskey culture" and experiments with drug culture and a life of dissipation.[22] The "endless flirtation with failure" is the younger generation's wholesale rejection of the Protestant work ethic and American society's overwhelming emphasis on sobriety, frugality, and success.

Fiedler rightly predicted that Burroughs would become an important literary figure for the counterculture. In *The Electric Kool-Aid Acid Test* (1968), Tom Wolfe points out that many hippies and "deadheads" consider Burroughs to be required reading; the culmination of Burroughs's guru status is his appearance, among many others, on the Beatles' *Sgt. Pepper's* album cover. When gauging Burroughs's popularity among younger readers, critics have suggested that the counterculture was attracted to the novelist's particular strain of anti-authoritarianism and his iconoclastic rebellion against established cultural norms; others have cited Burroughs's reputation as a self-styled expert on drugs and their effects.[23] However, it could also be argued that the younger generation was attracted to the less rigid conception of masculinity that was frequently depicted in Burroughs's work. In Burroughs's fiction, a particular mythic construction of Western masculinity—the rational, sober, static subject—is radically called into question.

The most radical version of alternative maleness can be found in Burroughs's *The Soft Machine* (1961). This early work can be read as an extension of Wilhelm Reich's theory of sexuality. The novel explores the pliability of the male body ("the soft machine") and its desires; in doing so, the novel negates the traditional parameters of masculine identity and the traditional format of the novel. While keeping the valence of the body as a mechanized entity, Burroughs foregrounds the attempt to remake the male body, and thus the novel itself becomes a site of praxis and lived experience. The novel's seventeen fragmentary routines are loosely organized around the Reichian theme of sexual repression and how it has been used by elites as a means of social control throughout history. Much like *Naked Lunch*, the novel begins with references to morphine addiction and the tactical strategy of drug pushers ("Invade. Damage. Occupy"). However, the drug references are juxtaposed with sexual references to the male body and its addictions; the notion of penetration becomes the novel's leitmotif, as the porous male narrator is willingly penetrated by hypodermic needles, chemicals, foreign objects, and male organs.

The novel's subject matter could also be described as a fictive exploration of Reich's notion of "genital character." In *The Function of the Orgasm* (1942), Reich argues that a majority of the population suffers from "orgastic impotence" and "the damming up of Living Energy in the organism" (361). For Reich, the blockage leads to "biopathic symptoms and social irrationalism" (360). The solution to the state of "chronic bioenergetic stasis" is the cultivation of "genital character," an "un-neurotic character that does not suffer from sexual stasis" (360). In Reich's project of sexual liberation, genital character gradually replaces "neurotic character" and "compulsive moral regulation," and in the process the patient achieves mental and physical well-being. In *The Soft Machine*, the various narrators explore different states of genital character, but Burroughs's routines are entirely devoid of Reich's utopian beliefs. Many of the routines contain vivid descriptions of the external world from a somatic point of view. For the narrator of "Early Answer" (the fifth routine), the experience of homosexual sex in Mexico triggers a sense memory from the narrator's sexual history:

> They was ripe for the plucking forgot way back yonder in the corn hole—
> lost in little scraps of delight and burning scrolls—through the open
> window trailing swamp smells and old newspapers—rectums naked in
> the whiffs of raw meat—genital smells of the two bodies merge in shared
> meals and belches of institutional cooking—spectral smell of empty
> condoms down along the penny arcades and mirrors. (61)

The various olfactory references ("swamp smells," "whiffs of raw meat," "genital smells") suggest that the images have been triggered by the narrator's sense memory, an important part of Reichian therapy. However, the passage also has masculine gender coding: the narrator's aggressively unsentimental and un-erotic view of sexual coupling and his gratuitous emphasis on grotesque details ("raw meat," "belches of institutional cooking") suggest a macho sensibility. The masculine coding is significant in that it supposedly allows the straight reader to experience the narrative fantasy without feeling tainted by the feminine. In other words, homosexual sex becomes an entirely masculine activity. Thus, Burroughs's version of softness—the porous male body—is Dionysian in that he makes the alteration of consciousness his primary quest. The male narrator of Burroughs's fiction explores the sensual, the irrational, and the nonlinear, yet has little or no interest in the embodied feminine: women. Similarly, the narrator of *The Soft Machine* often assumes the feminine position in homosexual sex, but is in no way womanly or effeminate. This anomalous sexual attitude in Burroughs's fiction—"macho softness"—is an important trope because it untangles the braid of effeminacy and homosexuality that is so commonplace in American literature of the 1950s and early 1960s.

TIMOTHY LEARY: SELLING TRANSFORMATIVE MASCULINITY TO THE MAINSTREAM

Unlike Burroughs, who was ambivalent about his status as an icon of the counterculture, Timothy Leary enjoyed playing the role of spokesperson and advocate for the psychedelic revolution. Most scholars who have written about Leary view him as the Johnny Appleseed of acid culture—an iconoclastic rebel who challenged the social mores and the traditional values of mainstream America in the 1960s and 1970s. However, there has been little discussion of how Leary's psychedelic agenda and political rhetoric were anchored in a particular conceptual understanding of gender and culture. The trajectory of Leary's career and thought are relevant to this study because they illuminate the rise of Dionysian masculinity and document the movement's cultural and intellectual influences.

Leary's intellectual transformation really begins in the early 1960s. At the early stages of his career, Leary (born 1920) was linked to the "robotic" masculinity of the World War II generation:

> I was at that time [1962] a successful robot respected at Harvard, clean-cut, witty, and, in that inert culture, unusually creative. Though I had attained the highest ambition of the young American intellectual, I was

> totally cut off from body and senses. My clothes had been selected to fit
> the young professional image. Even after one hundred drug sessions I
> routinely listened to pop music, drank martinis, ate what was put before
> me. (*Flashbacks* 113)

In Leary's eyes, his robotic masculinity is a product of the uptight
and repressed culture of the 1950s, a culture that favored social conformity, the drinking of alcohol, and the virtue of self-control. Like
many other countercultural intellectuals, Leary is fond of mocking
the social attitudes of the 1950s. Leary's conception of his own body
and self is also revealing: he highlights his overtly cerebral personality and emphasizes how he was entirely divorced from the Dionysian
aspects of his body. His reference to eating "what was put before me"
conjures up the image of Leary as a Pavlovian dog who mindlessly responds to various cultural stimulants. Despite Leary's LSD intake—
over a hundred sessions—he is still a square in many respects.[24]

The masculine transformation of Leary—from robotic body
to soft body—occurs when Leary has sex while taking psilocybin
during the spring semester of 1962. In his autobiography, *Flashbacks*
(1983), Leary frames the event as epiphanic and life changing: the
psychedelic drugs are a miraculous cure for his rigid and robotic
body. In Reichian terms, the drugs penetrate his "character armor"
and "muscular armor" and produce a heightened state of awareness
and a receptive erotic body. Leary's account of his first sexual experience while under the influence of psilocybin emphasizes the theme
of somatic transformation:

> We were sea creatures. The mating process in this universe began with
> the fusion of moist lips producing a soft-electric rapture, which irradi-
> ated the entire body. We found no problem maneuvering the limbs, ten-
> tacles, and delightful protuberances with which we were miraculously
> equipped in the transparent honey-liquid zero-gravity atmosphere that
> surrounded, bathed, and sustained us. (113)

When describing the sexual encounter, Leary omits the masculine
theme of aggressive penetration and instead uses aquatic language
("sea creatures," "tentacles") that emphasizes the supple and jelly-like
qualities of his reborn masculine body and self. In Leary's rhetoric,
the image of the soft, receptive, and mutable male body replaces the
hard-shell body and becomes a new cultural ideal for the younger
generation of the 1960s.

Leary's conversion to Dionysian soft-bodied masculinity implies gender essentialism, but also entails establishing a new relationship to the mythic cultural feminine. In the hard-boiled tradition, the feminine is regarded as antithetical to the masculine, and the male hero often has a paranoid fear of femininity and any form of feminine contamination. In *Flashbacks*, Leary challenges this by embracing the feminine principle and the feminine side of his personality and biological self. In an account of his own conception, Leary juxtaposes opposing masculine and feminine narratives of reproduction/creation:

> At the moment of climax, Tote [Leary's father] deposited over 400 million spermatozoa into my mother's reproductive tract. . . . According to traditional biological scenarios the 400 million sperm, one of which was carrying half of me, immediately engaged in some Olympic swimming race, jostling, bumping, frantically twisting in [an] Australian crawl of flagellating tail-stroke to win the competition, to rape poor, docile-receptive Miss Egg. Reproduction allegedly occurred when the successful jock-sperm forcibly penetrated the ovum. . . . I passionately reject this theory of conception. I was not reproduced! I was *created* by an intelligent, teleological process of Natural Election. . . . The selection of the fertilizing sperm and the decision about the final chromosome division was made by the Egg. It was the *She* of me that had the final say. . . . Miss Egg, far from being a passive, dumb blob with round heels waiting to be knocked up by some first-to-arrive, breathless, sweaty, muscular sperm, was a luminescent sun, radiating amused intelligence, surrounded by magnetic fields bristling with phosphorescent radar schemes and laser defenses. (10–11)

In this comic counternarrative of conception, Leary identifies with the feminine side of his self; in doing so, he rejects the biological narrative of masculine domination and penetration. For Leary, sexuality is a harmonious blending of opposing gender principles.

Throughout *Flashbacks*, Leary is influenced by Jungian psychology and the project of integrating the repressed feminine aspects of his personality and self (anima). Similarly, the masculine rhetoric of the psychedelic cultural revolution often revolves around the theme of embracing and cultivating the mythic cultural feminine. This goal, of course, is not a new ideal; Romantic poets have long been fascinated with the notion of reclaiming the feminine side of their nature and self. However, Leary's true innovation is to wed his romanticism to a praxis that comes in the form of a pill (or a tab).

While a lecturer in psychology at Harvard, Timothy Leary frequently wrote to various writers and intellectuals, inquiring if they would like to participate in psychological research that involved taking hallucinogenic drugs in a safe and controlled environment. In the early 1960s, Leary contacted Arthur Koestler, philosopher, scientist, World War II survivor, and author of the famous anti-totalitarian novel *Darkness at Noon*. Koestler agreed at first but later changed his mind after having an unpleasant experience with psilocybin at the University of Michigan. In *Flashbacks*, Leary recalls Koestler's account of his "bad trip" in Ann Arbor in the fall of 1960:

> It started off very well. I lay down on the couch and soon began to experience the kind of phenomena that mescaline mystics have reported. Luminous patterns of great beauty. If I had allowed myself, I probably would have shared the vision of Elijah as he was swept up to heaven. But I felt this was buying one's visions on the cheap, so I forced my eyes open. No easy paths for me. I congratulated myself on my sober self-control. Mine was a rational mind, not to be fooled by little pills. (56)

Leary then describes how the mushrooms "awakened Koestler's memories of past experiences as a political prisoner, memories of torture, brainwashing and extorted confessions" (ibid.). What sticks out in this account is Koestler's determination to hold on to "rational" control at all costs. Koestler, a trained scientist, is desperately attempting to retain masculine autonomy, as he refuses to allow his mind to be penetrated by "little pills." From a gender point of view, Koestler does not want to be seduced by the Dionysian experience of ecstasy and religious revelry; his reluctance ("buying . . . visions on the cheap") appears to stem from the belief that anything good in life must be earned through sweat and toil. Koestler's negative reaction to hallucinogenic drugs is instructive because it mirrors the objections of many Old Left intellectuals (Howe, Podhoretz, Rahv).[25]

Koestler's traditional response to psychedelic drugs is also revealing because it reflects the cultural milieu of the late 1950s and early 1960s. To those acquainted with hallucinogenics, Koestler's stubborn attempt to hold on to rationality seems somewhat comical; however, in the pre-psychedelic era of the early 1960s, Koestler's cautious attitude toward these drugs was often the norm. The preference for maintaining rational control was often considered a wise and proper choice by many in the scientific and academic communities. Hence, in urging the greater use of psychedelic drugs, Leary and his supporters in the Psychology Department at Harvard faced serious resistance. First, how does one prescribe a drug to someone who is not necessarily ill in the first place? There was no precedent for such a practice in Western medicine; in fact, the a priori goal of psychologists and physicians was to bring the mentally ill patient to a state of normality or rational stasis. The fields of psychology and psychotherapy were heavily influenced by Freudian thought, and their established lexicon was prejudiced against the "visionary" and "enraptured" experiences that the psychedelic drugs often produced. When Leary began promoting the therapeutic value of LSD, he was aware of the ingrained prejudices that existed within the field of psychology: "we [Leary and his colleagues] were not limited by the pathological point of view. We were not to interpret ecstasy as mania, or calm serenity as catatonia . . . nor the visionary state as model psychosis" (*High Priest* 66).

It is relevant to this study to see the debate about whether psilocybin produces anxiety or ecstasy as not merely a question of semantics and psychological interpretation; the debate itself has been colored by certain mythic conceptions of gender. The scientific perspective, which is based on materialist and rationalist doctrines, could also be described as a masculinist perspective with antifeminine prejudices built into its theories. Hence, women and various forms of taboo femininity—hysteria, extreme emotionalism—were frequently discouraged and pathologized in psychological discourse. Furthermore, it is reasonable to assume that certain antifeminine attitudes also existed in the lay population as well.

Similarly, when Leary begins his campaign to promote the cultural acceptance of LSD and other psychedelic drugs, he often encounters resistance from cultural authorities and the general public's ingrained prejudices against the drug and its mind-altering potential. Hence, Leary, a master of media stunts and propaganda, uses gender tropes to make the drug appealing to younger members of the counterculture:

> To middle-aged America, it may be synonymous with instant insanity, but to most Americans under twenty-five the psychedelic drug means ec-

stasy, sensual unfolding, religious experience, revelation, illumination, contact with nature. . . . many fifty-year-olds have lost their curiosity, have lost their ability to make love, have dulled their openness to new sensations. (*The Politics of Ecstasy* 123)

Leary's account of the younger generation's perception of LSD is revealing in that it links the drug to a Dionysian experience that could also be described as embracing the mythic cultural feminine. That is to say, the subject who willingly takes the drug becomes a feminized subject in a Weiningerian sense: open, receptive, mutable. While taking LSD, the Apollonian and rational side of one's personality is muted and temporarily suspended, and the subject experiences what psychologists describe as a "psychotic" and irrational understanding of reality. Leary's rhetoric also promotes his cause by stigmatizing the older generation as sterile and dull.

In a culture that favors traditional masculine values of rationality, diligence, and sobriety, Leary's promotion of the mythic cultural feminine is a fairly controversial activity. Given the cultural milieu of the early 1960s, Leary and his colleagues were bound to encounter skepticism and prejudices like the ones that Koestler voiced. Hence, the debate about the therapeutic value of LSD during this time can be linked to an alternative conception of masculine identity that directly challenges the traditional masculine values. To many in the older generation, LSD represents a threat to society because it engenders irrational and irresponsible behavior and because it appears to promote the deconditioning of the work ethic. As Koestler's reaction suggests, the older generation (especially the Old Left) was often skeptical about forms of enlightenment that came without toil and ascetic denial. To them, the wonder drug must certainly be an ersatz form of enlightenment.

At first, some New Left intellectuals also had reservations about LSD and its feminizing effects; Abbie Hoffman accused Leary of making young people "a bunch of blissed out pansies ripe for annihilation" (*Autobiography* 269). Although Hoffman was not a member of the Old Left, his initial objection expresses the Old Left's fear that LSD would make the younger generation apolitical and devoted to narcissism and self-indulgence.[26] To counter this charge, Leary in *The Politics of Ecstasy* (1968) argues that dropping LSD is a political act because it de-indoctrinates the users and thus makes them more apt to rebel against traditional cultural norms.[27]

By the late 1960s, psychedelic drugs become associated with an entire nexus of received social attitudes: cultural openness, anti-authoritarian beliefs, antiwar sentiments, environmentalism, multi-culturalism. In a fascinating turn of events, one's opinion of psyche-delic drugs, within certain circles, becomes a way of gauging one's political orientation. Abbie Hoffman, despite his initial skepticism about Leary and LSD, remarks on the connection between the LSD experience and certain social attitudes: "To this day, I still don't trust people who have not opened themselves up enough for the experi-ence. On some anal retentive level they are saying they fear looking inside, and grasp at any rationalization in reach to say 'No!'" (91).[28] In the cultural zeitgeist of the 1960s, somatic and psychological re-ceptiveness become the leitmotifs of the younger generation, and the notion of a stiff impenetrable body becomes a symbol of dysfunction rather than a cultural ideal for men.

Much of Leary's psychedelic agenda—especially his belief in the therapeutic value of LSD—was fairly radical in the early 1960s; however, Leary's research was also controversial because it reexam-ined philosophical concerns about human nature and the essence of maleness: Can aggressive behavior, once thought to be innate, be unlearned? Could aggressive masculinity be reformed and remade? For Leary, psychedelic drugs offered new possibilities and a new way of experientially exploring these issues. Leary's notion of "transac-tional psychology" was predicated on the notion that human nature was changeable, and his early research with LSD sought to provide empirical proof for the premise that LSD could radically alter the cultural, psychological, and physiological makeup of the individual who ingested it.

In the early 1960s, Leary convinced a prison psychiatrist at the Massachusetts Correctional Facility, a maximum-security prison, to allow him to conduct his transactional research on various inmates. The prison provided an interesting psychological laboratory in that the inmates were thought to be hardened criminals who were dif-ficult to reform. From a gender point of view, the prison was thought to be a bastion of aggressive hypermasculinity, and the first pool of

volunteers included two murderers, two armed robbers, an embez-
zler, and a heroin pusher. In *Flashbacks,* Leary reveals that, when he
first began to take psilocybin pills with inmates, he was quite terrified
of their reactions and the prospect of being locked up in the same
room with them for an extended amount of time.

Leary compared his project to the concept of imprinting, which
had been developed by Konrad Lorenz, a German ethologist who was
famous for his work with geese. "Imprinting" refers to the early rapid
learning, seen particularly in birds, "by which the neonatal animal
becomes attached to the mother and, by generalization, to members
of the animal's own species" (Kaplan and Sadock 71). Unlike most
forms of learning, imprinting is often associated with punishment
or a painful experience. After various experiments, Lorenz discovered that the young goslings became attached to the first warm and
moving animal that was presented to them. Lorenz also discovered
that he could become a surrogate parent to the goslings when they
were being hatched. When the goslings were introduced to their real
mother, they ignored her and continued to focus on Lorenz.

Although many other psychologists were reluctant to apply
Lorenz's findings to humans, Leary believed that humans were also
capable of being imprinted. Leary argued that taking psilocybin left
"neurological imprints" that could modify ingrained human behavior, and "in a positive, supportive environment, new non-criminal
realities . . . [could be] re-imprinted" (*Flashbacks* 90). In this passage,
Leary is misreading Lorenz's notion of imprinting because adult humans are not in a neonatal state; therefore, they cannot engage in the
same form of rapid learning that Lorenz identified in animals. Nonetheless, Leary's pilot study produced some compelling results: "only
25% of those who took the drug ended up in jail again, as compared
to the normal rate of 80%" (Lee and Shlain 75).[29]

Although Leary's prison project was originally presented as
psychological research, it can also be viewed in relation to hard and
soft masculinity. The low rate of recidivism suggests that psychedelic
drugs aid the process of rehabilitation and that the drugs could be
used as an antidote to different forms of aggressive masculine behavior. Leary's famous mantra ("Turn on, tune in, drop out") originally
signified "dropping out" of the "tribal game" (Leary's phrase for con-

formity and social norms). In this case, the word "tribal" also carries with it the notion of obsolescence and the suggestion that certain forms of aggressive behavior (i.e., the warrior ethos) were no longer necessary or productive. Like Fiedler, Leary also noted how the drug seems to have a feminizing effect on the subjects who take it; the LSD patient becomes less aggressive and more receptive to aesthetic and emotional experiences. When Allen Ginsberg first took psilocybin, he remarked on the drug's spiritual effect. He was seized by "messianic feelings": "We're going to teach people to stop hating... [and we are going to] start a peace and love movement" (Lee and Shlain 77).

Leary's efforts at promoting the therapeutic value of LSD were only partially successful. In the spring of 1963, amid much controversy, Leary was fired from Harvard for shirking his professorial duties (missing an Honors Program committee meeting). Richard Alpert (later known as Ram Dass), Leary's colleague in the Psychology Department, was also fired, allegedly for giving LSD to a male undergraduate with whom he was sexually involved. Thus, the Harvard LSD controversy of 1963 was also fueled, in some respects, by certain gender issues. In one sense, the administrators believed that Leary and Alpert were corrupting youth (Harvard undergraduates). However, Harvard's dismissal of Alpert also indicates that the educational authorities were concerned about the notion that LSD could trigger latent homosexual impulses in heterosexual men and women.[30]

When Leary left his academic career behind and embraced the role of cultural messiah, he became more alienated from his former colleagues and the establishment, and, as a result, his political rhetoric became increasingly divisive. One of his favorite targets was the older male population—his own generation. Leary's critique of the establishment and its elders contains some familiar ageist clichés of the "don't trust anyone over thirty" variety; however, his vituperative attacks also contain a gender subtext. Leary, a master of sound-bite mantras and crude binaries, uses some familiar masculine myths to attack the aging male population.[31]

In "Chemical Warfare—The Alcoholics vs. the Psychedelics" (1968), Leary mocks the older generation with hyperbolic rhetoric: "We have the astonishing spectacle of a small, menopausal, middle-class minority, tolerant [of] alcohol and addicted to external power"

(*The Politics of Ecstasy* 91). Leary's language ("menopausal . . . minority") suggests that the older generation is both impotent and womanly; moreover, Leary claims that his political views are based on Darwinian "hormonal politics": members of the younger generation are "carrying seed [and] are concerned with perpetuation of seed. It isn't conceivable to me that a young man or woman of twenty-five would do anything to blow up this planet" (262). In contrast, the older generation of males is more apt "to blow the thing up for some concept of status or prestige" (ibid.). Although he claims that his political theories are based on Darwinian precepts, Leary is recycling familiar gender tropes (e.g., impotency and sterility) that revolve around phallic conceptions of masculinity. In the Depression, Michael Gold argued that homosexuals and members of the leisure classes were effeminate and prone to sterility. Leary updates and modifies the trope by adding Lawrencean romanticism: the youthful male counterculture becomes the "seed bearers" and the enlightened protectors of the species while the older male generation is associated with violence and various forms of mental illness: "One of the terrible things, of course, about the menopausal society is that the older you get the more brain damaged you are" (273).

For Leary, gender and cultural attitudes are closely related to one's age and one's drug of choice. Alcohol produces aggressive masculinity, loutish behavior, and unwanted pregnancies. In contrast, Leary thought that psychedelic drugs produce a more spiritual and less hostile response in men ("psychedelic drugs . . . stimulate quiet, serene, humorous, sensual, reflective responses" (*Flashbacks* 178). Leary's virulent criticisms of the older generation are based on the assumption that those men are hopelessly addicted to alcohol, aggression, and power. Moreover, Leary's optimism about the younger generation is linked to its members' enthusiasm for mind-expanding drugs and his utopian belief that the psychedelic revolution will lead to the decline of alcoholism and the creation of a more benevolent and tolerant society.

Leary's cultural assault on the establishment can also be read as an updated version of Mailer's *The White Negro*; the hip group ("the Indians, the Negroes, the young, and the creative") is pitted against the squares ("the old-timers"). However, in Leary's version, squareness is specifically linked to aggressive masculinity and whiteness: "The history of the white, menopausal, mendacious men now ruling the planet earth is a history of repeated violation of the harmonious laws of nature, all having the direct object of establishing [a] tyranny of the materialistic aging over the gentle, the peace-loving, the young, the colored" (*The Politics of Ecstasy* 363). In Leary's Dionysian masculinity, the mythic cultural feminine—in this case, nature—is being violated by aggressive white masculinity. Moreover, white rulers are also linked to philistinism and the Reichian condition of emotional "deadness": "They are bores. They hate beauty. They hate sex. They hate life" (365). Leary's version of transformative masculinity attempts to critique the male propensity for aggression; however, in doing so, Leary is not willing to dispense with the most elemental masculine obsession: the myth of phallic potency. In the gender rhetoric of the 1960s, the critique of aggressive masculinity is often followed by the reaffirmation of phallic masculinity. Hence, in this crucial respect, the Dionysian mode of masculinity is not markedly different from its predecessors.

Although the critique of aggressive masculinity is a crucial component of Leary's psychedelic agenda, his gender politics are not as progressive as one might assume. In the mid-1960s, Leary's views on homosexuality are not different from that of the medical and psychological establishment of the time; Leary views homosexuality as a "psychological or learned distortion" and the result of various "symbolic screw ups." In his interview with *Playboy* magazine, Leary refutes the claim that LSD stimulates latent homosexual feelings. Conversely, Leary promotes LSD as a potential cure for homosexuality ("it's not surprising that we've had many cases of long-term homosexuals who, under LSD, discover that they are not only genitally but genetically male, that they are basically attracted to females"; *The Politics of Ecstasy* 133).[32] Throughout the *Playboy* interview, Leary's promotion of LSD is buttressed by hyperbolic claims about the drug's ability to enhance the sexual experience ("In a carefully prepared, loving LSD session, a woman can have several hundred orgasms"). Given the predominantly masculine cultural arena (*Playboy*), Leary is perhaps mindful of the fact that any serious critique of aggressive masculinity is bound to evoke criticism and, in many cases, a charge of effeminacy. Hence, Leary makes a sure bet: fantasies of phallic plenitude and superhuman potency.

If Leary's idiosyncratic version of Dionysian masculinity is predicated on phallic fantasies, how is it different from the robotic masculinity of the 1950s or the hard-boiled masculinity of the 1930s? The answer lies in Leary's radical embrace of the feminine concept of mutability. The mutable male subject and the changeability of human nature become crucial tropes of Dionysian masculinity in the 1960s; all the leading intellectuals and public figures who are associated with the counterculture—Timothy Leary, Julian Beck, R. D. Laing, Jerry Rubin, Charles Reich—share this belief while the members of the Old Left adopt a more cautious view of human nature. The transformative masculinity of the 1960s was also unique because it was quite successful at promoting a full-scale critique of aggressive hypermasculinity.

Leary, both as a trained psychologist and as a media-savvy celebrity, was quite skillful at promoting his idiosyncratic form of Dionysian masculinity; his media stunts and his outrageous political positions prompted President Richard Nixon to label him "the most dangerous man alive." From a gender point of view, Leary's LSD-inspired cultural revolution is a fascinating historical moment because it promoted a serious reevaluation of traditional masculinist myths and the warrior ethos. Leary's cultural agenda was anchored in the notion that the mutability of the masculine mind and body was both stimulating and desirable, and his rhetoric was successful in that it made various forms of irrationality appear attractive and vital while he mocked the cultural preference for rationality. In the aftermath of the psychedelic experiment, rationality, as a cultural and masculine ideal, lost much of its cultural prestige.

With regard to relations between the sexes, it is important not to overstate the transformation of gender mores; the male embrace of the Dionysian ethos did not significantly alter male attitudes toward women, and counterculture males were, by and large, not especially enlightened about sexual politics. However, the Dionysian mode of masculinity did legitimize the adoption of certain feminine attitudes that the previous generation would have considered womanly. Psychedelic culture aided the creation of a less rigid conception of maleness; some forms of masculinity could embrace emotional receptivity and the principle of feminine allure—in dress and manner—without being considered effeminate. However, the most significant development of the 1960s and the psychedelic revolution was the severe critique of certain forms of aggressive masculinity. The traditional mythic forms of masculinity—especially the hard and rigid varieties—were seriously challenged and debunked.

Although Leary continued to publish nonfiction essays and books throughout the 1960s—*The Politics of Ecstasy* (1968) was popular worldwide—it is evident that his assorted writings were merely intended as a preface to his larger socio-aesthetic project: the alteration of consciousness. Not surprisingly, various member of the Old Left and the older generation remained quite hostile to Leary's proselytizing for psychedelic culture. Moral objections aside, the Old Left's reservations about psychedelic culture can also be read as a nostalgic attachment to the primacy of the literary text in American cultural life. On a different level, the objections of the Old Left can also be viewed in masculinist terms: the debate about the ethical merits of LSD can be read as a debate about the porousness of the male body and the extent to which the male body can be transformed and remodified. The Old Left, with few exceptions, remained skeptical about the counterculture's attraction to the mutable male subject.

THE WAR ON RIGIDITY: THE LIVING THEATRE'S *THE BRIG* AND *PARADISE NOW*

Like Timothy Leary, Julian Beck and Judith Malina of the Living Theatre also had grandiose plans for the alteration of human nature and society. Both Leary and the Living Theatre were interested in combating masculine hardness and in devising a cultural program that championed the soft body as a new social ideal for the younger generation. While Leary was primarily working within a quasi-scientific framework with the Massachusetts Correctional Facility, the Living Theatre was primarily interested in devising aesthetic and performative events that ritualized the path from hardness to softness.

The avant-garde theatre troupe rose to international fame by producing a series of controversial theatrical works that attempted to marry politics and theatrical expression and thereby eliminate the traditional distinction between life and art. By the late 1960s, the Living Theatre conceived of theatre as a utopian forum for revolutionary praxis, a social laboratory that could alter human nature and enact various radical forms of political and social change. This was not an unreasonable project in 1968. The social unrest in Prague, Paris, Chicago, and Mexico City suggested that a global revolution was approaching. At this historic moment, students, hippies, and other members of the New Left were receptive to the company's radical utopian ideas and the visceral aesthetic of its physical performances. By the spring of 1968, the Living Theatre was at the forefront of the sexual revolution and the antiwar movement, and the leaders of the company were convinced that a political revolution would be linked to a radical change in sexual attitudes.

When considering the Living Theatre's utopian project of the 1960s, two productions—*The Brig* (1963) and *Paradise Now* (1968)— exemplify the company's pacifist politics and its attempt to create affective performances that morally transform the audience.[33] Both promoted an anarchist view of U.S. history and America's political and social institutions. The company's anarchist principles were largely derived from the writings of Paul Goodman, and in practice they mostly consisted of didactic slogans ("Abolish the state! Abolish the police!") that emphasized an optimistic view of human nature and encouraged the spectator to resist authority and social and political hierarchies. The theatre was conceived of as an ideal place for anarchist revolution because it facilitated the momentary transgression of social and political norms. However, it is important to note that the Living Theatre was not interested in creating ephemeral works of art; it wanted to mold spectators into revolutionary subjects who would take action when they left the sanctuary of the theatre.

The Living Theatre's utopian/anarchist vision was also rooted in a critique of traditional masculinity. The radical company conceived of theatre as a utopian space where rigid and aggressive forms of masculinity could be reformed through a nonverbal experience of sexual liberation. Like the work of Burroughs and Kerouac, the Living Theatre's utopian project was inextricably linked to the psychoanalytical theories of Wilhelm Reich. Though the Viennese psychologist died in the 1950s, his ideas enjoyed a great resurgence in the turbulent 1960s. Reich maintained that there is a one-to-one correspondence between acts of violence and sexual repression: if an individual—in this case, an audience member—could experience genuine sexual liberation, then this transformed individual would be less likely to commit acts of violence in the future. At the height of the Vietnam conflict, Reich's theories, which seemed to offer a mythic solution to the ubiquitous problem of masculine aggression, became extremely popular with the counterculture ("make love, not war"). The utopian experience of sexual gratification became a way of mitigating aggressive tendencies and breaking down one's "character armor" (Reich's term for various defense mechanisms in our personalities). In Reich's post-Freudian theory, the orgasm is a quasi-mystical experience that morally and physically transforms the individual; the orgasm is the teleological end of the Reichian sexual revolution and the solution to the problem of human aggression.[34]

The Reichian theory of the body sheds light on the utopianism of the Living Theatre. By merging the somatic and the political, Beck's theatrical writings promote Reich's call for sexual revolution.[35] Hence, political issues are sexualized and discussed in terms of body types. The hard body is associated with rigidity ("musculature armor") and the state of "unfeelingness." Hard-shell masculinity is a conception of maleness that positions itself in opposition to the various forms of feminine softness; the hard body is impervious to emotionalism and sentimentality, and the ideal of the soft body is presented as an antidote to rigidity. In Reichian theory, hypermasculine aggression is caused by the damming of sexual energy, and the orgasm allows for the release of the blocked-up energy and results in a softening of the body and the establishment of non-aggressive being. Thus, the Living Theatre's utopian project attempts to theatricalize ("act out") certain therapeutic aspects of Reich's psychoanalytic theory.

The transition from hardness ("character armor") to softness ("genital character") in Reichian theory is not as easy as it sounds. For Reich, all orgasms are not equal. For example, two partners in a loveless marriage do not achieve genital character when they have sex. Furthermore, the truly therapeutic and authentic orgasm ("orgastic potency") must occur during the act of a man penetrating a woman. For Reich, mere ejaculation does not signify orgastic potency:

> Orgastic potency is the capacity for surrender to the flow of biological energy without any inhibition, the capacity for complete discharge of all dammed-up sexual excitation through involuntary pleasurable contractions of the body. Not a single neurotic individual possesses orgastic potency; the corollary of this fact is that the vast majority of humans suffer from character neurosis. (*The Function of the Orgasm* 79)

A devout materialist, Reich sought to move away from abstract language ("unconscious," "ego," "id"). Instead, Reich wanted to ground his psychoanalytic theory in the materiality of the body. Hence, Reich focuses on physiological terms ("contractions of the body"). Reich's definition of orgastic potency implies that most people are "neurotic" and do not achieve orgastic potency (mental well-being) in their everyday lives.[36] The Living Theatre's productions attempted to redress the sexual imbalance that Reich identified in his writings.

The Living Theatre's interest in creating somatically affective theatre is evidenced in its production of Kenneth Brown's *The Brig*, an important avant-garde theatrical event when it was first staged off-Broadway in the early 1960s. *The Brig* is loosely based on the author's experiences in the marine corps, and its subject matter ideally suited the Living Theatre's commitment to Artaud's notion of the Theatre of Cruelty. Unlike most plays, *The Brig* is virtually devoid of characterization and conventional dramatic conflict. That is to say, the play has no plot; *The Brig*'s action revolves around attempts to brutalize and punish the prisoners who are incarcerated, and the production focused on dramatizing the prisoners' visceral experiences of pain and trauma. Julian Beck's set design featured a massive chain-link fence that separated the performers from the audience. The set emphasized total spatial control (see fig. 8), an environment where every action of the prisoners was regimented and carefully monitored. In this repressive milieu, even the attempt to speak was regulated ("Sir, prisoner number three requests permission to speak, Sir"). The narrative of the play featured no character development, only the dramatization of the acts of socially conditioning the prisoners.

The production was intended as an anarchist-cum-Artaudian critique of brutality in the military, and the play's political message was presented in clearly gendered terms; *The Brig* featured an all-male cast and dramatized the hypermasculine rituals of the marine corps in excruciating detail. Since characterization was a minor concern, the malleability of the male body became the central focus of the production. Judith Malina's "Director's Notes" document how the play's dramatic action is essentially the male soldier's body receiving blows and experiencing pain:

> The moment before impact: the prisoner draws upon his will . . . that is he *hardens* himself both muscularly and psychologically. . . . [Then,] the moment of impact. . . . This is the moment in which the prisoner has lost his total rigidity because he can now save himself with resiliency. But resiliency is a feminine (ergo: cowardly) attribute. (in Brown, *The Brig* 98–99; emphasis in original)

Malina draws attention to the hard and soft permutations of the male body in pain. At first, the male body is rendered rigid through various punitive acts (*"hardens* himself"). However, she also indicates that the male body is made soft and elastic by the blows ("the prisoner has lost his total rigidity because he can now save himself with resiliency"). Malina also indicates that the soldier's experience of pain is meant to arouse empathy: "When the first blow is delivered in the darkened Brig before dawn and the prisoner winces and topples from his superbly rigid position, the contraction of his body is repeated *inside* the body of the spectator" (98). This comment emphasizes the didactic aspect of *The Brig*'s depiction of brutality and underscores the attempt to create a theatre of somatic affect—a theatrical experience that is viscerally experienced by the audience.

It is clear that the blows administered in the production were not typical stage punches. The filmed version of the play reveals that the batons used were real, and the actors do experience excruciating pain when they are struck. The veracity of the physical pain on stage was offered as proof of the Living Theatre's commitment to Artaudian aesthetics. Malina's "Director's Notes" also uses an excerpt from Artaud to justify the production's pacifist interpretation: "I defy any spectator to whom such violent scenes will have transferred their blood—the violence of blood having been placed at the service of the violence of thought—I defy that spectator to give himself up, once outside of [the] theatre, to ideas of war, riot, and blatant murder."[37]

Hence, through acts of physical degradation and extreme pain, the Living Theatre attempted to create a therapeutic theatre of somatic gesture. Dramaturgically speaking, this is entirely different from a conventional character-driven play: the theatrical intent was not to entertain the audience, but to shock the audience with theatrical displays of physical brutality. If the audience reacted and was affected in some way, then the production was successful. In this sense, the Living Theatre assumed that the audience would be horrified by the raw depiction of brutality. However, in retrospect, there is no way of gauging the audience's actual responses to the production's critique of violence and aggressive masculinity. One can merely conclude that the Living Theatre assumed that its visceral brand of Artaudian theatre would emotionally transform the audience.

By depicting brutal acts of violence in plain view of the audience, the Living Theatre attempted to blur the distinction between theatricality and real life. The Living Theatre's production of *The Brig* cannot be called utopian because it did not present an alternative conception of a better world. Instead, the production was a dystopic and hellish view of military life. However, the Living Theatre's critique of masculine aggression in *The Brig* was the beginning of a didactic trajectory in that the production attempted to affect the audience viscerally and morally transform it.

After *The Brig*, the Living Theatre became more fascinated with the notion of directly involving the audience in the performance. Though *The Brig* contained moments where the actors improvised routines and moved away from the prescribed text, the production still maintained the traditional barriers between the performers and the audience. In future productions, the Living Theatre gravitated toward a more flexible theatrical aesthetic that explicitly contested the separation between life and art. With *The Brig*, the Living Theatre was still limited by the chain-link fence and the footlights that separated the performers from the spectators. *Paradise Now* would transcend these limitations; this utopian production was the apex of the Living Theatre's attempt to create a performance of social praxis and a ritual that did not stem from a text that was conceived by a playwright.

From its inception, *Paradise Now* was an extremely ambitious production that radically challenged the existing conceptions of theatre aesthetics. Created on the eve of the May 1968 rebellion in Paris, the production attempted to reflect the revolutionary fervor of the student protests and the Prague Spring. When the production was brought to New Haven, Connecticut, in August 1968, it received an enormous amount of publicity because it marked the company's return to North America after several years of exile. With great fanfare, the production toured theatres and college campuses during the fall of 1968 and the spring of 1969.

Given the limited appeal of avant-garde theatre productions, the Living Theatre's 1968 tour received massive attention from the print media (*Newsweek* and *Time*) and national television (CBS's *Camera Three*).[38] The mainstream press was curious about the company because it had produced several provocative shows that had generated a great deal of media attention in Europe and the company had not performed in North America for five years. Moreover, the Living Theatre's confrontations with the police (in New Haven and Philadelphia) and the fact that several performances were canceled by educational authorities (at MIT and USC) created yet more publicity and confirmed the company's established reputation for scandal and controversy. It is therefore no surprise that the Living Theatre often played to sold-out houses. The performances at the beginning of the tour—at the Yale School of Drama and the Brooklyn Academy— were attended by elite members of the theatrical world (critics and theatre scholars) and received extensive coverage in the scholarly press.[39] Both *Theater* and *The Drama Review* (*TDR*) devoted entire issues to the Living Theatre's North American tour, and each publication included interviews with Beck and Malina, roundtable discussions, reviews, and photos from the productions of *Frankenstein, Mysteries, Antigone,* and *Paradise Now.* In short, the Living Theatre's tour of 1968–1969 was arguably the most widely covered avant-garde theatre event in U.S. history and a defining moment for the counterculture of the late 1960s. In the annals of American theatre, there has never been anything quite like it before or since.

Unlike *The Brig, Paradise Now* was a collectivist theatrical creation that was loosely based on a mélange of mystical texts from disparate cultures: the I Ching, the Tibetan Book of the Dead, Kabbalah, Hasidic rings, tantric doctrines, yoga and breathing exercises, excerpts from works by Reich and Laing. The religious texts were juxtaposed with secular humanist texts, and the goals of the production were to free the audience from all forms of political and sexual repression and to promote a spontaneous, nonviolent, anarchist revolution.[40] The latter was supposed to be achieved through a revolution of sensibility that would begin in the traditional theatrical space and then spill out into the streets at the end of the performance.

In place of a traditional dramatic text, *Paradise Now* fostered audience participation and utilized elements of chance to create a loosely structured theatrical happening. Although the production was meant to signify a departure from text-based dramaturgy, *Paradise Now,* in performance, still resembled a tightly controlled theatrical event with a specific didactic purpose. The play consisted of eight revolutionary "rungs," a situation that dialectically moved toward a specific thematic concept and form of praxis. The ladder of eight rungs implied a "vertical ascent toward permanent revolution" (Neff 206). Each rung consisted of a rite, a vision, and an action. The "rites" and "visions" were performed by the Living Theatre actors, and "the actions [were] performed by the spectators with the help of the actors" (ibid.). The religious chants and yoga exercises were considered ideal because they are explicitly body-centered and nonrational.

In the first rite (the Rite of Guerrilla Theatre), the actors mixed with the spectators and began repeating various phrases ("I am not allowed to travel without a passport," "I don't know how to stop the wars," "You can't live if you don't have money," "I am not allowed to smoke marijuana").[41] The actors repeated the phrases several times with great urgency and frustration. The confrontational exercise immediately broke down the traditional barrier between the audience and the performer and challenged the audience to react to the situation. The actors' repetition of the fifth phrase ("I am not allowed to take off my clothes") culminated with the performers removing articles of clothing in a frenzy. The act of stripping down to the legal limit—g-strings, loincloths, bikinis—signified "an assault on culture" and a dialectical progression toward praxis ("the revolution of culture"). The first rung ended with the actors slowly rising from the ground, chanting a quotation taken from R. D. Laing's *The Politics of Experience:* "If I could turn you on, if I could drive you out of your wretched mind, if I could tell you, I would let you know" (138). The chant was a theatrical call to arms, and it encouraged the audience to "freak out," take the stage, and participate in Dionysian revelry. Thus, "modern man" became "natural man": an individual who could travel without a passport, live without money, and take his/her clothes off. The rite also implied an attempt to reclaim the paradisiacal state of being that existed in the garden of Eden.

The nudity of the actors was not considered gratuitous because it was thought to be consistent with the production's prelapsarian themes. In the 1960s, nudity was often considered both a revolutionary act and a gesture of radical political commitment; the act of stripping was also a typical manifestation of the Living Theatre's Reichian sensibility, which attempted to unite the political and the somatic. Much like the musical *Hair* (1968), the show's celebration of nudity and stripping became its signature motif; in some cases, female audience members who had heard about it would buy new underwear before attending the show.[42] The latter suggests that, for some, *Paradise Now*'s political message was overshadowed by the production's prurient appeal.

The subsequent rungs were concerned with the holiness of all human beings, the promotion of racial unity, the removal of sexual taboos, the exorcism of violence, the mythic destruction of the ego, and the establishment of principles of peace and nonviolence. The various rungs used different forms of confrontational devices (cultural assaults) that were designed to push the audience toward praxis (participation in the ritual).

The most controversial rung was undoubtedly the Rite of Universal Intercourse (rung 5). In this scenario, the scantily clad actors and some spectators—clothed and unclothed—formed a large "body pile," a mass of bodies that caressed one another in order to break the "touch barrier" (see fig. 9). The undulating body pile signified the ephemeral triumph of Reichian somatic consciousness: they were soft bodies purged of rigidity and aggressive tendencies. In symbolic terms, the spontaneous and collective body piles reinforced the Living Theatre's mantra, "the ego is the guide to behavior [while] sensation is the guide to experience." Psychologically speaking, "behavior" was considered pejorative because it implies robotic actions that are merely a product of the existing culture; sensation was considered to be superior to behavior because it is authentic and rooted in the emotions and the body. The theatrical cultivation of sensation also implied the unlearning of "civilized" behavior. The Living Theatre's preference for sensation often resulted in anti-intellectualism: to be physical or emotional was considered "real" and authentic, and to be circumspect or rational (which included nonparticipation in the rites) was to be square and complacent.

Paradise Now also included a rite that aimed at creating a trance-like state (the Rite of the Mysterious Voyage; or, The Flip-Out). The actors formed a circle around a male actor and began chanting. As the chant reached an explosive intensity, the actor was transformed by the sound and movement of the circle of performers. According to Neff, the purpose of the trance was "to allow the pain and tantrum and madness to possess one, to push into dangerous psychic areas and flow with these demonic forces without holding back" (213). Hence, the rite was an attempt to theatricalize the return to a primitive and quasi-nonrational state. The exercise was partly influenced by R. D. Laing's radical contention that "madness need not be all breakdown. It may also be a breakthrough. It is potential liberation and renewal as well as enslavement and existential death" (93). Laing's sympathetic view of madness was a product of the anti-psychiatry movement of the 1960s, which maintained that madness and psychological break-down also had a healing dimension that was often not recognized by the medical establishment. By the same token, the Living Theatre believed that it could create Laingian secular rituals that would induce a temporary destruction of the ego and lead the actor on a mental voyage to a more enlightened state of consciousness. Much like tribal initiation rituals, the Living Theatre believed that these intensely physical and nonrational exercises could produce a mystical breakthrough for the actor and the audience.

Paradise Now also included rungs (the Rite of Opposing Forces) that attempted to dramatize the creation of soft bodies. In this non-verbal improvisation exercise, a male Living Theatre troupe member lay down in the center of the theatre and completely relaxed his mind and body: "His body is limp, his mind is in a free space" (Neff 214). As the actor breathed deeply, a group of actors slowly approached him and "perform[ed] ritual acts on him": "They touch, caress, lift, shake, strike, and stroke him . . . they move his hair and his limbs; they kiss him, they make sounds in his ears, on his face and on various parts of the body." The sum of the ensemble's actions signified the process of rebirth: "[b]ringing both positive and negative forces which they try to pass through the body" of the actor (ibid.). The exercise culminated with the actor rising from his passive and receptive state and embracing "transcendent energy" and the state of "Here and Now" (ibid.). This improvised scenario was another attempt at the theatre of nonverbal somatic gesture: it represented the creation of the new soft male subject and the destruction of the masculine ego and its attendant state of rigidity. It also was an attempt to create a secular ritual: the actor's hard masculine body became a mass of formless clay that was shaped, fondled, and caressed by the male and female members of the cast. Thus, the hard male body became pliable and mutable, and the scenario of negative and positive energy passing through the male body implied the ritualized acceptance of feminine softness.

Paradise Now ended symbolically with the Vision of the Undoing of the Myth of Eden. In this scenario, the actors reconstructed the garden of Eden and the tree of knowledge. However, in the Living Theatre's version, the tree of knowledge was transformed into the "tree of life," as the actors and spectators left the stage, exited the theatre, and poured into the streets, shouting: "Theatre is in the street. . . . the street belongs to the people. . . . free the theatre. . . . Free the street. . . . Begin" (Neff 217). In several cases, the actors, still nude, carried members of the audience on their shoulders as they exited from the theatre. During the New Haven performances of 1968, several actors and spectators were met by the police and charged with indecent exposure. The police, who presumably missed the performance, were not persuaded by the Living Theatre's radical appeals for immediate cultural revolution.

Paradise Now was a collection of physical routines, exercises, and situations that used language and experiences to jar the audience and make them question their relationship to the performers and the performance itself. The political radicalism of *Paradise Now* was conveyed in the utopian creation of soft bodies, the embrace of nonrationalism, and the repudiation of certain types of language.

The Living Theatre's distrust of traditional verbal theatre was rooted in Julian Beck's belief that conventional theatrical dialogue merely reproduced certain predetermined forms of behavior. In some cases, Beck advocated an antagonistic relationship to language itself: "The breakdown of language equals [the] breakdown of values, of modes of insight, of the sick rationale. Breakdown of language means invention of fresh forms of communication"; 27). Instead, Beck strove to create physical and nonverbal situations that would "shake things up, change, [and make us] give ourselves over to what we don't comprehend" (ibid.). In place of language, Beck used nonverbal situations (body piles, yoga exercises) that attempted to convert hard and rigid bodies into supple and pliable bodies that would no longer be ruled by the intellect. Beck's faith in anti-rationalism suggests that the company's utopian vision was tinged with romanticism: the company promoted a mythic return to a supposedly benevolent and egoless world of pure sensation.

A photo from the Living Theatre's production of *Paradise Now* at the Yale School of Drama (see fig. 10) displays male audience members leaving the theatre space while exuberantly naked; the post-performance images, which reveal the social acceptance of male nudity, male camaraderie, and homoeroticism, are evidence that the Living Theatre's utopian project of creating less hostile male bodies was successful on this occasion. As praxis, the utopian gender experiments of *Paradise Now* produced some startling results and elicited some remarkable reactions from the audience. Neal Weaver, a theatre critic for *After Dark*, a New York dance publication, notes that the collapse of social and sexual mores also extended to the lobby and the bathrooms: "Exhausted by dancing, I seek out the men's room in search of a drink of water. I see a woman going in. But I realize that this barrier, too, has broken down. Men and women are sharing the same facilities, without self-consciousness, or embarrassment. Each goes about his business, ignoring the others" (56).[43] Weaver's account captures the transformative power of *Paradise Now* and how the production often inspired gaiety and a generosity of spirit within the performative space: "The whole atmosphere is changed now. It is no longer a theatre, but a party, a village fair, a debate, a ballgame, a salon, a happening" (55). Like this one, most historical accounts of

Paradise Now (Dekoven, Tytell, Croyden, Biner, Mantegna) tend to emphasize the production's benevolent side. However, not all of the audience reactions were so benign.

The Living Theatre's attempt to promote sexual liberation—without regard for differences in the social construction of sexuality and gender—and the notion that the theatre could be transformed into a fully liberated zone where audience members could say or do anything they pleased also could create a hostile environment for female audience members and the company's actresses. John Lahr's account of the Brooklyn Academy performance of *Paradise Now* reveals how the Living Theatre's utopian rhetoric about sexual liberation ("Do what you want! Free theater! Do what you want!") elicited incidents of sexual assault during the Rite of Universal Intercourse: "An actress stopped by a member of the audience; he reaches for her bikini and pulls it to her knees. Exposed, she waits for him to let go, her eyes needles of betrayal, her flesh lusterless. She is not ashamed of nudity, but in her defiant righteousness there is no innocence" (264). The novelist Leslie Epstein, then a reviewer for the *New American Review*, notes a similar incident: "A few seats from me a man reached beneath the brassiere of the loveliest girl in the cast, who was standing in the aisle, and began kneading her breasts from behind" (241). John Tytell notes that Jenny Hecht, a popular actress in the Living Theatre, "believed that she had to be as generous and open with spectators as possible in order to convince anyone of her radical stance, and consequently she would give of herself as often as she was asked" (259).

The most notorious incident occurred during the last performance of *Paradise Now* at the Brooklyn Academy: "On the night of their final New York performance, one of the cast was screwed on stage—random, violent, impetuous. More uncontrolled, in fact, than the Utopian dream at the base of Beck's revolution" (Lahr 263). In this account, Lahr is referring to an act of sexual assault. However, the identity of the female cast member is unclear, and the circumstances surrounding this incident still remain murky.

Many of the more recent ex post facto scholarly accounts of the Living Theatre (Dekoven 2004; Shank 1988, 2002; Tytell 1995) tend to downplay or elide the cases of sexual assault that occurred during the performances of *Paradise Now*. For example, Tytell briefly mentions that Malina was assaulted by "a group of short-haired young men" (244–45). The brevity of Tytell's account suggests a desire to avoid the unpleasant. In contrast, Judith Malina's account of the event in her memoir *The Enormous Despair* is more forthright:

> In the Paradise performance, during the first rung, I am attacked on stage by a hostile group of men. It was during the chanting of "If I Could Turn You On"; the stage was very crowded; there was hardly any room to dance; when this group grabbed me in the middle of the crowd, I chanted to them and accepted their mocking advances with as graceful/ as paradisial responses as I was able to muster. But it was soon out of my hands. Beyond a certain point, I saw it happen: that they were no longer compassionate. Then they begin to fight among each other, and in fighting to get at me beyond my capacity to either yield or resist. Hundreds of people surround us but the crowd is oblivious. I was no longer addressing them. They were only addressing each other and I was their quarry. They lost all sense of my existence. "Hold her!" one said to the other, as if I weren't there. (94–95)

Lahr and Malina may be discussing the same incident, which occurred during the performance on October 21, 1968.

Reports of sexual assault appear in various reviews of the performances at the Brooklyn Academy of Music (see Epstein and Lahr). Leslie Epstein, who is not referring to the assault of Malina, writes: "On stage, another man, fully clothed, pulled a participant from the Rite of Universal Intercourse and dragged her on her bare back to the wings, where he knelt between her legs. If he took her, no jury could convict him of rape. We had all been solicited" (241). Epstein's rhetoric demonstrates how the Reichian banner of sexual liberation often produced a hostile environment where men ("we") were inclined to use their own "liberation" as a justification for sexual harassment and, in some cases, sexual violence. To some male audience members, the Living Theatre's message of sexual liberation signified little more than the fantasy of unlimited access to the female body. These incidents also reveal the phallic subtext of the Living Theatre's critique of rationality and rigidity. In the rhetoric of transformative masculinity, the liberation from sexual repression is conceived of as an egalitarian struggle that is identical for both men and women. Such assumptions ignore the political and historical distinctions between the sexes and that sexual liberation is not a value-free concept, given the fact that women have often been subjected to male aggression and violence. Although adopting the banner of sexual liberation, the Living Theatre wrongly assumed that the immediate removal of sexual taboos would necessarily result in benevolent forms of social change.

The sexual assaults indicate some ethical blind spots in the Living Theatre's utopian vision as well as a problematic aspect of Dionysian ethos: the tendency to privilege emotion over rationality can be used to justify various aggressive actions. The company's belief that heightened emotionality would necessarily lead to a softer and more receptive masculinity was certainly a problematic assumption that often inspired heated exchanges and, in some cases, violent incidents between Living Theatre actors and audience members.

The Living Theatre's reputation for abusing and insulting the audience was legendary. At one theatrical event, Julian Beck confronted a female spectator, ripped a fur stole off her back, threw it on the floor, and shrieked at her: "'The weight of your furs makes it impossible for the needs of the people to touch you!' I threw things all over the room, put human relationship in crisis. I despair of the intellectual ever really taking part in the real revolution when it comes to it. We walk around its edges" (Beck 168). Beck's shock tactics were meant as an attack on bourgeois consumerism and as a critique of the complaisant intellectual who thinks too much and does not act. Beck argued that his aggressive behavior was justified because he was striving to put "human relationship[s] in crisis." In many cases, the Living Theatre prized emotional commitment over rational discourse and was fond of sexualizing discussions about political tactics: "The artist who talks about revolution especially non-violent revolution is just blowing words: aesthetic masturbation: (to fuck takes a certain amount of courage!) Action is valid" (ibid.). In this case, Beck's phallocentric "liberation" rhetoric suggests that political commitment should be measured in Reichian terms.

It is not surprising that the Living Theatre's shock tactics and anti-intellectualism were often met with resistance.[44] In a performance at Bennington College (then a women's college), various audience members objected to the Living Theatre's confrontational tactics. One female spectator shouted back at the actors: "But I agree with you. . . . why are you yelling at me? [Another female spectator was less restrained.] . . . Don't scream at me you fucking idiot! . . . I don't hate you because you are black. I hate you because you are spitting in my face" (Neff 110). During the same performance at Bennington, Rufus Collins, one of the Living Theatre's most volatile actors, "slapped a girl across the face during a heated confrontation" (111). Such displays were condemned by other Living Theatre company members; however, in the utopian rhetoric of the Living Theatre, they could be read as authentic expressions of "sensation," "passion," and "unrepressed emotion." Incidents like those at the performance at Bennington College demonstrated that the Living Theatre's utopian critique of aggression was sometimes nothing more than empty slogans, as certain actors of the company seemed curiously blind to their own capacity for aggression. Unlike *The Brig,* the Living Theatre's assault on hardness in *Paradise Now* was directed at the audience; the company's experiment in Artaudian praxis implied that the path to liberation requires the acting out of aggression. This trend also suggested that the realization of transformative masculinity requires the lived experience of hardness ("acting out" aggressive behavior) within the framework of performance.

The Living Theatre thrived on the unexpected and the stripping away of the veneer of civility that usually characterizes theatrical events. Although the Living Theatre espoused a critique of hypermasculinity in its productions, the actors were often aggressive toward their audiences. This contradiction is at the heart of transformative masculinity, which was predicated on the primacy of the expression of emotion ("don't talk, do it") as a means of breaking down all forms of rigidity and restraint. The Living Theatre's fanatical reverence for the expression of emotion coupled with its rejection of rationality often created an environment where antagonism was welcomed as an authentic way of breaking the ingrained passivity of the audience; in such an atmosphere, conventional notions of civility were considered irrelevant and passé.

The Living Theatre's attempt to critique rigid masculinity was ultimately more popular with the younger members of the audience. The Old Left and liberal members of the theatre establishment (Eric Bentley, Harold Clurman, Robert Brustein), who tended to be older, remained critical of *Paradise Now* and its desire to create an unrepressed atmosphere of touch and frenzy. Such critics were quick to point out the Living Theatre's moral contradictions: how its aggressive stance toward the audience could not be reconciled with its commitment to nonviolence and pacifism.

Bentley, a noted Brechtian scholar and theatre critic, was a vocal critic of the Living Theatre and the notorious Rite of Universal Intercourse:

> You know they [the Living Theatre] act as if we're all squares, as if we're all afraid of sex, for instance, and they're not. They talk down to us. . . . It's hard for me to imagine that the fifteen or twenty orgasms happening on the evening I attended at Yale, in the midst of the fruit-of-the-loom underwear, was an experience of any great human beauty or meaningful intimacy. . . . What I saw at Yale was a very juvenile petting party. What a poor way to have orgasms, in one's underwear with a bunch of strangers! And a larger bunch of strangers peering at one and cracking jokes. (qtd. in Feingold 112)

Like many other Old Left critics, Bentley was appalled by the Living Theatre's shock tactics and sexual antics.[45] However, Bentley's response also indicates the extent to which the Old Left—in Reichian rhetoric, the hard and robotic bodies—was put on the defensive ("they act as if we're all squares, as if we're all afraid of sex"). However, in retrospect, it might be inferred that the Living Theatre's embrace of phallic potency as a shock tactic was a rearguard tactic: it prevented critics from labeling the actors effeminate. The Living Theatre was vulnerable to such charges because its performances put the male body on display and fully embraced the notion of feminine allure.

For other critics, the utopian promotion of softness would lead to a decline of aesthetic and artistic standards. For Brustein, the Living Theatre's influence on American theatre was regrettable:

> The new theater may be as great a danger to dramatic art as the old theater. It already embodies similar defects. Its anti-intellectualism, its sensationalism, its sexual obsessiveness, its massacre of language, its noisy attention-getting mechanisms, its indifference to artistry, craft, or skill, its violence, and, above all, its mindless tributes to Love and Togetherness (now in the form of "group gropes" and "love zaps") are not adversary demands upon the American character but rather the very qualities that have continually degraded us, the very qualities that have kept us laggard and philistine in the theater throughout the past three decades. ("The Third Theater Revisited")

In a sense, the Living Theatre encouraged this response. Unlike its previous productions (*The Brig, The Connection*), *Paradise Now,* which relied heavily on audience participation, was not very concerned with conventional notions of professionalism and artistic standards. In a review of *Paradise Now,* Harold Clurman, a veteran Old Left theatre critic, called the members of the Living Theatre "fanatics of amateurism." Bentley, Clurman, and Brustein remained unconvinced by the Living Theatre's utopian appeals. However, Brustein's response also evoked the practical and theoretical limits of transformative masculinity and its inability to derationalize certain members of the theatre establishment and the audience.

The Living Theatre's program for *Paradise Now* at the Brooklyn Academy of Music contains a succinct statement of the production's therapeutic aim: "If we can reduce the amount of aggression in one person, or change one person from being more rigid to less rigid, then the effort was worth the while" (qtd. in Tytell 245). It is impossible to say if the production met its Reichian criterion for success because there is no accurate way to document if hard and aggressive bodies who participated in *Paradise Now* were made soft by the proceedings.

Although *The Brig* was not intended to be a utopian production, it could be argued that its results were more satisfactory than those produced by *Paradise Now.* The chief difference is that the audience was separated by a chain-link fence and therefore was not encouraged to interact with the performers. The Living Theatre's didactic intent was to make the audience feel brutality rather than love. *The Brig* produced no known or reported incidents of assault. In *Paradise Now,* when literally all barriers between the performers and the audience were removed, the Living Theatre could not ensure that its rituals would produce utopian behavior. On many occasions, the results were positive and benevolent; however, during some performances, the theatre space became unmanageable and bedlam ensued.

The sexual assaults that occurred at some performances of *Paradise Now* reflect a familiar trend of the time: gestures of liberation were often juxtaposed with hypermasculine behavior. The emergence of the so-called soft male of the counterculture did not necessarily produce a more enlightened or progressive view of women and their bodies. In many respects, the sexual politics of the New Left and counterculture in the late 1960s often resembled the chauvinism of the previous generation.

The production of *Paradise Now* can be viewed as a cultural microcosm that documents the conflicting attitudes in the gender kulturkampf of the late 1960s. In one sense, Fiedler's anxieties about the feminization of youth culture and literary culture were realized. In the utopian rhetoric of the Living Theatre, the traditional male subject—rational, static, impenetrable—was negated and rendered obsolete. Much to the Old Left's dismay, the new male body was put on display and made malleable and pliable. Although the historic taboos against mutability and feminine allure were temporarily lifted, Fiedler's paranoid vision was also misleading in that it failed to anticipate transformative masculinity's devotion to the cult of phallic plenitude and the residual appeal of hard masculinity.

The ascendancy of utopian transformative masculinity may have been fairly short-lived—it died with the counterculture in the early 1970s—but its legacy remained: its critique of hard-shell masculinity was successful in that the myths of traditional masculinity were perceived as less appealing and less viable. Both the older and the younger generations began to reexamine their adherence to these myths. In the following decades, the masculine myths that had been deflated would have to be reinvented. In the 1980s, Susan Jeffords would call this trend "remasculinization."[46]

The gradual erosion of traditional masculine myths was part of a larger paradigm shift in gender attitudes in the late 1960s and early 1970s; the radical transformation of maleness and the attempt to demythologize traditional masculine myths were important in that these trends enabled other alternative conceptions of masculine and feminine identities to emerge and become manifest in popular culture. The most significant new identities arrived with gay liberation and the women's movement, radical movements that were explicitly predicated on critiques of traditional masculinity.

5

The Gender Upheavals of the Late 1960s and Early 1970s: The Black Panthers, Gay Liberation, and Radical Feminism

The last performance of *Paradise Now* was at the Sportspalast in Berlin on January 10, 1970. After sixteen months of touring, the event was somewhat anticlimactic because the thirty-member theatre troupe was experiencing internal dissension. In the aftermath of the tour, a press release announced that the radical company had, "for the sake of mobility, . . . [split] into four cells" (Biner 225). One cell went to India to seek spiritual renewal while another went to Paris to continue political engagement through community-based theatrical projects that would not be performed in "theatre buildings" for a "privileged elite" (226). Other members of the Living Theatre had become disenchanted with the company's commitment to nonviolence and pacifism. One member, Carl Einhorn, gravitated toward the Black Panther model of armed resistance. Like many leftists in the early 1970s, Einhorn became convinced that only violent revolution would produce lasting political change. By one account, Einhorn traveled to join Eldridge Cleaver and other Black Panthers who were living in exile in Algeria in 1970.[1]

Einhorn's fascination with the Black Panther movement also reflects an attraction to a different style of masculinity. While the

Living Theatre espoused the ideal of Dionysian soft-bodied masculinity, the Black Panther movement signified a revival of the mythos
of rugged masculinity. In the tradition of Norman Mailer's *The White
Negro,* the counterculture male viewed the African American radical as the symbolic embodiment of revolutionary commitment and
phallic hardness. This particular cultural trend is best exemplified in
the hypermasculine writings of Eldridge Cleaver, the Black Panthers'
minister of education in the late 1960s and early 1970s. For gender
historians, Cleaver's *Soul on Ice* (1968) is an extraordinary cultural
document because of its popularity with the New Left (it sold over
two million copies in the late 1960s and early 1970s) and the fact that it
succinctly articulates the mythic fascination with hypermasculinity
that distinctly emerged in the late 1960s and early 1970s. *Soul on Ice*
conveys the intersection of race and masculine identity and demonstrates the tremendous power of certain racial and sexual myths that
were synonymous with African American maleness.

Cleaver's political theory and literary criticism are anchored in
gender myths that are linked to both the Old Left and the New Left.
Intellectually, Cleaver's gendered reading of literature and culture
blends Michael Gold's theory of the white effeminate leisure class
and Norman Mailer's conception of the hypersexual African American male. However, Cleaver's account goes way beyond Gold's and
Mailer's masculinist conceptions of literature because he devotes
three chapters (section IV of *Soul on Ice*) to systematizing his idiosyncratic theory of gender politics, class identity, and black-white
relations. Central to Cleaver's Freudian-Marxist account of American race relations is the notion that one's class identity reveals par-
ticularities about one's sexual identity and sexual desire. For Cleaver,
"each class projects a sexual image coinciding with its class function
in society" (178). In Cleaver's racial caste system, "[t]he source of
the fragmentation of the Self in Class Society lies in the alienation
between the function of man's Mind and the function of the Body"
(ibid.). Moreover, Cleaver argues, "man as thinker performs an Ad-
ministrative Function in society . . . [and] Man as doer performs a
Brute Power Function." In other words, "the racial binary" consists
of the "Omnipotent Administrator" (who is usually white) and the
"Supermasculine Menial" (who is usually black).[2] In "our fragmented

class society," the basic impulse of the "Omnipotent Administrator[s]
is to despise their bodies and glorify their minds," while the lower
ranks of society ("Supermasculine Menials") are alienated from their
minds (179). Cleaver further argues that the working class is mired
in false consciousness: "the mind counts only insofar as it enables
them to receive, understand, and carry out the will of the [white]
Omnipotent Administrators" (180).

In Cleaver's racial caste system, social class status is inscribed
on the body; thus, the male Omnipotent Administrator is associated
with "weakness, frailty, cowardice, and effeminacy," while the Supermasculine Menial is linked to "strength, brute power, force, virility,
and physical beauty" (180). Cleaver's racial/class binary also extends
to women. Because the Omnipotent Administrator is "markedly effeminate," upper-class women must "possess and project an image
that is in sharp contrast": "ultrafemininity" (181). The elite women become "ultrafeminine" while the working-class women become coarse
and "subfeminine." Cleaver posits that the racial caste system also explains the nature of one's libidinal desires. The Omnipotent Administrator cannot help but envy the "bodies and strength of the most
alienated man beneath him": the Supermasculine Menial. Thus, the
Black Panther propagandist reaffirms the age-old myth that homosexuality is a byproduct of leisure culture. Moreover, the ultrafeminine white woman experiences sexual dysfunction and frigidity when
she is coupled with the effeminate Omnipotent Administrator; while
in his bed, she only finds "physical exhaustion" because her "psychic
bridegroom" is the Supermasculine Menial (185). For Cleaver, this
also explains the African American male's fascination with ultrafeminine white women: "she is his dream girl. She, the delicate, weak,
helpless, Ultrafeminine, exerts a magnetic attraction upon him" (187).
Cleaver even asserts that the relations between African American
males and African American females are doomed from the start because the "amazon [the African American female] finds it difficult to
respect the supermasculine menial"; she is psychically driven by the
"Primeval Urge to transcend the Primeval Mitosis" (Cleaver's quasi-
scientific term for same-race coupling). Though Cleaver is by birth
and experience a Supermasculine Menial, his self-education and his
faith in literary expression suggest an attempt to transcend the state
of alienation implied in his socially inscribed identity.

Cleaver's literary criticism ("Notes on a Native Son") is an attempt to theorize a masculinist understanding of the African American literary tradition and American literature. In this chapter, the young Black Panther discusses his response to Mailer's controversial essay *The White Negro* and how it influenced his view of America's race relations. Cleaver describes Mailer's essay as "prophetic and penetrating in its understanding of the psychology involved in the accelerating confrontation of black and white in America" (98). Mailer's influence is also evidenced in Cleaver's "Convalescence," a brilliantly comic essay that provides a racial interpretation of the history of American rock 'n' roll: "The twist . . . had created in the collective psyche of the Omnipotent Administrators and Ultrafeminines, an irresistible urge to just stand up and shake the ice and cancer out of their alienated white asses" (199–200). In this humorous essay, Cleaver charts the liberatory power of African American musical traditions and their ability to subvert the conservative mores of the postwar era.

Unfortunately, the playfully mocking humor of "Convalescence" is less evident in Cleaver's homophobic attack on James Baldwin in "Notes on a Native Son."[3] Cleaver begins his essay by praising Baldwin's literary brilliance: "a talent capable of penetrating so profoundly into one's own little world that one knows oneself to have been unalterably changed and *liberated,* liberated from the frustrating grasp of whatever devils happen to possess one" (97). According to Cleaver, the literary fissure between Cleaver and Baldwin begins when the young Cleaver objects to Baldwin's novel *Another Country:* "I began to feel uncomfortable about something in Baldwin. I was disturbed upon becoming aware of an aversion in my heart to part of the song he sang" (98). Later in the essay, Cleaver is repulsed by Baldwin's bisexual character, Rufus Scott: "the epitome of a black eunuch who has completely submitted to the white man" (107). Cleaver also takes issue with Baldwin's "flippant, schoolmarmish dismissal" of Mailer's *The White Negro* (98). For Cleaver, Baldwin's rejection of Mailer tacitly signifies the novelist's preference for non-phallic maleness and leisure-culture effeminacy. Thus, by praising Mailer's essay, Cleaver makes aggressive, phallic masculinity an essential requirement for all aspiring black male radicals. However, the most notorious part of the chapter is Cleaver's attempt to link Baldwin to "ethnic self-hatred" by equating the novelist's homosexuality with the castration of the African American male:

> The white man has deprived him [the black homosexual] of his masculinity, castrated him in the center of his burning skull and when he submits to this change and takes the white man for his lover as well as Big Daddy, he focuses on "whiteness" all the love in his pent up soul and turns the razor edge of hatred against "blackness"—upon himself, what he is, and all those who look like him. He may even hate the darkness of night. (103)

Cleaver's rhetoric suggests that black homosexuality is a sexual byproduct of slavery and miscegenation. To possess homosexual desire is a form of psychosis because it expresses an unconscious attraction to whiteness. After scapegoating the black homosexual, Cleaver foregrounds phallic, hard masculinity as the ideal form of African American maleness, which can unite the black community and ensure reproduction and the rejection of whiteness. Cleaver also associates Baldwin with "the Martin Luther King self-effacing love of his oppressors" (106). Thus, Cleaver uses masculine identity to demarcate specific political positions. Ideologically, Martin Luther King Jr. becomes a soft figure who endorses nonviolence and appeasement of the white establishment while the Black Panthers represent the militant, hypermasculine alternative.

Cleaver's political rhetoric also features other familiar gender tropes. One of the most powerful themes in his work is the image of the castrated African American male who has been killed by white oppressors. The opening chapter of *Soul on Ice* centers on the mutilated body of Emmett Till, a fourteen-year-old African American who was murdered in 1955 by a gang of white vigilantes in Mississippi for allegedly flirting with a white woman. Cleaver connects Till's mutilated body with a masculine call to arms: the black male must fight back and avenge Till's death by embracing his essential blackness: hypermasculinity. Thus, through the symbolic renunciation of the black homosexual, the African American male is encouraged to adopt a more aggressive and radical political stance.

Although many male writers have been described as phallocentric, Cleaver's rhetoric is phallocentric in the most obvious sense of the word. Cleaver defends his convictions by attacking those who question the articles of his faith. Thus, Baldwin, the homosexual, becomes a target because he skillfully debunked the myth of black sexual prowess in "The Black Boy Looks at the White Boy" ("to be an American Negro male is also to be a kind of walking phallic symbol"). Cleaver's autobiographical fiction, including his belief that the "rape [of white women] is an insurrectionary act," is predicated on the literary performance of tough and hard masculinity. Cleaver, a convicted felon who writes from his cell at Folsom Prison, has impeccable hypermasculine credentials. Although the narrative of *Soul on Ice* emphasizes moral reformation and the theme of enlightenment through knowledge ("That is why I write. To save myself"), Cleaver champions the most central myths of traditional phallic masculinity, including the trope of the hard and impervious male body. The prison doctrine of survival—one must penetrate but not be penetrated—becomes a political and ethical imperative in Cleaver's literary criticism. In the tradition of Michael Gold, Cleaver's attack on James Baldwin illustrates how a male writer's political discourse is effectively packaged in powerful gender myths that can have a gripping effect on the unsuspecting reader. In a visceral sense, Cleaver prompts his reader to conduct a virility test on the writer in question, and thus the reader's literary assessment is filtered through the mythos of masculine identity. Hence, in Cleaver's gendered reading of African American literature, to embrace Baldwin is to embrace impotence and a latent desire for whiteness.

Cleaver's belief in the primacy of phallic masculinity also led him to dabble in men's fashion. While living in exile in Paris in 1975, Cleaver promoted a line of menswear that showcased phallic trousers—pants that highlighted the male genitals by placing them in a sock-like codpiece (see fig. 11). In an interview with *Newsweek,* the former Black Panther explained the philosophy behind his sartorial creations: "I want to solve the problem of the big fig-leaf mentality. . . . clothing is an extension of the fig leaf—it put our sex inside our bodies. My pants put sex back where it should be."[4] Cleaver, the reborn capitalist, added: "My design has a tremendous future both artistically and commercially, because not just the intellect—the head and face—is honored. The other half of man's identity, the sex organs, is, too" (qtd. in Silva). Although Cleaver abandoned his radical black nationalism and converted to born-again Christianity and Mormonism, he remained an ardent promoter of hypermasculine conceptions of maleness. At news conferences in the late 1970s, he frequently modeled his codpiece trousers for the press corps (see fig. 11); however, much to Cleaver's dissatisfaction, many newspapers refused to run photos of him from the waist down.

Though Cleaver lost credibility with leftists and intellectuals in the late 1970s, the impact of his homophobic writings should not be underestimated. By several accounts (Weatherby, Field), the attack was devastating for Baldwin. He chose not to respond publicly when reporters quizzed him on the subject, and even in the 1980s, he spoke of "trying to undo the damage that Cleaver had caused" (qtd. in Field 465). However, privately, he remarked: "All that toy soldier has done is call me gay" (Weatherby 292). Baldwin also spoke of the attack with his biographer W. J. Weatherby: "I thought that we'd gone through all that with the Muslims and were past it. All he [Cleaver] wants is a gunfight at OK Corral. He should go and make movies with John Wayne" (ibid.). To some, Baldwin's unwillingness to respond to Cleaver's virulent attack seems surprising because Baldwin himself had "pulled rank" and mounted several literary attacks at various points in his career.[5] Baldwin's public response finally came in "No Name in the Street" (1972), four years after the publication of Cleaver's attack; he adopts a conciliatory tone with Cleaver:

> He [Cleaver] seemed to feel that I was a dangerously odd, badly twisted, and fragile reed, of too much use to the Establishment to be trusted by blacks. . . . I felt I was confused in his mind with the unutterable debasement of the male—with all those faggots, punks, and sissies, the sight and sound of whom, in prison, must have made him vomit more than once. Well I certainly hope I know more about myself, and the intention of my work than that, but I am an odd quantity. So is Eldridge; so are we all. It is a pity that we won't, probably, ever have the time to attempt to define once more the relationship of the odd and disreputable artist to the odd and disreputable revolutionary. (459)

Read today, what is striking is that Baldwin does not try to analyze or condemn Cleaver's egregious homophobia. Baldwin opts not to defend the concept of homosexuality nor his own homosexuality, and actually distances himself from transgressive forms of sexual difference (the "faggots, punks, and sissies" whom Cleaver presumably encountered in prison). With rapprochement in mind, Baldwin attempts to find common ground with Cleaver by asserting that their mutual strangeness ("odd and disreputable") could produce solidarity in the racial struggle. Given the fact that Baldwin was publishing in 1972—the heyday of gay liberation—his decidedly nonconfrontational response to Cleaver's homophobia seems strange. However, Baldwin's reluctance to highlight the issue of sexual difference was actually a fairly typical response for writers who were brought up in the pre-Stonewall era. Both the critique of homophobia and the defense of sexual difference in American literary culture were quite rare before 1970. However, all this would change with the emergence of gay liberation, a loud and radical social movement that made outspokenness a moral and political imperative.

GAY LIBERATION AND THE HARD/SOFT DEBATE

Although gay writers and intellectuals were not necessarily at the forefront of the Stonewall riots—the protest was a spontaneous uprising led by radical gay activists and queer citizens who quickly became radicalized during the confrontations with police—the event and its aftermath spawned the creation of numerous activist organizations and self-styled liberation fronts that would, over time, dramatically alter and redefine the political and social identities of gays and lesbians. The liberation movement fostered social and cultural transformation precisely because it promoted an ongoing public forum on taboo issues (homophobia) and topics (homosexual stereotypes) that were strenuously avoided by the American media during the pre-Stonewall era.

Though gay liberation, as a political movement, was linked to the New Left—many of the movement's most important figures (Jim Fouratt, Karla Jay) were active in the antiwar movement—the counterculture and the New Left were actually slow to embrace gay liberation. Fouratt, a gay Yippie activist and a close friend of Abbie Hoffman, notes that, during the Stonewall confrontations with the police, he received little support from his straight comrades in the

New Left.[6] This is not surprising, given the fact that many of the New Left's political leaders routinely included homophobic references in their political rhetoric and in their interviews with the media. In a fictional interview with himself in *Revolution for the Hell of It* (1968), Hoffman discusses the counterculture's willingness to use the American media to disseminate its political message, and the opposing styles of Fidel Castro and Andy Warhol:

> Well I think I would like to combine his [Warhol's] style with that of Castro's. Warhol understands modern media. Castro has the passion for social change. It's not easy. One's a fag and the other is the epitome of virility. If I was forced to make the choice I would choose Castro, but right now in this period of change in the country the styles of the two can be blended. It's not guerilla warfare but, well, maybe a good term is monkey warfare. If the country becomes more repressive we must become Castro. If it becomes more tolerant we must become Warhols. (59)

This passage demonstrates how political identity was often gendered and sexualized in the 1960s and the extent to which the hard/soft dichotomy and anti-homosexual attitudes were embedded in the rhetoric of the New Left. As the 1960s progress and the counterculture becomes more disenchanted with the political viability of nonviolent tactics, it is clear that Hoffman and other counterculture luminaries will gravitate toward Castro-like "virility" (the myth of phallic potency) and the traditional tropes of hard masculinity. The Yippie leader's use of the epithet "fag" conveys that homophobic references were not uncommon in the parlance of the New Left. In the post-Stonewall era, the gay liberation movement would "raise consciousness" about the politics of sexual difference and pose a challenge to the anti-homosexual discourses that were ubiquitous in the popular culture.

While gay liberation presented a critique of the repressed hypocrisy of mainstream America, its project of raising consciousness also fostered various forms of self-criticism. Influenced by New Left political rhetoric, a hypermasculine faction of gay liberation quickly emerged. The writings of several of these young gay activists was avowedly anti-effeminate. In "I.D., Leadership and Violence" (1970), a keynote speech for the National Gay Liberation Front Student Conference in San Francisco, Charles P. Thorp, a gay militant, addressed the question of violence as a means of resistance and issued a gay call to arms: "Violence as a means of oppression is being used and we are told to accept that. Bull Shit. If violence shall oppress us so shall it liberate. Our community is a Community of Lovers and because of oppression we've become an Army of Lovers" (Jay and Young 363). In other passages of this speech, Thorp quoted lines from his poem "(we shall) overcome" and veered into the familiar terrain of macho hyperbole:

> we are bursting dreams
> you will not escape in sleep
> for violent fairies will
> visit you even in your dreams and
> castrate you at night
> as you have castrated so many of my people. (362)

Similarly, Craig Alfred Hansen, another gay activist, offered a hypermasculine critique of bourgeois gay camp culture. In an essay that was published in *Gay Sunshine,* Hansen describes camp lifestyle as the "princess syndrome" and argues that the term characterizes the "fem-identification, the fantasy imagery, the egocentricity, and the cultural conservatism of the tired old gay trip" (266). Hansen adds that the "fairy princess creates a romanticized, ego-centric, and spurious inner world—fairyland—set against outer reality because he lives a frustrated life of emotional deprivation and isolation due to feelings of inadequacy and worthlessness in the real world" (267). Hansen's Marxist-cum-macho rhetoric echoes Michael Gold's obsession with the leisure-culture pansy of the 1920s and 1930s; however, Hansen presents the argument from a gay perspective and adds a few ageist clichés that were commonplace in the 1960s:

> [W]e should expose our Princess Floradora Femadonna so that our younger brothers will not fall into the lavender cesspool and be swept down the sewers of fantasyland. We must make our younger brothers realize that the princess trip is a rotten one, a self-deluding flight into the past that never was, artificiality, and an escape from reality. It is a selfish, self-serving, irrational and materialistic journey which shuns real human relations for past images and things material. (269)

Much like his counterculture comrades, Hansen argues that young liberated gays should reject the values of the over-thirty generation and he equates gay camp culture with decadence and commodity fetishism.

While Hansen's critique of the princess syndrome presents an aggressively nonpluralistic view of gay identity, other critics viewed the embrace of hardness as an appropriate response to growing up in a homophobic culture. Martin Levine, the author of *Gay Macho: The Life and Death of the Homosexual Clone* (1998), argues that "gay men enacted a hypermasculine sexuality as a way to challenge their stigmatization as failed men, as 'sissies,' and . . . many of the institutions that developed in the gay male world of the 1970s and early 1980s catered to and supported this hypermasculine code—from clothing stores and sexual boutiques, to bars, bathhouses, and the ubiquitous gyms" (5). Levine also stresses how the physical manifestations of hardness became highly visible soon after the beginning of gay liberation:

> [The gay macho] clone was, in many ways, the manliest of men. He had a gym-defined body; after hours of rigorous body-building, his physique rippled with bulging muscles, looking more like competitive body-builders than hairdressers or florists. He wore blue-collar garb—flannel shirts over muscle T-shirts, Levi 501s over work boots, bomber jackets over hooded sweatshirts. He kept his hair short and had a thick mustache or closely cropped beard. (7)

The hyperbolic style of gay macho, especially the embrace of working-class models (the burly construction worker, the Marlboro man cowboy), can also be read as a conscious repudiation of the sartorial aesthetics of leisure-culture effeminacy. The hard-bodied homosexuality that emerged in the 1970s became a highly visible subculture that acted out and performed an alternative narrative of same-sex passion in the public realm.

At the other end of the ideological spectrum, the newly formed effeminist movement lobbied against hardness and the tyranny of the hypermasculine ideal within gay culture. One effeminist, Perry Brass, offered a critique of gay bar culture and "cruising." Brass's analysis of gay courting rituals ("Cruising: Games Men Play") was influenced by radical feminism. Brass equates cruising with male chauvinism and argues that gay men often mimic the oppressive behavior of straight culture. In contrast to Hansen, Brass offers an

analysis of the phenomenon of gay hardness: "Because we are forced
to live in a society that condemns us as half-men, many of us feel that
we must become men-and-a-half. This means to shut out all of the real
tenderness and sensitivities associated with femininity" (265). Some
effeminists embraced Sue Katz's critique of masculine sex. For Katz,
a radical lesbian, the term "sex" implied an "institution" in American
cultural life. The popularity of the missionary position implied the
capitalist obsession with productivity: "[sex] is goal-oriented, profit-
& productivity-orientated. It is a prescribed system, with a series of
building activities aimed at the production of a single goal: climax"
(qtd. in Teal 285). In "Smash Phallic Imperialism," Katz notes, "I
cannot separate the word 'sex' from the phallic tyranny I suffered
from for so many years" (Jay and Young 260). As an alternative to
male-female sex, Katz proposes that women adopt the "formless and
amorphous" experience of non-goal-oriented "sensuality." Terence
Kissack notes that, when the effeminists applied Katz's critique of sex
to gay men, it implied that "a whole new set of sexual desires and gendered behaviors were deemed off-limits. Butch/femme, leather, sado-
masochism, and other forms of sexuality were set beyond the pale."[7]
Thus, in some cases, the effeminist critique "produced a catch-22
situation in which gay male sexuality became simultaneously a site
of liberation and oppression" (Kissack 121).

These opposing views of gay male sexuality created heated debate and tension during the early phases of gay liberation. However,
as the 1970s progressed, a more inclusive and less rigid conception of
gay identity would emerge, and the new pluralistic conception would
embrace both antipodes of the hard/soft dichotomy. For example, the
Village People, a successful gay pop group in the mid-1970s, presents
a less divisive conception of gay identity and the hard/soft divide.
The group's iconography features butch stereotypes—a policeman,
a construction worker, a Native American warrior—yet their lyrics
offer a playful critique of butchness ("Macho Man") and suggest that
hardness is merely a playful aesthetic guise that can be divorced from
oppressive behavior.

Gay liberation initially had great success as a consciousness-
raising entity. It fostered dialogue about homosexual stereotypes and
anti-gay sentiments that had been internalized by gay men and lesbi-

ans. However, the political movement's efficacy in making changes in mainstream heterosexual society is more difficult to assess. In the early 1970s, various gay activist organizations had some success at establishing dialogues with some political movements that had homophobic reputations. On May Day in 1970, Jim Fouratt, a leading spokesperson for the Gay Liberation Front, publicly challenged the Black Panther movement to examine its anti-gay attitudes: "We call upon every radical here to OFF the word faggot, to OFF the sexism which pervades this place and to begin to deal with their own feelings about homosexual brothers and sisters. We demand that you treat us as revolutionaries."[8] Fouratt's public challenge to the Black Panthers was certainly a risky political proposition, given the Panthers' penchant for machismo and homophobic posturing. However, Fouratt's willingness to address the thorny issue of homophobia paid off as the two radical organizations managed, through dialogue, to find common ground in the revolutionary struggle. A few weeks later, Huey Newton, supreme commander of the Black Panther Party, wrote a reply to Fouratt's challenge: he urged fellow Panthers to confront their "insecurities about homosexuality" and welcome Gay Liberation activists as fellow revolutionaries (qtd. in Teal 151–53). In the same letter, Newton also expressed solidarity with the women's liberation movement and offered an analysis of gay bashing: "Our first instinct is to want to hit the homosexual in the mouth. . . . We want to hit the homosexual in the mouth because we are afraid that we might be homosexual" (ibid.).[9] Donn Teal, a gay activist and historian, argues that, in this statement, Newton was the "first . . . nationally known heterosexual male to recognize the equality of women and . . . homosexuals" (153).

Gay liberation's rapprochement with the Black Panther movement exemplifies the attempt to establish political ties with other radical leftist organizations. Gay activist organizations also confronted mainstream organizations that openly expressed anti-gay attitudes and practices. While not all of these protests and interventions produced tangible results, gay liberation's ongoing protest against the American Psychiatric Association (APA) was a remarkable success. In 1970, gay liberation organizations attended APA conventions in San Francisco, Los Angeles, New York, and Chicago and protested the panels that discussed the "treatment" and "correction" of homosexuality. During the sessions, gay activists would disrupt the proceedings by shouting "barbarism," "medieval torture," "disgusting."[10] The efforts of gay activists resulted in the removal of homosexuality as a psychiatric disorder from the APA's diagnostic manual.[11]

Over time, the radical actions of the various gay liberation organizations provided a more diverse conception of gay identity by challenging the one-dimensional stereotype of the effeminate gay man and the widespread belief that homosexuality is a form of mental illness. When a more pluralistic image of gay identity emerged, the notion that effeminacy and homosexuality were synonymous was openly challenged in the mainstream culture. With the rise of gay liberation, the image of gayness in American literary culture was also profoundly transformed. Perhaps the most significant trend was the radical interrogation of the efficacy of silence in public and political matters. During this time, gay and lesbian writers and intellectuals became more apt to be politically engaged and to identify themselves as gay when they participated in public debates. This social trend would become more pronounced during the ongoing AIDS crisis in the 1980s, 1990s, and 2000s.

While gay liberation was certainly a radical cultural movement that transformed the gay community, it did not pose a direct threat to mainstream heterosexual culture and the phallic-identified males of the New Left. Thus, gay liberation's collective coming-out party was welcomed by most New Leftists (e.g., Jerry Rubin, Timothy Leary, Abbie Hoffman) who had espoused homophobic beliefs in the pre-Stonewall 1960s. However, the women's movement of the late 1960s and early 1970s was a different matter because it represented a more direct challenge to the cherished myths of masculinity and to males on both sides of the hard/soft divide.

RADICAL FEMINISM AND THE HARD/SOFT DICHOTOMY

Many assume that the emergence of the soft male in the 1960s signaled a sea change in gender relations and implied a different way for men to relate and interact with women. However, in the various histories of the counterculture there is little actual evidence to support this claim. In many respects, the sexism of the New Left resembled the sexism of the Old Left. The decline of the hard-shell model of masculinity did not result in a more enlightened view of women. The key transformation of gender relations and male attitudes came with the rise of the women's movement itself, and the male response to it.

The women's movement grew out of the New Left and the antiwar movement. Women, who were crucial to the civil rights and antiwar movements, began to resent the sexism of New Left men and women's second-class status within the movements. The key splintering point for many early feminists centered about the issue of whether gender oppression could be disentangled from the class struggle and the broader aims of traditional left-wing politics (i.e., ending the Vietnam War, racism, and poverty). In the 1930s, gender oppression had often been conceived as a byproduct of capitalism that would be reformed after the revolution arrived. However, the radical feminists of the late 1960s were not willing to tolerate an interregnum of male supremacy and sexism. Crucial to the women's movement was the desire to challenge the political and sexual hegemony of New Left men. Hence, in the cry for liberation, the politics of the bedroom suddenly took center stage. Political discourse was deeply sexualized, and women's liberation was often framed as the act of resisting the sexual tyranny of men.

In 1970, there was an outpouring of feminist manifestos and theoretical works. Germaine Greer's *The Female Eunuch* (1970) begins with an account of how the second wave of feminism is different from its ideological predecessors; Shulamith Firestone's *The Dialectic of Sex* (1970) begins with a description of the ubiquitous sex class system and an argument for why profound social change—a revolution—is both necessary and desirable. Like the books of Greer and Firestone, Kate Millett's *Sexual Politics* (1970) is an ambitious theoretical work that analyzes patriarchal structures from a feminist point of view. However, unlike Greer's and Firestone's, Millett's revolutionary work begins with literary criticism. Central to Millett's criticism is the suggestion that males and females read sexual fantasy differently.

Millett begins *Sexual Politics* with a close reading of Henry Miller's novel *Sexus* (1965). Her choice of Miller is important because it implies that the genre of masculine fantasy has great cultural significance for the burgeoning feminist movement. In a sense, Millett's choice of opening suggests that male fantasy is so pervasive in American culture that it constitutes a material reality that a feminist revolutionary cannot afford to ignore. Millett, a scholar of literature and masculinist fantasies, goes on to cite erotic passages from various male writers from different cultures—Norman Mailer, D. H. Lawrence, Jean Genet—and then rigorously decodes the male understanding of sex. In each case, Millett's interest is the chimerical guises inherent in masculine accounts of heterosexual intercourse and how male fantasy often informs and shapes our understanding of sexual representations. For Millett, fictional depictions of sexual encounters are not devoid of ideological significance: each sex scene contains an implicit account of power relations, or "sexual politics." Millett notes, "Coitus can scarcely be said to take place in a vacuum; . . . it is set so deeply within the larger context of human affairs that it serves as a charged microcosm of the variety of attitudes and values to which culture subscribes" (23). In Millett's view, "politics" refers to "power-structured relations, arrangements whereby one group of persons is controlled by another" (ibid.). Thus, the author's approach to revolutionary praxis proceeds through the matrix of the bedroom: the reader learns that one's understanding of sex—both in fiction and in reality—is a political act that has specific ideological implications. To illustrate her conception of sexual politics, Millett cites a sexually explicit scene from Miller's *Sexus* at the very beginning of her book:

> I would ask her to prepare the bath for me. She would pretend to demur but she would do it just the same. One day, while I was seated in the tub soaping myself, I noticed that she had forgotten the towels. "Ida," I called, "bring me some towels!" She walked into the bedroom and handed me them. She had on a silk bathrobe and a pair of silk hose. As she stooped over the tub to put the towels on the rack her bathrobe slid open. I slid to my knees and buried my head in her muff. It happened so quickly that she didn't have time to rebel or even pretend to rebel. In a moment I had her in the tub, stockings and all. I slipped the bathrobe off and threw it on the floor. I left the stockings on—it made her more lascivious looking, more the Cranach type. I lay back and pulled her on top of me. She was like a bitch in heat, biting me all over, panting, gasping, wriggling like a worm on the hook. As we were drying ourselves, she bent over and began nibbling at my prick. I sat on the edge of the tub

and she kneeled at my feet gobbling it. After a while I made her stand up, bend over; then I let her have it from the rear. She had a small juicy cunt, which fitted me like a glove. I bit the nape of her neck, the lobes of her ears, the sensitive spot on her shoulder, and as I pulled away I left a mark of my teeth on her beautiful white ass. Not a word was spoken. (180)

Millett's critique of Miller begins by demonstrating how men and women read and understand erotic literature differently. The author notes that the reader of Miller's prose "is vicariously experiencing . . . a nearly supernatural sense of power—should the reader be male" (6). Millett then argues that "the passage is not only a vivacious and imaginative use of circumstance, detail, and context to evoke the excitations of sexual intercourse, it is a male assertion of dominance over a weak, compliant, and rather unintelligent female. It's a case of sexual politics at the fundamental level of copulation" (ibid.). Millett also notes that the male ego experiences various forms of gratification when reading Miller's prose: "Several satisfactions for the hero and reader alike undoubtedly accrue upon this triumph of the male ego, the most tangible one being communicated in the following: 'she had a small juicy cunt, which fitted me like a glove'" (ibid.). Millett's incisive close reading of Miller's passage discusses how and why the passage foregrounds a male perspective of sexual coupling and how the literary representation of the sexual act glorifies phallic prowess and male power over women.

Millett's attempt to politicize sexuality, as well as the literary representation of sexual acts, is significant at this historical moment because sexuality was often treated as a personal matter that was beyond the locus of political struggle. Crucial to Millett's reading of Miller's gendering of fantasy is the mythos of hardness as an erotic ideal: the male narrator as an aggressive figure who penetrates the soft female. Moreover, softness is read as undesirable and politically suspect because it reinforces the theme of feminine passivity. Millett also emphasizes Ida's silence during the act of copulation. Ida—who in Millett's reading is servile, weak, and powerless—embodies the degraded status of women in the psyche of the male narrator. Millett also concludes that Miller's frank discussion of sexual matters should not be confused with social progress: "To provide unlimited scope for masculine aggression, although it may finally bring the situation out into the open, will hardly solve the dilemma of our sexual politics" (313). Nonetheless, Millett posits that "Miller does have something highly important to tell us; his virulent sexism is without question a contribution to social and psychological understanding which we can hardly afford to ignore" (ibid.).

Millett juxtaposes her reading of Miller's *Sexus* with a homosexual sex scene from Jean Genet's *The Thief's Journal* (1964). In this excerpt, the narrator describes a sexual encounter with his hypermasculine lover Armand:

> A few days later, when I met him near the docks, Armand ordered me to follow him. Almost without speaking, he took me into his room. With the same apparent scorn he subjected me to his pleasure. Dominated by his strength and age, I gave the work my utmost care. Crushed by that mass of flesh, which was devoid of the slightest spirituality, I experienced the giddiness of finally meeting the perfect brute, indifferent to my happiness. I discovered the sweetness that could be contained in a thick fleece on torso, belly, and thighs and what force it could transmit. I finally let myself be buried in that stormy night. Out of gratitude or fear I placed a kiss on Armand's hairy arm. "What's eating you? Are you nuts or something?" "I didn't do any harm." I remained at his side in order to serve his nocturnal pleasure. When we went to bed, Armand whipped his leather belt from the loops of his trousers and made it snap. It was flogging an invisible victim, a shape of transparent flesh. The air bled. If he frightened me then, it was because of his powerlessness to be the Armand I see, who is heavy and mean. The snapping accompanied and supported him. His rage and despair at not being *him* made him tremble like a horse subdued by darkness, made him tremble more and more. (134)

Millett argues that Genet's sexual politics are fundamentally different from Miller's. The first difference is obvious: the passage foregrounds the "feminine" experience of sex; the feminine male narrator is seduced by the hypermasculine figure, Armand. Millett, however, goes on to argue that Genet's sexual politics are fundamentally different from Miller's in that Genet is offering an implicit critique of our sexual-social practices: "Genet submits the entire social code of 'masculine' and 'feminine' to a disinterested scrutiny and concludes that it is odious" (19). Millett's reading of Genet's sexual politics emphasizes the claim that Genet's intent is essentially didactic: "Genet is urging [that], unless we eliminate the most pernicious of our systems of oppression, unless we go to the center of the sexual politic and its sick delirium of power and violence, all our efforts at liberation will only land us again in the same primordial stew" (22). Within her reading is the assumption that the soft male narrator is pitiful because his submission to Armand is so complete; moreover, the phrase "primordial stew" suggests that the sexual politics of the 1960s are archaic and barbaric.

While Millett's suggestion that Genet is a didactic reformer of sexual mores is not persuasive, I am interested in her juxtaposition of Miller's and Genet's depictions of sexual coupling and her claim that Genet's sexual politics are fundamentally different from Miller's phallocentric perspective. However, Miller's and Genet's depictions of sexual coupling are not really as distinct as Millett's reading suggests. Namely, both authors depict phallic hardness as an erotic ideal. Moreover, both Miller and Genet feature laconic hypermasculine males who are aggressive ("What's eating you? Are you nuts or something?") and seemingly devoid of feminine tenderness during the act of intercourse. The allure of hardness in Genet's homosexual passage calls into question Millett's suggestion that Genet finds the "social code of 'masculine' and 'feminine' [to be] odious." On the contrary, the male narrator of *The Thief's Journal* seems to relish the feminine role that he assumes ("I experienced the giddiness of finally meeting the perfect brute"). While Millett certainly deplores masculine hardness, she also remains suspicious of effeminate males who assume the passive role in sex. Her misreading of *The Thief's Journal* wrongly pegs Genet as an effeminist critic of hard masculinity. Moreover, Millett's reading of Miller and Genet assumes that the erotic narrative of dominance and submission—and the sexual politics that it implies—is necessarily objectionable and in desperate need of reform. The latter issue would polarize second wave feminists in the 1970s.[12]

Millett's critique of the cult of phallic potency in *Sexual Politics* had a significant effect on literary critics and on male and female authors who wrote in the aftermath of the epoch of radical feminism. Her criticism and the work of other feminist critics forced writers to become more self-conscious about their depictions of male-female relations, and in turn opened the door for writings that explored female subjectivity and charted the erotic empowerment of women. As Ann Snitow has noted, the depiction of sexual encounters in fiction written by women underwent a social transformation in the 1970s.[13] On the other hand, the female response to male fantasy was not as uniform as Millett's reading suggests. While her critique of male fantasy and masculine sexual practices was certainly persuasive, female desire itself is not as straightforward and predictable as Millett's analysis suggests. For example, in erotic terms not all women find hardness to be inherently objectionable and softness to be undesirable. Moreover, the master narrative of masculine dominance and feminine submission is a cultural trope that possesses enormous mythic appeal for gays and straights alike; in short, hardness and softness are cultural myths that did not simply wither away during the feminist cultural revolution of the early 1970s. Whether radical feminists liked it or not, the hard/soft dichotomy continued to play an important role in the feminist debates of the early 1970s.

Hardness and softness were central to the feminist struggle, yet often deeply contested. Much like the gay liberation movement of the early 1970s, the women's movement wrestled with the issue of adopting a politically correct gender style. Since women had been socially conditioned to be soft and ladylike, did that imply that women must embrace masculine hardness to earn their independence and liberation? Were women who embraced masculine traits—aggression, independence—in danger of becoming the same as men? For many early feminist theorists, women needed to unsex themselves and embrace a masculine style because this was the only way to remove the cultural noose of feminine passivity.

The debate over gender style was both a material and a literary concern for the radical feminist movement. Some feminists adopted clothing and hairstyles that rejected feminine allure. For example, Cell 16, a radical feminist group, advocated short hair to emphasize the rejection of male standards of beauty. In print culture, gender style was contested in literary creations that attempted to reappropriate language that perpetuated gender stereotypes. Some radical feminists adopted a macho prose style that championed the trope of masculine assertion. Joreen Freeman's "The Bitch Manifesto" (1969), a classic exercise in reverse discourse, attempts to reclaim the dreaded epithet from masculine culture by making "bitch" synonymous with the feminine performance of aggression ("A Bitch takes shit from no

one. You may not like her, but you can't ignore her"; Crow 226). Freeman's manifesto calls into question the notion of feminine passivity
by attacking the taboos against feminine aggression. While stopping
just short of unadulterated female masculinity, Freeman advocates
a synthesis of gender antipodes: "What is disturbing about a Bitch is
that she is androgynous. She incorporates within herself qualities traditionally defined as 'masculine' and 'feminine'" (227). In the radical
feminist writings of the early 1970s, "androgynous" is a gender ideal
because it represents a synthesis of masculine and feminine traits.
Although "The Bitch Manifesto" celebrates female independence
and individuality, it ends with a plea for sisterhood and solidarity:
"Bitches have to learn to accept themselves as Bitches. Bitches must
learn to be proud of their strength and proud of themselves. They
must move away from the isolation that has been their protection
and help younger sisters avoid its perils" (232). Thus, in "The Bitch
Manifesto," the guise of masculine hardness is usurped by a radical
feminist and redefined.

Unlike "The Bitch Manifesto," Valerie Solanas's notorious
"SCUM (Society for Cutting Up Men) Manifesto" (1968) has little interest in directly attacking the gender stereotypes that afflict women;
apart from her brief critique of "Daddy's Girl," Solanas's chief concern is the demystification of phallic masculinity and its effects. Like
other feminist satires, the "SCUM Manifesto" attempts to politicize
women by attacking particular masculine myths that are embedded in American popular culture. Solanas's central premise is that
phallic masculinity is nothing more than an elaborate masquerade
that is designed to prop up the chronically insecure male. Since the
male is secretly female ("an incomplete female"), he must project his
feminine side ("vanity, frivolity, triviality, weakness") onto women.
Thus, for Solanas, the drag queen represents the uncloseted essence
of masculinity: a male who no longer represses his feminine nature
and his inner desire to be feminine.

Like other works of radical feminism, the "SCUM Manifesto"
reappraises the social value of sex and women's participation in erotic
relations with men: "Sex is not part of a relationship; on the contrary,
it is a solitary experience, non-creative, a gross waste of time. The
female can easily—far more easily than she may think—condition

away her sex drive. . . . Sex is the refuge of the mindless. And the more mindless the woman, the more deeply embedded in the male 'culture'" (213).

Solanas's critique of sex is echoed in Dana Densmore's "On Celibacy." In the first issue of *No More Fun and Games*, Densmore, a member of Cell 16, argues that sex is "inconvenient, time-consuming, energy draining, and irrelevant" (qtd. in Echols, *Daring to Be Bad* 164). In both cases, intercourse is deeply politicized; the anti-sex position represents a rejection of the myth of phallic potency and an attempt to challenge the hyperbolic rhetoric of the sexual revolution. The most provocative claim is Solanas's suggestion that female sexuality can be refashioned, that a woman can "condition away her sex drive." Thus, in Solanas's manifesto, the feminist rebellion against masculine culture is taken to its logical extreme: the withdrawal from sexual ties with men is reconfigured as the ultimate act of feminist empowerment.

Like "The Bitch Manifesto," Solanas also valorizes feminine aggression. The SCUM women are praised as "dominant, secure, self-confident, nasty, violent, selfish, independent, proud, thrill-seeking, free-wheeling, [and] arrogant," while the "Daddy's Girls" are stigmatized as "nice, passive, accepting, 'cultivated,' polite, dignified, subdued, dependent, scared, mindless, insecure [and] approval seeking" (Crow 217). Hence, Solanas's rhetorical strategy is to critique women's ties to male society and their willingness to interact with male society and function as "ego boosters, relaxers, and breeders" (218). However, unlike "The Bitch Manifesto," Solanas is so tough that she resists making direct appeals to "sisterhood": "Why should the independent [women be] confined to the sewer along with the dependent who need Daddy to cling to?" (ibid.). Although Solanas scorns phallic masculinity, her manifesto is clearly a call for women to embrace hypermasculine assertion.

As a work of satire, the "SCUM Manifesto" is rhetorically effective in that it deconstructs the reader's received notions of masculinity and femininity. However, we should be mindful that Solanas's understanding and depiction of sexual difference has homophobic overtones. In Solanas's macho hierarchy, the lowest figures are the effeminate males ("faggots," "drag queens") and the soft, apolitical females who cling to "Daddy" (patriarchy). Moreover, Solanas's homophobic rhetoric is not a trifling concern: the anti-gay attitudes expressed in the "SCUM Manifesto" prefigure her violent attack in 1968 on Andy Warhol, an effeminate gay artist who doubtlessly occupied the lowest position on her hypermasculine scale of values.[14]

If Valerie Solanas represents the face of hypermasculine feminism and the attempt to embrace masculine hardness, radical feminism also contained a rearguard movement that moved in the opposite direction: cultural feminism, which gained popularity in the mid-1970s. Cultural feminism is a reclamation of women's essential femininity and an attempt to establish a viable alternative to patriarchy: women's culture. One example of this particular trajectory of the feminist movement was Robin Morgan, a cultural feminist and polemicist who embraced essentialism in the mid-1970s and argued that second wave feminism was being corrupted by its cultural addiction to maleness and the "male style." In "Lesbianism and Feminism: Synonyms or Contradictions?" (reprinted in *Going Too Far* [1977]), Morgan attempts to position feminism as a movement that is defined by its complete and total opposition to the cultural inheritance of masculinity. In this controversial keynote speech, Morgan describes "the male style as . . . a destroyer from within." Thus, Morgan promotes her particular brand of essentialism by arguing that women are fundamentally different from men:

> Every woman here knows in her gut the vast differences between her sexuality and that of any patriarchally trained male's—gay or straight. That has, in fact, always been a source of pride to the Lesbian community, even in its greatest suffering. That emphasis on genital sexuality, objectification, promiscuity, emotional non-involvement, and coarse invulnerability, was the *male style*, and that we, as women, placed greater trust in love, sensuality, humor, tenderness, commitment. (181)

Morgan's strategy is to unite feminists of various stripes by claiming that women are inherently different from men. However, in terms of the hard/soft dichotomy, her argument can also be viewed as a backdoor attempt to reclaim feminine softness. Hence, women, who place a "greater trust in love, sensuality, humor, tenderness, commitment," are diametrically opposed to men and their innate hardness and hypersexuality ("promiscuity, emotional non-involvement, and coarse invulnerability"). Thus, Morgan's cultural feminism is also predicated on the idea that women, as mothers, are more nurturing and have closer ties to nature. However, what is most surprising about Morgan's essay is her insistence that male culture and all men are inimical to feminism: the "straight men, the gay men, the transvestite men, the male politics, the male styles, the male attitudes, are being arrayed once more against us" (181). Morgan's willingness to lump all the disparate forms of masculinity in the antifeminist camp signifies the politics of radical exclusion. And like Solanas, Morgan also veers into homophobic terrain when she expresses her contempt for both drag queens and effeminate men. Drag queens earn her contempt because they often act out and perform the trope of outmoded feminine submission. While cultural feminism obviously deplored masculine hardness, it also in some cases remained deeply suspicious of all forms of male softness; hence, men who were sympathetic to feminism sometimes occupied a dubious position in cultural feminism.

Cultural feminism, a hodgepodge of gender essentialism, female empowerment rhetoric, matriarchal worship, and neopaganism, was in some cases fraught with internal contradictions. Although Morgan subscribes to the notion that women are innately more nurturing and caring than men, her softness is often merely a rhetorical trope, as she never gives up her aggressive prose style and her penchant for abuse and rancor. Throughout "Lesbianism and Feminism," her favorite target is a transvestite who identified with radical feminism and wanted to attend a feminist conference held at UCLA in 1973.[15] Although Morgan's rampant homophobia was not the norm within the cultural feminist movement, her invocation of the politics of exclusion represents the contradictions within the women's movement in the early 1970s and the cultural inheritance of the hard/soft binary. When debating the role that progressive men should play in the feminist movement, some sectarian feminists were quick to invoke the homophobic rhetoric of the hard/soft dichotomy to justify the politics of exclusion.

Although cultural feminism attempted to reclaim feminine softness as an ideal, this does not imply a revival of the trope of feminine submission. Instead, the recovery of softness was reconfigured as an act of female empowerment. Kate Millett's radical attempt to deconstruct the phallic bias of heterosexual sex becomes political praxis: a plan to remake the nature of female sexuality itself. When the sexual practices of a straight feminist are aligned with the dictates of cultural feminism, the politicized woman can have nongenital sex or she can be on top during the act of heterosexual coitus; masturbation is valorized as an alternative to the phallic economy, and lesbianism becomes the most radical gesture of all. However, the act of trying to marry sexual desire to ideology is problematic because it overvalues phallic masculinity and its mythology; cultural feminism is ultimately questionable because it constantly defined itself as an alternative to masculinity, and in doing so failed to take into account that hardness and softness are not laws of nature, but cultural myths that can be refashioned by the feminist critic.

Unlike Morgan, the Combahee River Collective (CRC), a black feminist group also loosely linked to the cultural feminist movement, rejected biological essentialism—the notion that biological maleness determines oppressive male behavior—and attempted to view racism and sexism as socially constructed cultural myths.[16] A key component of CRC's political project was consciousness-raising activities that sought to deconstruct cultural myths that are associated with race, gender, and class.

Thus far, my discussion of second wave feminism has focused on the various extremes of the hard/soft divide. However, radical feminism was an extremely diverse movement that also featured theorists and activists who rejected the polarities of the hard/soft binary. Shulamith Firestone, the author of the feminist classic *The Dialectic of Sex*, advocated a blending of the two discourses in a "cultural revolution": "a reintegration of the male (technological mode) and the female (aesthetic mode) to create an androgynous culture" (218). In Firestone's utopian vision, the rise of "androgynous culture" implies the abolition of cultural categories (the masculine, the feminine) and the end of "culture itself." In many respects, Firestone's approach to the hard/soft dichotomy is more flexible because she recognized that hardness and softness are merely cultural myths that can be divorced from one's particular sexual identity. Moreover, in *The Dialectic of Sex*, there is no fanatical attempt to align sexual practices and political identity, and Firestone resists the urge to become prescriptive about sexuality ("Eroticism is *exciting*. No one wants to get rid of it"). In Firestone's cultural revolution, the feminist revolutionary has agency; she views phallic masculinity as just another cultural myth that can be retained or discarded in the act of creating an inclusive and pluralistic androgynous culture.

SECOND WAVE FEMINISM AND NEW LEFT MALES

Second wave feminism had a significant impact on New Left men in the early 1970s, and many radicals were forced to reassess their chauvinist attitudes and their sexual politics. Some radical men embraced feminist ideas in theory, but incorporating them into their everyday lives was somewhat more problematic. In *The Autobiography of Abbie Hoffman* (1979), the famous co-founder of the Yippie (Youth International) Party describes how his response to feminism stemmed from the politics of the bedroom. Hoffman's decision to get a vasectomy in the early 1970s represents his attempt to embrace the ideals of feminism and to assume more responsibility for his sexual politics ("I would be putting my balls where my mouth is"; 280). However, unlike most vasectomies, Hoffman's vasectomy would be a public event and a political statement. Hoffman decided that he would make a short documentary film about the operation ("a political and cultural act"), and he argued that the decision to get a vasectomy stemmed from the fact that he felt that "the whole contraception business just didn't seem fair because it often implied that birth control was 'a woman's responsibility'" (279). In the chapter "Sex, Women, Getting a Vasectomy, and All That Sticky Stuff," Hoffman describes the plot of the film: "Larry Rivers filmed the entire sequence of events. The film shows me speaking of the reasons. It shows me playing with my children and 'climaxes' with the actual operation" (ibid.). However, Hoffman also describes how his agitprop vasectomy film was not terribly effective with its intended audience: "[The short film] was interesting and compelling theater, [but] it fails on a propaganda level. Guys instinctively grab their nuts when they see it" (280).

After discussing the vasectomy film project, Hoffman writes about the evolution of his gender politics, including his active sex life within the circles of the New Left and his eventual conversion to macho feminism ("I consider myself a macho-feminist") in the early 1970s. Hoffman's version of feminism used "macho discourse" to criticize men who didn't embrace the women's movement and the new gender roles: "Guys and gals that cling to old roles, I see as 'sissies' afraid to meet the challenge and adventure of a new attitude. When it comes time to clear away the dishes only cowards stay seated at the table" (281).

The case of Abbie Hoffman's agitprop vasectomy and macho feminism is instructive in that it expresses the legacy of both hard masculinity and Dionysian masculinity from the 1960s, and the various contradictions that the two trends imply. Hoffman is a key figure because he, in many respects, is the embodiment of both traditions. On one hand, Hoffman is a product of the Old Left. He is the son of radical left-wing Jewish parents, and his toughness evokes his devout commitment to progressive politics and social change. And his use of the word "sissies" reflects his inheritance of the Old Left's vocabulary. Hoffman has intellectually accepted a progressive idea (feminism), but at the same time, on a psychosocial level, he is disavowing that he is in any way soft or effeminate for doing so. His version of feminism includes a specific rejection of feminine softness and effeminacy. His phrase "macho feminism" represents the cultural inheritance of hard masculinity and is an attempt to remake hardness by linking it to feminism. In this case, the medical remaking of the body suggests that one can be hard and tough and embrace feminism at the same time.

On the other hand, Hoffman is obviously indebted to the Dionysian masculinity of the counterculture. He wholeheartedly embraces the cult of unseemly confession, the feminine notion of mutability, and LSD-enhanced self-transformation. His creative political activism and his willingness to refashion his evolving political philosophy and his male body represent the most compelling aspects of the counterculture's dynamic revolution of values. Hoffman's willingness to stage his vasectomy for public consumption evidences his acceptance of the growing influence of second wave feminism and the notion that the personal is political; moreover, it suggests that Hoffman, as a spokesperson of the counterculture and the New Left, wanted to take a stand and make the issue a matter of public debate. Hoffman's political gesture was part of a social trend in the early 1970s, as progressive men were being encouraged to assume greater responsibility in sexual matters.[17]

Hoffman's account of the agitprop vasectomy is also revealing because his conversion to feminism is juxtaposed with a brief history of his active sexual life during the 1960s and his fear of siring unwanted children. It is telling that Hoffman does not make an argument for the broader universal aims of the women's movement (equal rights, equal pay, etc.); his encounter with feminism is fundamentally personal and stems from the sexual politics of the bedroom. Hence, his vasectomy film project can be read as a public atonement for his own (and the New Left's) sexism. The decision to film the event also reflects the paradigm shift in masculine attitudes toward intimate matters. For the Old Left, sexual intercourse between a man and a woman was considered an unequivocally private matter, and to discuss such things publicly was regarded as unseemly. Filming the event was symbolic in that it reflected the counterculture's new attitudes toward the politics of sexuality and the radical attempt to abolish the distinction between the public and the private. Hoffman's autobiography includes other disclosures that previous generations would have avoided (e.g., "I am not ashamed to say that I jerk-off").

The male audience's response to Hoffman's publicity stunt also reflects certain social trends in the 1970s. Hoffman's attempt to demystify the procedure of a vasectomy and thereby make the operation more socially acceptable was largely unsuccessful ("Guys instinctively grab their nuts when they see it"). However, the male response is telling because it raises some important issues. Culturally and historically, the psychological and social hostility toward vasectomies alludes to the tremendous residual power of the myth of phallic potency and how men are often unable to dispense with certain traditional conceptions of maleness (e.g., the male as reproducer). Despite the counterculture's progressive rhetoric and its popular critique of aggressive masculinity (Leary's *The Politics of Ecstasy*; the Living Theatre's *Paradise Now*), its sexual politics often resembled its ideological predecessor—hard masculinity—in that the New Left had great difficulty relinquishing the fantasy of phallic potency. After the apex of hard masculinity in the 1930s and 1940s and despite the rise of Dionysian masculinity in the 1960s, phallic masculinity has remained a popular way of defining maleness in American culture, and, in some respects, it continues to be an impediment to social change. Although Hoffman's agitprop vasectomy film failed as propaganda, it represents an attempt to redefine maleness and the cultural meaning of hardness.

Hoffman's attempt to reinvent hardness (macho feminism) can be contrasted with another distinct social trend: the ongoing radical embrace of transformative masculinity within a certain sector of the counterculture in the 1970s. This faction of males, who had been radicalized by the antiwar movement, welcomed the women's movement and gay liberation and attempted to further enlarge the parameters of American maleness by rejecting the cultural values of the previous generation ("the establishment"). This trend is especially visible in Jerry Rubin's *Growing (Up) at Thirty-Seven* (1976), a memoir that charts the ex-Yippie's attempt to adapt to American life after the demise of 1960s radicalism. Rubin's extremely confessional narrative documents his flirtation with various alternative subcultures and the rise of the "personal growth movement" of the 1970s. While living in San Francisco, Rubin devised his own self-styled crash course in New Age spirituality and soft-bodied masculinity: "In five years, from 1971 to 1975, I directly experienced est, gestalt therapy, bioenergetics, rolfing, massage, jogging, health foods, tai chi, Esalen, hypnotism, modern dance, meditation, Silva Mind Control, Arica, acupuncture, sex therapy, Reichian therapy, and More House—a smorgasbord course in New Consciousness" (20). In other passages, Rubin affirms the central importance of yoga. His reflective narrative associates traditional American culture with emotional reticence and somatic hardness; thus, his ambitious project of perpetual rejuvenation stresses the compensatory need to transform the body and the limited conception of maleness that he has inherited. With each activity and revelation, the key theme is the pliability of the mind, body, and spirit; for Rubin, mutability becomes the highest ideal and the embodiment of personal and inner growth.

Rubin's odyssey through the alternative cultures of the 1970s includes phallic and non-phallic forms of masculinity and a discussion of the evolution of his own attitudes toward homosexuality: "In *Do It* [1970] I described homosexuality as sick. The gay community attacked me publicly, forcing me for the first time to examine my sexual bias" (121). When describing his transformation, Rubin cites the importance of radical massage therapy, a countercultural fad in the 1970s: "Studying massage helped break my shyness about my body. Doing massage, we looked at each other's genitals and massaged each other. Nakedness and touching felt natural; there was no sense of shame or judgment. Men and women massaged my body, including my genitals, and I massaged other people's bodies. Everything felt good!" (115). Rubin's new gender sensibility includes a reconsideration of homoerotic boundaries within the existing culture of the time: "To make love with a man would be like making love with a mirror image of myself, a legitimate aspect of general sexual self-pleasure. I now embrace, touch, and kiss men on the lips. I enjoy kissing and holding male friends, but I have never become turned on to a man's genitals" (121). Rubin's reevaluation of traditional masculinity and male sexuality also includes a rejection of phallocentric masculinity and overcoming the perceived stigma of having a small penis: "In reducing my obsession with sex, I am developing a new relationship to my cock. I love it and my entire masculinity is not bound up in my cock. I no longer need to relate to women solely through it" (115). In *Growing (Up)*, Rubin never tires of revelatory moments and the act of making once-private matters public. In his case, the cult of laconic hardness produces a distinct counterreaction: a narrative of expressiveness and perpetual confession.

In many respects, Rubin's transformative masculinity represents the desire to challenge the traditional conception of maleness and, above all, to reject the rigid gender norms of his parents' generation. Rubin notes that the "excesses of each decade are corrected by the excesses of the next decade," and "[e]ach decade rejects the previous one to establish its own identity" (18). Rubin's project of perpetual transformation makes Weininger's conception of feminine mutability an article of faith. If the Old Left was reluctant to embrace new gender norms, a radical sector of the counterculture became devoted to transforming them. Although Rubin's program of perpetual rejuvenation appears obsessive today, his desired goal of breaking the cultural grip of hard masculinity is significant. While the complete liberation from gender stereotypes and gender myths may not always be possible, Rubin's project is important in that it attempted to enlarge society's conception of masculinity and create cultural space for a more pluralistic conception of maleness. Prior to gay liberation and the women's movement, there was no sustained cultural effort to redefine the traditional form of maleness that dominated cultural life in the 1950s and early 1960s.

Epilogue: The End of Innuendo

I began this project with the goal of writing a history of macho criticism and the politics of masculinity in American literary culture. This book began with Michael Gold's promulgation of the gender myths that operated in the literature of the 1920s and 1930s. In many respects, Kate Millett's *Sexual Politics* signified the end of Gold's project and the inauguration of a new trajectory of literary criticism. While the differences between Gold's hypermasculine version of Marxism and Millett's radical feminism are fairly apparent at this point in the book, their similarities are perhaps not as obvious; in an odd way, their antithetical projects can be read as complementary. Though Millett's feminist project attempted to turn macho criticism on its head, it can also be linked to Gold's project in several important ways. Both acknowledged that gender myths are explicitly political and that male fantasy constitutes a material reality that cannot be ignored by the revolutionary. Both posited a gendered revolution of literary sensibility and advocated a form of literary criticism that proclaimed the need for new subject matter, a new audience of readers, and a new way of reading.

Gold attempted to revolutionize American literature by promoting proletarian realism, a genre that was just emerging in the 1920s and 1930s. Politically, Gold's proletarian realism was aimed at the male body and attempted to remasculinize both the male reader and the male writer. To accomplish his project, Gold attacked the genteel tradition and various writers whom he considered effete. Millett's feminism was equally ambitious in that it took aim at a select group of twentieth-century male writers who depicted sexual relations from a masculine point of view (Henry Miller, Norman Mailer, D. H. Lawrence). Unlike Gold, Millett did not rely on homophobic rhetoric; nonetheless, her criticism was extremely polemical when it first appeared and, like Gold's criticism, aroused much debate in American literary culture.

Millett and Gold are also similar in that they both foregrounded the hard/soft binary as they read literature. While Gold's project was an attempt to defeminize American literature by making it more masculine and more working-class, Millett's focused on the demystification of masculine hardness and its chimerical allure. To achieve this aim, Millett's feminism emphasized consciousness raising and the attempt to pry female subjectivity away from its psychosocial connection to masculine dominance. The end result of Millett's project was an attempt to remake literary culture through the locus of the female body and through the transformation of female sexuality.

When considering Gold's and Millett's revolutionary projects and the various gender upheavals of the mid-twentieth century, we can identify coexisting narratives of success and failure. "Success" implies visibility in the popular culture and the emergence of gender self-consciousness: the moment when the unspeakable becomes speakable and fully manifest in public discourses. The narrative of visibility is apparent in literary culture. In the aftermath of second wave feminism (and Millett's work), feminist literary criticism has become firmly established in American literary culture and in academic culture at large. There is now a new audience of readers and critics who read literature through the critical prism of feminist theory. As a result, writers of all sexual persuasions have become much more self-conscious about gender issues and the multivalent ways that gender can be represented and understood in literature. The success narrative entails that literary culture is increasingly aware of gender myths and more self-conscious about the perpetuation of gender stereotypes.

Most notably, gay liberation prompted what could be described as the end of innuendo. Gayness has become increasingly visible in literary culture, and homophobia has become a political issue and a matter of public morality that is openly debated with great urgency. To fully understand and appreciate the historic importance of gay liberation, we need to consider the ubiquitous presence of the culture of innuendo in the 1930s–1960s. The culture of innuendo was so pervasive that it is difficult to find a writer from these decades who openly self-identified as homosexual. Any queer writer who challenged the culture of innuendo could face public scorn and commercial suicide. However, there was at least one notable exception to the trend: Allen Ginsberg's outspoken and unapologetic queerness in *Howl* (1956) is the boldest public rejection of the closet that I can recall.[1]

With the emergence of gay liberation, the old gender order gradually changed. Gay liberation insisted on visibility and created a viable cultural space for gay and lesbian writers, gay and lesbian issues, and what might be called the "queer sensibility." The critique of homophobia has manifested in literary culture and in the public realm in recent decades. However, it is also important to realize that the culture of gender self-consciousness can also produce gendered ghettos: if a writer is too openly gay or lesbian, he or she will probably be pigeonholed and placed in a literary ghetto (gay, lesbian, or queer).

But any discussion of contemporary literary culture should not be limited to a critique of gender ghettos. We should also examine the forms of cultural production that have managed to garner attention and success with straight and mainstream audiences. Tony Kushner's *Angels in America* (1991), Moisés Kaufman's *The Laramie Project* (2001), and Ang Lee's *Brokeback Mountain* (2005) are examples of this trend. How and why do certain "gay" works find a larger audience? What enables these works to transcend the traditional sex and gender barriers? These are important questions that should be considered.

THE GENDER DUSTBIN OF HISTORY

The narratives of success, or "progress," are really only half of the story; the narratives of failure and neglect are equally important. The literary culture of the mid-twentieth century is littered with failed and forgotten gender revolutions. One of the most apparent failures was the sustained attempt to remasculinize the man of letters in the 1930s. In the aftermath of the financial crisis of 1929, Gold attacked

American literary culture's suspicious ties to leisure culture and affluence. For Gold and many other Old Left writers, the muscular working class was the way forward because it was the perfect antithesis to leisure-culture effeminacy. In most historical accounts of the 1930s, Gold's hypermasculine conception of Marxism has been assigned to the gender dustbin of history, since the homophobia of the Old Left is a topic that most historians prefer to ignore. However, Gold's homophobic critique did not actually remain in the dustbin. In a fascinating ideological reversal, Joe McCarthy recycled Gold's homophobic rhetoric in the 1950s and used it to attack homosexuals and affluent left-wingers who supported the New Deal ("pinks, pansies, and punks"). McCarthy's reappropriation marks the beginning of the American Right's long and enduring love affair with hardness and homophobic hyperbole. In the political culture of the late 1940s and early 1950s, softness ("soft on Communism") became the worst possible insult. However, McCarthy's alliterative name-calling is also revealing in that it sheds light on the failure of the remasculinization project of the 1930s. In the aftermath of World War II, literary culture and the literary male were still—in the eyes of the general public—wedded to notions of affluence, effeminacy, and leisure culture.

The failed attempt to butch up the man of letters in the 1930s can be juxtaposed with another forgotten gender kulturkampf: the counterculture's war on the hard body of the Old Left. With the rise of the new sensibility in the 1960s, various icons of the New Left and counterculture (Norman O. Brown, William Burroughs, Timothy Leary, the Living Theatre, to name a few) conducted an assault on rigidity and the culturally inherited hard body. The utopian attempts to remake the hard body—to make it more affective, more pliable, less aggressive—have largely been forgotten. However, the counterculture's critique of traditional hard-bodied masculinity was more pervasive than many of us realize. By the mid-1970s, the age-old myths of traditional masculinity were often regarded as bogus and morally bankrupt. With the ascendancy of the women's movement and gay liberation, the mythos of hard-bodied masculinity was openly questioned and devalued in literary culture and in popular culture. In the post-Vietnam era, the beleaguered hard body of traditional masculinity was repackaged and reclaimed by right-wing ideologues.[2]

Much like literary culture, American political culture has often
been structured and influenced by the mythology of hardness and
softness. Soft masculinity (the so-called "wimp factor") is frequently
demonized in U.S. presidential campaigns. McCarthy's obsession
with anti-Communism and softness in the early 1950s was closely
connected to the theme of anti-intellectualism. The Eisenhower-
Stevenson electoral campaigns of 1952 and 1956 were couched in
gendered rhetoric. Adlai Stevenson, the effete intellectual, was pitted
against Dwight Eisenhower, the former football player and victorious
five-star general. Some fifty years later, the Bush-Kerry campaign
of 2004 revisited many of the same themes. John Kerry, despite his
record of distinguished military service, was labeled an elite and soft
intellectual, while George W. Bush successfully mastered the narrative of hard masculinity and folksy anti-intellectualism. The election
of 2008 was also influenced by the hard/soft binary. John McCain's
military service and ability to endure torture in Vietnam established
his notable hard credentials, while Barack Obama was predictably
labeled soft on terrorism and crime. However, the surprise of 2008
was not only Obama's remarkable ability to transcend the racial divide, but also his ability to overcome the rhetoric of the hard/soft
binary and anti-intellectualism, both of which often surface in U.S.
political campaigns. It was also evident that, after eight years of President Bush, anti-intellectual arguments had less credibility with the
voting public. To be a politician even in the twenty-first century is
to confront the dictates of the hard/soft binary. A presidential can-
didate must fashion a gendered response that addresses the popular
culture's preference for hardness and the ingrained prejudices against
leisure-culture effeminacy. Any serious presidential campaign cannot afford to ignore these concerns.

American literary culture mirrors American political culture
in that an aspiring writer must also produce a gendered identity in
his/her literary works. One of the most popular responses in the
twentieth and twenty-first centuries has been the embrace and celebration of hypermasculine myths. But despite the grandiose plans
of various male critics, attempts to remasculinize the American male
writer have had, at best, limited success. It is doubtful whether the
masculine critics have improved the status of the intellectual or the

literary artist in the culture at large. In toto, literary culture, despite its elaborate guises and transformations—anti-genteel, hard-boiled, proletarian—has had great difficulty severing itself from its "pale-face" origins. For many in the nonliterary public, the practice of writing remains a feminizing activity that is divorced from "real" and meaningful work. Hence, for many contemporary male writers, the act of writing itself has evolved into a curious act of disavowal—as a way of anticipating and mitigating the general public's persistent fear of leisure-culture effeminacy. Hyperbolic macho criticism, at its root, stems from this obsession.

Although *Pinks, Pansies, and Punks* has presented an extensive critique of hard masculinity and its mythic appeal, any serious cultural critic must also concede that the narrative of hardness—both as a physical ideal and as a cultural myth—continues to have tremendous popularity in the culture at large. How do we account for hard masculinity's remarkable resilience? The narrative of traditional masculinity—despite its obvious flaws and moral limitations—continues to be satisfying and attractive because it provides a mythic façade of strength, comfort, stability, well-being, and normalcy. Hard masculinity's enduring popularity in our cultural life should not be regarded as depressing. Academics and cultural critics who are obsessed with hard masculinity's grip on gender norms are missing a significant point: the narrative of hard masculinity should also draw attention to its repressed antithesis—affective soft-bodied masculinity. Because affective and porous forms of masculinity are continually repressed, they possess a vital residual presence within the male psyche. Moreover, the cultural and psychological need to project and perform hardness—to be always tough, rigid, sturdy, aggressive—inevitably becomes a taxing burden. Within a culture of manifest hardness, the longing for release and transformation is palpable. The narrative of psychoanalysis is illuminating: that which is repressed and denied is often more vital and potent than that which is deemed socially acceptable.

Notes

Introduction

1. Hearst magazines first serialized *To Have and Have Not* in 1934. The complete novel was then published in book form in 1937.

2. His essays "Toward Proletarian Art" (1921) and "Proletarian Realism" (1930) were widely read and anthologized in the 1920s and 1930s.

3. For an extended discussion of the genteel tradition, see the chapter on the 1930s.

4. The macho lives while the coward wishes he could.

5. Andrew Dvorsin notes that, when Rahv and Phillips founded the *Partisan Review* in 1934:

> [T]he aims of the magazine announced [in] its opening editorial were to defend the Soviet Union, to combat fascism and war, and to promote a literature which would express the viewpoint of the working class. But in 1937, the aims of the magazine, which had folded once and now reappeared with a new editorial board, including Mary McCarthy, Dwight Macdonald, and F. W. Dupee, were to concern itself with the intellectuals, rather than with the proletarians. (xiii)

6. See Rahv, "Proletarian Literature: A Political Autopsy," in his *Essays on Literature & Politics*.

7. For an account of the alleged accident, see Leon Edel, *Henry James: A Life*. When James was running from a Newport fire, he became "jammed into the acute angle between two high fences." The incident lasted "twenty odious minutes," and it is believed that this is what prevented James from taking part in the Civil War. In the twentieth century, Ernest Hemingway also made references to James's impotence. In *The Sun Also Rises*, Hemingway suggests that James became impotent during a bicycle or horse-riding accident. Edel's biography

contains a complete list of all the literary references to James's supposed impotence (721–22). Edel notes, "Critics in the 1920s, tended to see a relationship between the accident and his celibacy, his apparent avoidance of involvements with women and the absence of overt sexuality in his work. As a consequence there emerged a 'theory' that the novelist suffered a hurt during those 'twenty odious minutes' which amounted to castration" (58).

8. I will discuss the theme of Jewish masculinity on pp. 11–12.

9. In *The Heart of Whiteness: Normal Sexuality and Race in America*, Julian B. Carter examines how the upper-class white male body is often linked to neurasthenia ("nervous exhaustion") in nineteenth-century medical discourse. Carter argues that intellectuals ("brainworkers") were believed to be especially susceptible to this condition: "Such 'brainworkers'—upper-class Anglo intellectuals and writers—were the prototypical neurasthenics. Nervous collapses were almost commonplace among the great thinkers of the day: the roster of famous intellectual neurasthenes includes Herbert Spencer, Charlotte Gilman Perkins, William and Henry James, and Henry Adams" (48–49).

10. For detailed discussions of race and whiteness, see Gail Bederman, *Manliness and Civilization*, and Carter, *The Heart of Whiteness*. Both works discuss the origins of neurasthenia in the medical discourse of the nineteenth century and how the condition was often linked to upper-class and middle-class white bodies. The solution to the anemic neurasthenic body was a return to nature and an embrace of the "strenuous life"; Whitman, as poet and icon, embodies this tradition.

11. Rahv's essay does not refer to female writers and exclusively focuses on the male body that produces literature. Other anti-genteel critics did consider the contributions of female writers. In Malcolm Cowley's *After the Genteel Tradition* (1936), Willa Cather is read as an anti-genteel writer.

12. See Boyarin, Itzkovitz, and Pellegrini, *Queer Theory and the Jewish Question;* and Paul Breines, *Tough Jews.*

13. Mosse, *Nationalism and Sexuality* 36, 145–46.

14. Sengoopta, *Otto Weininger* 62.

15. Mosse argues that Weininger's *Sex and Character* was "one of the most influential racist tracts of the twentieth century, profoundly affecting the views of Adolf Hitler and many other racists" (145).

16. Various forms of the hard/soft binary also operate within the Asian American literary tradition. See Espana-Maram, *Creating Masculinity in Los Angeles's Little Manila;* and Eng, *Racial Castration.*

17. The idea that aggression in men is desirable is central to Lewis Terman and Catharine Miles, *Sex and Personality.* I will discuss their psychological study in the chapter on the 1930s.

18. There are several scholarly works that introduce versions of the hard/soft dichotomy, including Jeffords, *Hard Bodies: Hollywood Masculinities in the Reagan Era;* and Cuordileone, *Manhood and American Political Culture in the Cold War.*

19. I offer the hard/soft binary as a tool for identifying and deconstructing the popular gender myths that exist within Anglo-American literary culture. My hope is that it will not be used to reify existing gender stereotypes (e.g., "leisure-culture effeminacy").

20. This phrase is borrowed from Laura Mulvey's famous essay "Visual Pleasure and Narrative Cinema."

21. Halberstam, *Female Masculinity* 1.

22. Jeff Solomon's article on Truman Capote is an excellent beginning. Solomon persuasively unveils the macho pecking order that existed within New York literary culture in the 1940s and 1950s. He analyzes the rhetoric of female critics (Hardwick, Trilling) who performed toughness in their hostile reviews of Capote's early fiction. See Solomon, "Capote and the Trillings."

23. Jeffords, *The Remasculinization of America: Gender and the Viet Nam War,* and Jeffords, *Hard Bodies: Hollywood Masculinities in the Reagan Era,* focus primarily on the 1980s; Robinson, *Marked Men: White Masculinity in Crisis,* focuses on the 1970s and 1980s; Kimmel, *Guyland: The Perilous World Where Boys Become Men,* focuses on the generation of males (sixteen to twenty-six years old) who are coming of age in the twenty-first century. David Savran's groundbreaking study—*Taking It Like a Man: White Masculinity, Masochism, and Contemporary American Culture*—is unique in that it covers a much larger period (1950s–1990s). Another popular trend in masculinity studies is scholarly works that focus on one specific decade; several important studies have focused on the 1950s and the Cold War: Davidson, *Guys Like Us: Citing Masculinity in Cold War Poetics;* Cohan, *Masked Men: Masculinity and the Movies in the Fifties;* Gilbert, *Men in the Middle: Searching for Masculinity in the 1950s;* Corber, *Homosexuality in Cold War America;* and Cuordileone, *Manhood and American Political Culture in the Cold War.* Cuordileone's study is the definitive work on Cold War masculinity; it discusses "the hard/soft dualism" to foreground the importance of gender in postwar American political culture. Cuordileone argues that "the political dynamics of the early cold war years were fought to an unusual extent on the terrain of manhood and sexuality" (xxiii). My survey of existing scholarship has identified a need for work that offers a wider historical perspective and a critical overview of the mid-century decades (i.e., 1930s–1970s).

24. In addition to Bederman and Chauncey, my study was also influenced by Sherry, *Gay Artists in Modern American Culture: An Imagined Conspiracy.* Sherry's remarkable book documents the shrill rhetoric of paranoid homophobes who imagined that a cabal of homosexual artists ("homintern") was taking control of and degrading American cultural life in the 1950s and 1960s. Sherry's study often focuses on anxieties within the cultural milieu of modern music and the various gay composers of the mid-century (Virgil Thomson, Aaron Copeland, Samuel Barber, Gian Carlo Menotti, and others) who dominated cultural production during that time. I was also deeply influenced by Savran, *Taking It Like a Man.* Savran's salient chapter on the 1960s examines Leslie Fiedler, "The New Mutants" (1965)—the Beats, the hippies, and the counterculture—and Fiedler's provocative claim that American literature was being demasculinized by a wave of soft male authors who took delight in being feminized, humiliated, and penetrated. Savran's probing study also examines the veiled discourse of masochism and its various permutations in American literary and popular culture.

25. Levine, *Gay Macho: The Life and Death of the Homosexual Clone,* charts the emergence of the subculture in the late 1960s and early 1970s. Levine's sociological study documents "the rise of a specifically masculine gay subculture,

an articulation of male homosexuality that stressed gender conformity to traditional masculinity" (i.e., gay men who are "real men"; 1).

26. Although Sontag published in the *Partisan Review* (the preferred journal of the Old Left) in the early 1960s, her political and aesthetic views eventually
aligned her with the New Left and the counterculture. For evidence of Sontag's
political views and embrace of the New Left, see her essay "What's Happening in
America."

27. Richard Hofstadter has written about this in *Anti-Intellectualism in
American Life*.

1. "Healthy Nerves and Sturdy Physiques"

1. *New Republic* (Dec. 17, 1930): 141.

2. See Castonovo, *Thornton Wilder*; Harrison, *The Enthusiast: A Life of
Thornton Wilder*; Aaron, *Writers on the Left*; Michael Folsom, "The Education of
Michael Gold," in Madden, *Proletarian Writers of the 1930s*; Bloom, *Left Letters:
The Culture Wars of Mike Gold and Joseph Freeman*.

3. Rahv's "Paleface and Redskin" was written in 1939.

4. See Homberger, *American Writers and Radical Politics*; Aaron, *Writers
on the Left*; Bogardus and Hobson, *Literature at the Barricades*. Both Homberger
and Aaron are not that interested in gender concerns, especially the contributions of radical women writers in the1930s. Aaron's classic study of American
left-wing writing does cover the Gold-Wilder affair, but ignores the gendered
aspects of the controversy. Bogardus and Hobson's book is an excellent collection of essays from various critics and writers (Irving Howe, Alan Wald, James T.
Farrell); however, it is only marginally concerned with gender politics and masculinity. Michael Denning's definitive study, *The Cultural Front*, does discuss
gender concerns (radical female novelists); however, it is not concerned with the
question of the literary Left's hypermasculinity (e.g., the Gold-Wilder controversy). Szalay, *New Deal Modernism: American Literature and the Invention of the
Welfare State*, covers the aesthetic debates of the 1930s, but does not consider the
literary Left's gender politics. Dickstein, *Dancing in the Dark*, is an excellent cultural history of the 1930s, and it contains a chapter on female writers ("Gender
Trouble: Exposing the Intellectuals"), but it is not concerned with the literary
Left's hypermasculine rhetoric and homophobia.

5. Several scholars have examined Gold's importance in American liter-
ary culture, but most are not really interested in examining the significance of
Gold's gender politics. Dickstein, *Dancing in the Dark*, discusses Gold's influence
on the literary culture of the 1930s, but does not cover the Gold-Wilder affair.
Alan Wald's volume *Exiles from a Future Time* contains an excellent chapter on
Gold's influence in the 1930s, but Gold's gender politics are a minor concern.
For a warts-and-all portrait of Gold, see Bloom, *Left Letters*. William Maxwell's
study *New Negro, Old Left: African-American Writing and Communism between
the Wars* examines Gold's literary relationship with African American radical
Claude McKay. While several scholars (Wald, Bloom, Maxwell) acknowledge
Gold's homophobia, Gold's conception of gender is not a central concern in their
scholarship.

6. Burgam, "Three Radical English Poets" 330.

7. The phrase "genteel tradition" was first coined by the philosopher George Santayana in an essay in 1911. His use of the term reflected a critique of American Puritanism's idealist strain. In the 1920s and 1930s, the phrase was adopted by literary critics and authors (Sinclair Lewis, Malcolm Cowley), but their use of the term is distinct from Santayana's in that they focus on figures (William Dean Howells, Henry Van Dyke) who were influential in American literary culture in the period before World War I. Although Howells (1837–1920) and Van Dyke (1852–1933) lived well into the twentieth century, their literary influence began to wane in the twentieth century and especially in the period after 1914. For more on the genteel tradition, see Van O'Connor, *An Age of Criticism*. Also see Carpenter, "The Genteel Tradition: A Re-interpretation." For Howells's influence on American literature, see De Mille, *Literary Criticism in America*.

8. In *Criticism and Fiction* (1910), Howells defends the omission of sexual passion:

> I hate what is cheap and meretricious, and hold in peculiar loathing the cant of the critics who require "passion" as something in itself admirable and desirable in a novel. . . . Most of these critics who demand "passion" would seem to have no conception of any passion but one. Yet there are several other passions: the passion of grief, the passion of avarice, the passion of pity, the passion of ambition, the passion of hate, the passion of envy . . . all these have a greater part in the drama of life than the passion of love. (267)

9. For a more detailed discussion of manliness and masculinity, see Gail Bederman, *Manliness and Civilization*. Bederman indicates:

> Unlike "manly," which referred to the highest conceptions of manhood, the adjective "masculine" was used to refer to any characteristics, good or bad, that all men had. As *The Century Dictionary* put it, "Masculine applies to men and their attributes." "Masculine" was defined as "having the distinguishing characteristics of the male sex among human beings, physical or mental . . . suitable for the male sex; adapted or intended for the use of males." During the early nineteenth century, "masculine" was most frequently employed to differentiate between things pertaining to men versus women—for example, "masculine clothing," "a masculine gait," or "masculine occupations." Thus, "masculine," more frequently than "manly," was applied across class or race boundaries; for, by definition, *all* men were masculine. (18)

10. The speech was given on December 12, 1930, at the tail end of the Gold-Wilder controversy. In Aaron, *Writers on the Left,* Lewis mentions that he objected to Gold's "anti-pansy line" (257).

11. Wright's scorn for literature that produces an affective response anticipates another macho text: Wimsatt and Beardsley, "The Affective Fallacy" (1949), a foundational text for the New Critics. I will discuss the gendered aspects of New Criticism in the chapter on the 1950s.

12. Wright may be referring to Carl Van Vechten, a gay writer and a patron of African American writers of the Harlem Renaissance. For a detailed discussion of Van Vechten's relationship to African American writers of the 1920s, see Herring, *Queering the Underworld*.

13. For a detailed history of medical and scientific ideas about homosexuality, see Terry, *An American Obsession: Science, Medicine, and Homosexuality in Modern Society*. Terry analyzes the formation of the Committee for the Study of Sex Variants (CSSV) in 1935 and George Henry's *Sex Variants: A Study in Homosexual Patterns* (1941). Henry's important study of homosexuality was based on the research of the CSSV. Terry's book also contains an analysis of Terman and Miles, *Sex and Personality*.

14. In the field of psychoanalysis, Freud speculated about the psychological differences between males and females, but his theoretical writings do not actually contain empirical data that verify his claims.

15. The 1930s were arguably the heyday of eugenics in California. By 1936—the year that *Sex and Personality* was published—there were over eleven thousand sterilizations in California (Minton, *Lewis M. Terman* 149). Terman was a member of the American Eugenics Society and actively promoted the Immigration Act of 1924, which attempted to limit immigration from eastern Europe, southern Europe, and Asia.

16. For a genealogy of sex role theory and its influence, see Pleck, "The Theory of Male Sex-Role Identity."

17. I will return to sex role theory when I discuss Nicholas Ray, *Rebel without a Cause* (1955), in the chapter on the 1950s.

18. In the preface to *Three of a Kind*, Cain mentions that his fiction is often described as "hard-boiled."

19. The best example of this point is Madden, *Tough Guy Writers of the Thirties*. This collection contains several essays on the hard-boiled, but none of them consider the genre's relation to masculinity or gender politics.

20. Cowley, *After the Genteel Tradition*, covered only two decades of American literature (1910–1930).

21. In *The Fervent Years: The Group Theatre and the Thirties*, Harold Clurman offers the following appraisal of Odets's significance in the 1930s: "Clifford Odets was the voice of his day, reflecting, even more than he proclaimed or knew, the urgent need of the people of his time and place. That this was so the correspondence between his work and the social-political scene gave ample proof" (181). In many respects, Clurman's interpretation of Odets has been mirrored by various theatre historians and scholars as they have assessed Odets's legacy. Odets scholars—Michael Mendelsohn, Gerald Weales, Gabriel Miller, Harold Cantor, Christopher Herr—have emphasized the sociopolitical aspects of his work and how his plays brilliantly captured the lived experience of the Depression. These critics are only peripherally concerned with Odets's conception of masculinity and with the gender politics within Odets's plays.

22. Odets had three plays running on Broadway in 1935: *Waiting for Lefty, Awake and Sing!* and *Paradise Lost*. In 1938, at the height of his popularity, he appeared on the cover of *Time* magazine.

23. See Harold Clurman's introduction to *Six Plays of Clifford Odets*.

2. Doughfaces, Eggheads, and Softies

1. See Kennan 17–32.

2. Qtd. in Costigliola 1339.

3. Qtd. ibid., 1333.

4. For an extended analysis of Kennan's gendered language, see ibid.

5. For a more detailed analysis of Schlesinger's *The Vital Center* and his use of gendered tropes, see Cuordileone, "Politics in an Age of Anxiety," and Cuordileone, *Manhood and American Political Culture* 1–36.

6. *Gung Ho* (1943) was directed by Ray Enright and produced by Universal Pictures.

7. See Daniel Leab's entry for *Crossfire* in the *International Dictionary of Films and Filmmakers,* 3rd ed. (Detroit, Mich.: St. James, 1997); also see Edward Dmytryk, *It's a Hell of a Life and a Hell of a Way to Make a Living* (New York: New York Times Books, 1978). The apparent interchangeability of various minority groups is also evident in *Home of the Brave* (1949), a Hollywood war film based on Arthur Laurents's Broadway play; the lead character, a Jewish soldier, becomes an African American soldier. I will discuss Laurents's play to illustrate Talcott Parsons's theory of racial scapegoating.

8. For an extended discussion of the invisibility of homosexuality in mainstream Hollywood films during the 1940s, see Russo, *The Celluloid Closet.*

9. Parsons 167–81.

10. Parsons's theory of sex roles will be examined further in my discussion of Nicholas Ray, *Rebel without a Cause* (1955), in the chapter on the 1950s.

11. The theme of scapegoating is most evident in the persecution of gays and lesbians who worked in the federal government. See Johnson, *The Lavender Scare,* which is the definitive study on the subject.

12. See D'Emilio, *Sexual Politics, Sexual Communities;* and Berube, *Coming Out under Fire.*

13. Also in 1948, Harry Hay established the Mattachine Society, the first political organization devoted to securing and protecting the civil rights of gays and lesbians. The date is cited in the introduction by Roscoe to Hay, *Radically Gay: Gay Liberation in the Words of Its Founder.* I mention this because many historians cite 1950 rather than 1948.

14. For a more in-depth discussion of *The City and the Pillar,* see Claude J. Summers, "The Cabin and the River," in his *Gay Fictions.*

15. See Vidal's introduction to *The City and the Pillar* (1995) and his memoir, *Palimpsest* (1995).

16. Wylie's tirades against women and overprotective mothers have interesting parallels with the gender theories of G. Stanley Hall and of Terman and Miles, which maintain that men and boys need to embrace their hypermasculine nature because they have been overly feminized by female teachers, or what Hall deemed "the prim pedagogue propriety of petticoat control" (157).

17. For other discussions of Wylie's momism, see Braudy, *From Chivalry to Terrorism* 503–505; Rogin, "Kiss Me Deadly."

18. The rage against mom and softness can also be found in pop psychology books. Lundberg and Farnham, *Modern Woman: The Lost Sex,* present an equally

paranoid view of relations between the sexes. Similar to Wylie's antifeminist rant, the authors posit that "contemporary women in very large numbers are psychologically disordered and . . . their disorder is having terrible social and personal effects involving men directly in all departments of their lives as well as women" (v).

19. These figures are now considered too high. Many critics have questioned Kinsey's methods of data collection and have posited that certain social groups (gays and prison populations) were overrepresented in his 1948 study.

20. For Kinsey's critique of Terman and Miles, *Sex and Personality*, see *Sexual Behavior in the Human Male* 637–38.

21. For a more detailed account of the firing of homosexual government employees, see D'Emilio, *Sexual Politics, Sexual Communities*; and Johnson, *The Lavender Scare*.

22. Sam Tanenhaus in *Whittaker Chambers* refers to Chambers's homosexuality and his "closed door" confession to the FBI; and K. A. Cuordileone's probing article "Politics in an Age of Anxiety" analyzes how soft masculinity functioned as a subtext in the trial. Allen Weinstein's study *Perjury* briefly mentions the rumors about homosexuality that were circulating at the time of the trial.

23. For an analysis of the 1952 election, see Hofstadter, *Anti-Intellectualism in American Life*.

24. Hofstadter's study documents the Right's penchant for anti-intellectual arguments in the 1952 and 1956 elections.

3. Highbrows and Lowbrows

1. See Veblen, *Theory of the Leisure Class*.

2. See Ehrenreich, *Hearts of Men*. Ehrenreich argues that "other-directedness was built into the female social role as wives and mothers" (33–34).

3. For other readings that emphasize the representation of sexual difference in *The Glass Menagerie*, see Paller, *Gentleman Callers*; Sarotte, "Fluidity and Differentiation in Three Plays by Tennessee Williams"; Lilly, "Tennessee Williams: *The Glass Menagerie* and *A Streetcar Named Desire*." For a gendered analysis of Williams the playwright, see Paller, *Gentleman Callers*; and Savran, *Communists, Cowboys, and Queers: The Politics of Masculinity in the Work of Arthur Miller and Tennessee Williams*. For a critical overview of *The Glass Menagerie*, see Bigsby, *Critical Introduction* 2:15–134.

4. See *Social-Sex Attitudes in Adolescence* (1953) from *The Educational Archives*, vol. 1: *A Guided Tour through the Darkened Classrooms of the Past* (Fantoma Films, 2001).

5. See the earlier discussion of Parsons in the chapter on the 1940s.

6. Reich, a psychoanalyst and a radical advocate of sexual liberation, will be discussed in greater detail later in this chapter and in the chapter on the 1950s.

7. For a critique of Mailer's racial politics, see James Baldwin, "The Black Boy Looks at the White Boy," in his *Nobody Knows My Name*. Baldwin's acerbic and heartfelt response to *The White Negro* condemns Mailer's and the Beats' attempts to romanticize black male sexuality. Baldwin notes that, for whites, the

black man—whether he likes it or not—becomes a "walking phallic symbol" and a projection of the white male's sexual panic. Throughout the essay, Baldwin adopts a tough-guy persona and uses masculine metaphors to describe how writers size each other up. His meeting with Mailer is described in Darwinian terms: "Two lean cats, one white and one black, met in a French living room. I had heard of him and he had heard of me. And here we were, suddenly, circling each other. We liked each other at once, but each was frightened that the other would pull rank" (172–73). For Baldwin, writing becomes the act of demonstrating masculine prowess. Elsewhere, Baldwin describes Mailer as a "gladiator" who "strides through the soft Paris night." Similarly, Baldwin does his own bit of male strutting in the essay: "I wandered through the underside of Paris, drinking, fighting, screwing. It's a wonder I was not killed" (177). Baldwin's macho posturing mimics Mailer's masculinist writing and serves as a public repudiation of the leisure-culture effeminacy stereotype. For an extended discussion of Baldwin's work and the themes of race and sexuality, see Reid-Pharr, *Once You Go Black;* and McBride, *Why I Hate Abercrombie & Fitch.* For a broader discussion of representations of black masculinity in American popular culture, see Harper, *Are We Not Men?*

8. The hyperbolic tone of "The New Mutants" suggests that Fiedler is appalled and dismayed by the reversal of gender roles and the emergence of the counterculture. However, Fiedler's later work *Cross the Border—Close the Gap* suggests that his anxiety about the feminizing of the Western male was somewhat exaggerated. It is perhaps more appropriate to read "The New Mutants" as a tongue-and-cheek jab at the younger generation with Fiedler playing the role of provocateur. In *Cross the Border—Close the Gap,* Fiedler abandons his devotion to high modernism and admits to an admiration for "pop culture" and the lowbrow genres (comic strips, horror films) that delighted him during his youth. Furthermore, Fiedler was arrested and charged with "maintaining premises where marijuana was used" in 1967; Fiedler's account of the incident, *Being Busted* (1969), reveals that the Buffalo police regarded him as a corrupter of youth and as a leading member of the counterculture.

9. For accounts of Beat women writers, see Johnson and Grace, *Girls Who Wore Black.*

10. Kerouac and Cassady had sex with men, but did not identify themselves as bisexual.

11. The Beats' alternative lifestyle was also appealing to women in the late 1950s. Joyce Johnson, a young novelist who had a relationship with Kerouac during that time, stresses how the "Beats ushered in sexual liberation, which would not only bring a new and permanent openness to American art and literature but transform life for everyone" (*Door Wide Open* xv). Her two memoirs, *Minor Characters* (1983) and *Door Wide Open* (2000), provide an intimate account of the life of a Beat girlfriend and a firsthand account of Kerouac's meteoric rise to media stardom in the fall of 1957. In *Door Wide Open,* Johnson discusses the intellectual support that she received from Kerouac and takes issue with the notion that Beat women were solely domestic enablers: "He'd written to a very young woman as an equal, someone strong enough to take the truth. He'd generously recognized the writer in her. And he'd never boxed her in. This was rare for the

sexist 1950s, even in Bohemian circles" (xxv). However, Johnson's memoirs also indicate that she performed the traditional role of nurturing mother; she provided a home and comfort for her peripatetic boyfriend, who was often between poetic sojourns. In one of her letters, Johnson, the twenty-four-year-old aspiring novelist, plays mother to Kerouac, the thirty-four-year-old wayward son ("Its been great seeing Jack again, I dig ironing his shirts, cooking for him"). The attitudes expressed in Johnson's letters are a reflection of the contradictory gender attitudes of the 1950s. On one hand, Johnson felt liberated by her Beat-inspired rejection of conventional values; however, in other letters, her sense of liberation is often overshadowed by the prevailing gender roles and patriarchal mores of the time. The contradictory attitudes expressed in Johnson's letters suggest that women were primarily attracted to the Beats' romantic and alternative lifestyle. However, the Beats' rejection of the domestic revival did not imply a critique of patriarchy nor of the gender expectations placed on women.

12. In *Subterranean Kerouac,* Ellis Amburn argues that Kerouac was deeply troubled by his bisexuality and that his ambivalence was often expressed through homophobia and attempts to disavow his own homosexual desires.

13. Savran, *Taking It Like a Man,* 70.

14. The Nausicaa episode of James Joyce's *Ulysses* also contains similar imagery. Along the shore of Sandymount, Leopold Bloom masturbates and experiences an orgasm as he watches Gerty MacDowell, "the virgin of the rocks," from a safe distance: "And then a rocket sprang and bang shot blind blank and O! then the Roman candle burst and it was like a sigh of O! and everyone cried O! O! in raptures and it gushed out of it a stream of rain gold hair threads and they shed and ah! They were all greeny dewy stars falling with golden, O so lovely!, O, so soft, sweet, soft!" (Joyce 789). Kerouac's "roman candles" metaphor may be an allusion to Joyce's passage.

15. Scholarship on the New Criticism has primarily focused on the New Critics' pedagogical legacy ("the close reading") and how their method of interpretation forecloses the possibility of historicizing or politicizing the literary text. Scholars have largely stayed clear of gendering the New Critics; John Crowe Ransom's masculinist approach to literary criticism in *The World's Body* has not received much scholarly attention. For an analysis of New Criticism and its critical and historical significance, see Leitch, *American Literary Criticism from the 30s to the 80s.* Also of interest: Spurlin and Fischer, *The New Criticism and Contemporary Literary Theory;* Jancovich, *Cultural Views of the New Critics;* Malvasi, *The Unregenerate South;* and Searle, "New Criticism." Clark, *Sentimental Modernism,* is the exception. It contains a gendered reading and feminist critique of Ransom's literary theory and criticism.

16. Although Ransom argues that criticism should emulate science ("Criticism must become more scientific, or precise and systematic"), Ransom and Tate were also deeply critical of science and industrialism; in other works, Ransom argued that the spread of industrialism and science had uprooted agrarian society and destroyed its traditional communal values. For an analysis of the New Critics' cultural values and their contradictory attitudes toward science, see Jancovich, Malvasi, and Leitch.

17. In England, the trend began in the 1920s. In *The Meaning of Meaning* (1923), I. A. Richards argues that literary criticism should emulate the scientific use of language. The New Critics often cite Richards in their writings.

18. For an analysis of the New Critics' critique of emotionalism and fascism, see Braudy, "Varieties of Literary Affection."

19. Ransom, *The World's Body*, could also be read alongside other hyper-masculine texts of the 1930s (e.g., Gold, Terman and Miles, Cain). In these texts, the fear of feminine contamination is a rhetorical obsession. I am discussing Ransom's text in this chapter because the heyday of New Criticism is the 1950s. Ransom had a profound effect on literary studies and pedagogical approaches to literature in the 1940s and 1950s.

20. Lowell 558.

21. Since the 1990s, gendered readings of Eliot's work have become popular. Kaye, "A Splendid Readiness for Death," explores homoerotic themes in Eliot's early poetry. Lamos, *Deviant Modernism;* and Laity and Gish, *Gender, Desire, and Sexuality in T. S. Eliot,* present gendered readings of Eliot's poetry. For a discussion of Eliot's theory of the "depersonalization of art," see Ellmann, *The Poetics of Impersonality.*

22. For an extended discussion of the "bewildering minute" in Eliot's prose and poetry, see Kermode's introduction to *The Waste Land and Other Poems.*

23. The various references to canto XV and Brunetto Latini (Dante's homosexual teacher) invite queer readings of Eliot's theory of poetics.

24. Eliot was not the only modernist to experiment with this project. Other modernists (James Joyce, Gertrude Stein) also theorized that artistic expression is not merely a reflection of the artist's personality. Also see Ellmann, *The Poetics of Impersonality.*

25. Quoted in Grant, *T. S. Eliot* 80.

26. Neither of Eliot's biographers suggest that "Tradition and the Individual Talent" was influenced by Aiken's review in the *Dial.* See Ackroyd, *T. S. Eliot: A Life;* Gordon, *T. S. Eliot: An Imperfect Life.*

27. Eliot remained hostile to homoerotic readings of his work and the suggestion that he was a closeted homosexual. In 1952, he threatened to sue for libel when John Peter, a little-known Canadian academic, argued in *Essays in Criticism* that "The Waste Land" was an elegy for a dead male beloved. Peter's article "described the elements of sexual guilt and misogyny in the poem, and pointed to a variety of literary allusions to pederasty and sodomy" (Ackroyd, *T. S. Eliot* 309). Eliot's attempt to police Peter's reading was, of course, at odds with his contention that an author's interpretation of his/her own work is not more valuable than the reader's interpretation.

28. In a remarkably detailed argument, Savran, *Taking It Like a Man,* examines the strong current of masochism in Ginsberg's poetry.

4. Reforming the Hard Body

1. Feuer's accounts of the free speech movement at Berkeley were published in the *New Leader* and the *New York Times Magazine.*

2. Although I often mention the New Left and the counterculture togeth-er, I do not wish to conflate the two social movements. However, the members of the Old Left (Fiedler, Howe, Rahv) and the Old Right (Feuer) often placed the New Left and the counterculture under one heading: "the New Left." The confusion stems from the fact that the term "counterculture" emerged in the late 1960s.

3. See Morris Dickstein's discussion of Leslie Fiedler's cultural criticism in *Gates of Eden: American Culture in the Sixties* 66–67.

4. Howe, Rahv, and Trilling are less concerned with gender issues, espe-cially those concerned with sexuality. For example, Trilling's study *E. M. Forster* makes no references to Forster's homosexuality.

5. Irving Howe, the leading spokesperson for what could be termed the Old Left's conservative cultural values, argued that Fiedler had responded to the counterculture's assault with "uncharacteristic forbearance" and silence. Howe offered this assessment of "The New Mutants":

> Fiedler denies himself any sustained or explicit judgments of this "futurist revolt," so that the rhetorical thrust for his essay is somewhere between acclaim and resignation.... about drugs Fiedler betrays no equivalent skepticism, so that it is hard to disagree with Lionel Abel's judgment that, "while I do not want to charge Mr. Fiedler with recom-mending the taking of drugs, I think his whole essay is a confession that he cannot call upon one value in whose name he could oppose it." (*Selected Writings 1950–1990* 277)

On the other hand, Susan Sontag, the champion of the new sensibility, argued that Fiedler's critique of the counterculture was "wrongheaded" because he stopped short of endorsing the revolt against masculinity and what she termed "the depolarization of the sexes." In other words, Sontag felt that Fiedler did not go far enough (i.e., he did not endorse the soft and androgynous forms of mascu-linity that were emerging in the 1960s).

6. See Hayden, *Reunion: A Memoir*; James Miller, *"Democracy Is in the Streets"*; and Gitlin, *The Sixties*. Each of these works focuses on the role of the Students for a Democratic Society (SDS) in the fight for social change in the 1960s, and each discusses the clash between the New Left and the Old Left. The differences are usually discussed in terms of political tactics: labor and the Old Left favored cooperation, and the New Left advocated confrontation. Hayden, Miller, and Gitlin also emphasize the notion that the Old Left was skeptical and defeatist about the possibility for radical social change. There are some interest-ing discussions of how the New Left differs from the counterculture. The New Left (Miller, Gitlin, Hayden) tends to be more conservative and square. Hayden notes in *Reunion*:

> I could no more be a hippie in 1967 than I could be a beatnik in the fif-ties. I loved the music of the times, but strictly as a background to my life. I went to few concerts, owned hardly any albums, rarely danced, and was privately frightened by the loss of control that drug advocates

celebrated. . . . During the cultural revolution, I remained the straight
man. (203)

Gitlin's book extensively covers the counterculture's cultural revolution and the
influence of pop music on American culture in the 1960s (*The Sixties* 205–21).
One of the best books on the counterculture is Roszak, *The Making of a Counter
Culture*. Roszak briefly discusses the counterculture's masculinity: "One of the
most remarkable aspects of the counter culture is its cultivation of feminine softness among its males. It is an occasion [for] endless satire on the part of critics
[e.g., Leslie Fiedler], but the style is clearly a deliberate effort on the part of the
young to undercut the crude and compulsive he-manliness of American political
life" (74). Gitlin, Hayden, and Miller provide an overview of the political and
cultural experience of the 1960s, but they do not provide a detailed or in-depth
analysis of masculine attitudes during that time nor discuss how the Old Left
and the New Left and the counterculture had different attitudes with regard to
gender and masculinity.

7. My use of the term "Dionysian" is also borrowed from the Performance
Group's production of *Dionysus in '69*, an adaptation of Euripides' tragedy *The
Bacchae* that was staged by Richard Schechner in 1968. Much like the Living Theatre's *Paradise Now*, the utopia-themed production attempted to bridge the separation between life and art. The play dramatized the conflict between Dionysus,
the Greek deity of wine and fertility, and Pentheus, the repressed king of Thebes,
who attempts to censor and outlaw the worship of Dionysus within the kingdom
of Thebes. In the Performance Group's version, Pentheus becomes a stand-in for
the establishment that favored strict sexual mores and traditional morality while
Dionysus is interpreted as a harbinger of the sexual revolution and the libertine
values associated with the counterculture. In homage to the spirit of Dionysus,
the production featured several provocative scenes that negated the traditional
physical barriers that traditionally separate the performers from the audience.
One of the most provocative scenes in the production was called "The Caress."
When Dionysus seduced Pentheus and took him into the pit, the cast of *Dionysus
in '69* slowly crawled into the audience area and began to "caress" individual audience members who appeared "responsive."

8. By citing Howe's "psychology of unobstructed need" and Sontag's new
sensibility, I am building on Morris Dickstein's paradigm for analyzing the intellectual and cultural history of the 1960s. Dickstein's analysis of Howe and Sontag
can be found in "The Rise of a New Sensibility; or, How the Fifties Broke Up" in
his *Gates of Eden: American Culture in the Sixties*.

9. Trilling's skepticism about sexual liberation is also evident in his moral
critique of the Kinsey Report. Both "Freud and Literature" and "The Kinsey Report" are included in Trilling, *The Liberal Imagination*.

10. Podhoretz was still affiliated with the literary Left in the 1960s. However, in the 1970s he began to drift toward the right. His book *Breaking Ranks*
describes his political odyssey and his conversion to neoconservatism. In the
early 1960s, he was enthusiastic about Norman O. Brown's discussion of polymorphous perversity in *Life against Death*. However, as the 1960s progressed,
Podhoretz became more skeptical about both sexual liberation and psychedelic

drugs. Podhoretz's drug of choice—alcohol—symbolically reflects his commitment to "whiskey culture" and the traditional gender mores of the Old Left.

11. See Adorno and Horkheimer, "The Culture Industry: Enlightenment as Mass Deception." Adorno and Horkheimer, Western Marxists, are extremely hostile to various forms of popular culture (Hollywood movies, jazz). The Old Left contributors to the *Partisan Review* (Howe, Rahv, Dwight Macdonald) favored high modernist literature and shared a disdain for popular culture.

12. For an expanded analysis of the new sensibility debate (Howe versus Sontag), see my article on Sontag's intellectual roots and her conception of gender politics ("depolarization of the sexes") in the 1960s, "Gendering Susan Sontag's Criticism in the 1960s: The New York Intellectuals, the Counter Culture, and the Kulturkampf over 'the New Sensibility,'" *Women's Studies: An Interdisciplinary Journal* 37.8 (Dec. 2008): 921–41.

13. Here is the full text of Howe's remarks:

> In this *kulturkampf,* the New York intellectuals [i.e., the Old Left] are at a severe disadvantage. Some have simply gone over to the other camp. A critic like Susan Sontag employs the dialectical skills and accumulated knowledge of intellectual life in order to bless the new sensibility as a dispensation for pleasure, beyond the grubby reach of interpretation and thereby, it would seem, beyond the tight voice of judgment. That her theories are skillfully rebuilt versions of aesthetic notions long familiar and discarded; that in her own critical writing she interprets like mad and casts an image anything but hedonistic, relaxed, or sensuous—none of this need bother her admirers, for a highly literate spokesman is very sustaining to those who have discarded or not acquired intellectual literacy. Second only to Sontag in trumpeting the new sensibility is Leslie Fiedler, a critic with an amiable weakness for thrusting himself at the head of parades marching into sight. (*Selected Writings 1950–1990* 276–77)

14. Note how the affective and feminized egghead of the 1950s morphs into an impotent and reactionary figure who suffers from "hypertrophy of the intellect" in Sontag's critique.

15. Dwight Macdonald, a critic for the *Partisan Review,* is also an Old Left defender of high modernism and high seriousness. His essay "Masscult & Midcult" examines the clash between high culture and popular culture. The Old Left's view that literature should be an occasion for high seriousness is borrowed from Matthew Arnold, *Culture and Anarchy* (1869).

16. In *Against Interpretation,* Sontag also attempts to elevate the intellectual status of film, which at the time was a fairly controversial critical position. The discipline of film studies, with its roots in popular culture, was considered the softest of the soft in academic circles in the 1950s and early 1960s. However, film studies did begin to gain a degree of academic respectability in the late 1960s and early 1970s.

17. In "The New York Intellectuals," Irving Howe applauds Simon's critique of Norman O. Brown and Marshall McLuhan. The Old Left scorned McLuhan because he prophesied the rise of the mass media (low culture) and the

decline of the written word and high culture. Howe's praise demonstrates how the cultural values of the Old Left and the Old Right were often fairly similar.

18. In the 1960s, Old Left male fashion tended to be traditional and conservative. Old Left intellectuals favored suits, neckties, and short hair (see the author photos of Howe, Rahv, Podhoretz, William Phillips, and other New York intellectuals during that time). Thus, the fashion sense of the Old Left can be contrasted with the often loud and colorful clothing of the counterculture and New Left. The choice of whether to grow long hair often visually marked the male writer / cultural critic's reaction to the new sensibility. Those who were against the new sensibility (Trilling, Howe, Rahv, Podhoretz) tended to favor short hair.

19. The New Left's politics of liberation was also based on a Marcusean reinterpretation of the Marxist conception of alienation. In *Eros and Civilization,* a synthesis of Marx and Freud, Marcuse argued that Western societies (especially the United States) were governed by the principle of scarcity (*lebensnot*), which implies that "the struggle for existence takes place in a world too poor for the satisfaction of human needs without constant restraint, renunciation, delay" (32–33). Marcuse called the mania for restrictions "surplus repression." In the 1960s, many members of the counterculture and the New Left latched on to Marcuse's concept of surplus repression. In the utopian rhetoric of some counterculture thinkers, the condition of alienation could be overcome by vacating rationality via experimental drugs and the expansion of consciousness.

20. *Naked Lunch's* notoriety greatly increased when the book, much like Ginsberg's *Howl* in the mid-1950s, was the subject of an obscenity trial in Massachusetts in July 1966. Transcripts from the trial reveal that the district attorney's charge of obscenity was closely linked to the novel's explicit descriptions of homosexual sex. On several occasions, the trial focused on the novel's homosexual content and the tacit assumption that certain depictions of homosexual sex were "utterly without redeeming social value" and an "affront to conventional community standards." While other authors (E. M. Forster, Thornton Wilder) showed discretion and tact when they alluded to homosexuality in their fiction, Burroughs makes no attempt to veil or disguise various homosexual acts. The fact that the Supreme Court of Massachusetts judged the book to be "not obscene" was seen as a victory for free speech and the foes of censorship. It has also been argued that the decision was groundbreaking in that it legitimized candid literary representations of homosexuality. It is also significant that the trial was the last major censorship trial in the United States. Similarly, literary critics who attacked *Naked Lunch* made no attempts to disguise their disgust with Burroughs's depictions of "unspeakable homosexual fantasies." John Willett, a reviewer for the *Times Literary Supplement* and translator of *Brecht on Theatre,* was outraged by the suggestion that Burroughs's fiction had a "moral message." Willett's review is also interesting in that he chooses to highlight passages that depict not only homosexual sex, but the taboo act of being penetrated. Willett's moral outrage appears to be based partly on the idea that certain queer forms of masculinity should not be represented in literature. Burroughs, as a literary author and cultural producer, seemed to specialize in upsetting the established conventions of literary and gender decorum and challenging the legal and cultural boundaries of what could and could not be represented.

21. See Michael Gold's essay "Hemingway—White Collar Poet."

22. In "Letter from a Master Addict to Dangerous Drugs," Burroughs writes of the United States: "Our national drug is alcohol. We tend to regard the use of any other drug with special horror." The letter is published in an appendix to *Naked Lunch*.

23. See Morgan, *Literary Outlaw*.

24. When Leary first started teaching at Harvard, he was considered clean-cut and conventional. Dr. Humphrey Osmond, a British psychiatrist, described Leary as "a nice fellow . . . but just a little bit square" (qtd. in Lee and Shlain 75). Aldous Huxley, who had just met Leary, agreed, "You may well be right" (ibid.).

25. Each of these intellectuals was critical of psychedelic drugs and the growing popularity of LSD in the 1960s.

26. Irving Howe makes a similar argument about LSD in "The New York Intellectuals."

27. Leary argues, "I used the term 'politics' to focus on the cultural-social implications of the psychedelic experience" (*The Politics of Ecstasy* 6). Leary also notes, "Young minds exposed to neurological freedom and the free spray of electronic information suddenly blossom like flowers in the spring" (3).

28. In *Flashbacks*, Leary praises Hoffman's open mind and willingness to experiment: "The thing I liked about Abbie was that he kept changing, taking risks, dropping acid, reprogramming his head. He became the ultimate contradiction—a psychedelic socialist" (269).

29. Leary's statistics and methodology have been questioned by scholars. Critics claim that Leary's results are simply too high to be credible (see Lee and Shlain, *Acid Dreams*).

30. Alex Haley also brings up the homosexuality issue in the famous *Playboy* interview with Leary in 1966.

31. In "Hormonal Politics: The Menopausal Left-Right," Leary often takes outrageous positions: "human beings born after the year 1943 belong to a different species from their progenitors" (*The Politics of Ecstasy* 169). Leary's hyperbole suggests that political affiliation is directly related to one's date of birth and that the older generation is quickly becoming culturally and politically obsolete.

32. In the 1970s, Leary, like many other counterculture intellectuals, revised his views and became an active and vocal supporter of gay liberation.

33. For an expanded analysis of the Living Theatre's productions of *The Brig* and *Paradise Now*, see my article "The Living Theatre and Its Discontents: Excavating the Somatic Utopia of *Paradise Now*," *Ecumenica* 2.1 (Spring 2009): 17–36. There, I explore the issue of praxis and the lived experience of the performance event: What actually happened in the theatre space when *Paradise Now* was performed? To what extent were the spectators transformed by the experience of participating in the Living Theatre's utopian experiment? I also analyze how the production has been documented by theatre historians and performance studies scholars. Central to my article is the following question: Have scholars attempted to elide the dystopian and ethically problematic aspects of *Paradise Now*?

34. Thus, Reichian psychoanalysts are skeptical about the efficacy of the Freudian doctrine of sublimation; in most cases, they maintain that "genital satisfaction" is preferable and therapeutic.

35. See Beck, *The Life of the Theatre*.

36. For Reich, homosexuality and other nontraditional forms of sexuality are not viable forms of orgastic potency. Reich's attitude toward homosexuality was complicated. On one hand, he opposed all legal restrictions against homosexuality. However, he also argued that "homosexuality [was not] a legitimate libidinal choice but a regression to an oedipal longing for a maternal penis that could only be found in the substitute object of an 'effeminate' male" (Corrington 35). Reich did not mention lesbian sexuality in his writings, but given his gender essentialism and his view of homosexuality, we can assume that he probably considered it to be a form of neurotic behavior. The homosexual intellectuals like Julian Beck who closely adhered to Reich's teachings in the 1960s tended to ignore or disregard his views on homosexuality.

37. See Artaud 82.

38. The unsigned review in *Time* was quite hostile; the reviewer asserted that the company "preaches love but . . . would rather rape an audience than woo it." The reviewer also asserted that the company was guilty of "arrogant moral snobbery" (Sept. 27, 1968: 66). In contrast, Jack Kroll of *Newsweek* was more tolerant of the company's radical politics and utopian vision: "*Paradise Now* and *Antigone* were exhausting, aggravating, sometimes exalting rituals which aimed to create psychic, moral, social and political change in their audiences and in the society which is an extension of those audiences" (Oct. 28, 1968: 445).

39. Criticism of the Living Theatre in the 1960s and 1970s can be divided into roughly three camps: wide-eyed defenders, angry detractors, and critics who alternate between the two camps. The detractors included Eric Bentley, John Simon, and Walter Kerr of the *Herald Tribune*. At the opposite end of the spectrum were the devout supporters of the Living Theatre who applauded the company's commitment to radical politics and avant-garde aesthetics. This group included the *Village Voice* and the criticism that was written by members of the Living Theatre itself (Julian Beck, Judith Malina, Pierre Biner) and works by dramaturges (Gianfranco Mantegna, Renfreu Neff) who documented the company's European and American tours. More recently, John Tytell, in *The Living Theatre: Art, Exile, and Outrage*, defended the political and aesthetic legacy of the Living Theatre. The final group includes the critics who began as supporters and ended as hostile detractors (Robert Brustein, Richard Gilman); they were enthusiastic about the company's early productions (*The Connection*, *The Brig*), but strongly objected to the shock tactics and didacticism in *Paradise Now* and the assumed decline of the Living Theatre's artistic standards. One of the most fascinating aspects of the Living Theatre's work was its ability to polarize both critics and spectators; the company's confrontational aesthetic style and aggressive sexual politics inevitably drove the audience into one of the camps. The hagiographic approach (Biner, Mantegna) to the Living Theatre was fairly common in the 1960s and 1970s. It came mainly in response to the hostile criticism that the Living Theatre's work often engendered. There are two notable exceptions: Christopher Bigsby's chapter on the Living Theatre in *A Critical Introduction to Twentieth-Century American Drama* provides a balanced critique of the company's work, and Arnold Aronson, *American Avant-Garde Theatre: A History* (New York: Routledge, 2000), also provides a less partisan approach. For a larger

historical view of alternative theatre in New York City in the 1960s, see Bottoms, *Playing Underground*.

40. To some leftists, the juxtaposition of secular political aims and religious texts was considered bizarre because European anarchism is rooted in anticlericalism and atheism. However, Julian Beck and Judith Malina largely ignored these criticisms and maintained that the religious texts were compatible with their Artaudian aesthetics and their desire to create ritualistic theatre that viscerally affects the audience.

41. All my citations are taken from Beck and Malina, *Paradise Now: Collective Creation of the Living Theatre Company*.

42. See Honor Moore, "The Visit: A Memoir of the Living Theatre at Yale," *Theater* 3 (1998).

43. See Weaver, "Mirror, Mirror, on the Wall, Who's the Avantest Garde of All." Weaver provides remarkably detailed accounts of each of the Living Theatre's productions of *Frankenstein, Mysteries and Smaller Pieces, Antigone,* and *Paradise Now*.

44. For examples of audience resistance, see Bigsby, *Critical Introduction*; and Neff, *The Living Theatre*.

45. Howe's critique of the new sensibility is similar to Bentley's critique of the Living Theatre's *Paradise Now*. See Howe, "The New York Intellectuals" 274.

46. See Jeffords, *The Remasculinization of America*.

5. The Gender Upheavals of the Late 1960s and Early 1970s

1. See Tytell, *The Living Theatre: Art, Exile, and Outrage*.

2. Tennessee Williams's short story "Desire and Black Masseur," written in 1954, brilliantly anticipates Cleaver's Freudian-Marxist account of American race relations in *Soul on Ice*. In Williams's version, the white Omnipotent Administrator (Anthony Burns) masochistically craves sexual and physical destruction in the powerful hands of the Supermasculine Menial (the black masseur).

3. Several scholars have discussed Cleaver's homophobic attack on Baldwin and its implications: Field, "Looking for Jimmy Baldwin"; Abugo Origiri, "We Are Family"; Reid-Pharr, "Tearing the Goat's Flesh."

4. Quoted in Horacio Silva, "Radical Chic," *New York Times,* Sept. 23, 2001.

5. Baldwin was no stranger to literary fights; his adept critiques of Richard Wright ("Everybody's Protest Novel") and Norman Mailer ("The Black Boy Looks at the White Boy") helped to solidify his prominent position in African American letters in the 1950s and early 1960s.

6. See Duberman, *Stonewall* 198.

7. Kissack, "Freaking Fag Revolutionaries" 121.

8. Quoted in Teal, *Gay Militants* 147.

9. For an extensive discussion of Huey Newton's gender politics vis-à-vis the gay liberation movement, see Reid-Pharr, *Once You Go Black* 121–45.

10. My account of the APA protests is taken from Adam, *The Rise of a Gay and Lesbian Movement*.

11. Adam also reveals, "When the APA Council accepted deletion of homosexuality from the diagnostic manual in a unanimous vote in 1973, the conserva-

tives forced a referendum on the issue. The result of this curious spectacle of defining pathology by plebiscite was a vote of 58 percent for deletion and 37 percent for retention in 1974" (82).

12. In *Daring to Be Bad,* Alice Echols explores the divisions within the feminist movement on this issue:

> It was generally assumed by radical feminists that female desire when liberated from male constraints and expectations would be untarnished by fantasies of dominance and submission. It was also assumed that one's sexuality could, with some work, be transformed into an unambiguous reflection of one's politics. But in the late 1970s quite a few feminists had discovered that sexuality was neither malleable nor so easily aligned with one's politics. The antipornography movement with its strictly egalitarian vision of sexuality pitched themselves into self-confrontation again. Some began to wonder if holding desire accountable to some abstract standard of political correctness didn't encourage us to renounce our sexuality as it is now. (290)

13. See Ann Barr Snitow, "The Front Line: Notes on Sex in Novels by Women, 1969–1979," *Signs: Journal of Women in Culture and Society* 4 (1980).

14. In some cases, the feminist support for Valerie Solanas reinforced homophobic themes. In "Goodbye to All That," Robin Morgan expresses her admiration for Solanas and her attack on Andy Warhol: "Free Valerie Solanas! . . . Valerie Solanas, then serving time on a conviction of having shot Andy Warhol (used-decadence salesman)" (*Going Too Far* 130).

15. The keynote address was delivered at the West Coast Lesbian Feminist Conference in 1973. The conference was deeply divided over the issue of whether a male transvestite could attend the event. Morgan describes the individual as "a smug male in granny glasses and an earth-mother gown (he was easily identifiable, at least—he was the only person there wearing a skirt)" (*Going Too Far* 171). Morgan's camp maintained that the "gate-crashing . . . male transvestite" should not be permitted to attend the event (ibid.). An opposing camp of feminists defended the transvestite and argued that he should be allowed to attend the conference.

16. See *Combahee River Collective Statement.* The CRC also attempted to "publicly address . . . racism in the white women's movement" in the 1970s.

17. The number of vasectomies in the United States increased significantly during the early 1970s.

Epilogue

1. Bold representations of uncloseted homosexuality can also be found in Gore Vidal, *The City and the Pillar* (1948), and Truman Capote, *Other Voices, Other Rooms* (1948); both are also significant examples of public homosexuality.

2. As I noted in the introduction, Susan Jeffords analyzes the revival of hardness in *The Remasculinization of America* and *Hard Bodies.* Savran, *Taking It Like a Man,* also examines this ongoing cultural trend.

Bibliography

Aaron, Daniel. *Writers on the Left.* New York: Avon, 1965.

Abugo Origiri, Amy. "We Are Family: Black Nationalism, Black Masculinity, and the Black Cultural Imagination." *College Literature* 24.1 (Feb. 1997): 280–94.

Ackroyd, Peter. *T. S. Eliot: A Life.* New York: Simon and Schuster, 1984.

Adam, Barry D. *The Rise of a Gay and Lesbian Movement.* Boston: Twayne, 1987.

Adorno, Theodor, and Max Horkheimer. "The Culture Industry: Enlightenment as Mass Deception." In Adorno and Horkheimer, *Dialectic of Enlightenment.* New York: Continuum, 1972.

Adorno, Theodor, et al. *The Authoritarian Mind.* New York: Wiley, 1950.

Aiken, Conrad. "Divers Realists." In *T. S. Eliot: The Critical Heritage,* ed. Michael Grant. London: Routledge and Kegan Paul, 1982.

Amburn, Ellis. *Subterranean Kerouac: The Hidden Life of Jack Kerouac.* New York: St. Martin's, 1998.

Arnold, Matthew. *Culture and Anarchy.* 1869. New York: Oxford University Press, 2006.

Artaud, Antonin. *The Theatre and Its Double,* trans. Mary Caroline Richards. New York: Grove, 1958.

Baldwin, James. *Nobody Knows My Name: More Notes of a Native Son.* New York: Dial, 1962.

———. "No Name in the Street." In his *Collected Essays.* New York: Library of America, 1998.

Beck, Julian. *The Life of the Theatre.* San Francisco: Limelight, 1986.

Beck, Julian, and Judith Malina. *Paradise Now: Collective Creation of the Living Theatre Company.* New York: Random House, 1971.

Bederman, Gail. *Manliness and Civilization.* Chicago: University of Chicago Press, 1995.

Bercovitch, Sacvan, ed. *The Cambridge History of American Literature,* vols. 6, 7, and 8: *Prose Writing, 1910–1950* (1994); *Prose Writing, 1940–1990* (1999);

Poetry and Criticism, 1940–1995 (1996). Cambridge: Cambridge University Press.

Berman, Paul. *A Tale of Two Utopias.* New York: Norton, 1996.

Berube, Allan. *Coming Out under Fire: The History of Gay Men and Women in World War Two.* New York: Macmillan, 1990.

Bigsby, Christopher. *A Critical Introduction to Twentieth-Century American Drama.* 3 vols. Cambridge: Cambridge University Press, 1982.

Biner, Pierre. *The Living Theatre.* New York: Horizon, 1972.

Bloom, James D. *Left Letters: The Culture Wars of Mike Gold and Joseph Freeman.* New York: Columbia University Press, 1992.

Bogardus, Ralph F., and Fred Hobson. *Literature at the Barricades: The American Writer in the 1930s.* Tuscaloosa: University of Alabama Press, 1982.

Bottoms, Stephen J. "The Effeminacy/Efficacy Braid: Unpicking the Performance Studies/Theatre Studies Dichotomy." *Theatre Topics* 13.2 (Sept. 2003).

———. *Playing Underground: A Critical History of the 1960s Off-Off Broadway Movement.* Ann Arbor: University of Michigan Press, 2004.

Boyarin, Daniel, Daniel Itzkovitz, and Anne Pellegrini, eds. *Queer Theory and the Jewish Question.* New York: Columbia University Press, 2004.

Brass, Perry. "Cruising: Games Men Play." In *Out of the Closets: Voices of Gay Liberation,* ed. Karla Jay and Allen Young. New York: New York University Press, 1992.

Braudy, Leo. *From Chivalry to Terrorism: War and the Changing Nature of Masculinity.* New York: Knopf, 2003.

———. "No Body's Perfect: Method Acting and 50s Culture." *Michigan Quarterly Review* 35.1 (1994): 191–215.

———. "Varieties of Literary Affection." In *The Profession of Eighteenth Century Literature: Reflections on an Institution,* ed. Leo Damrosch. Madison: University of Wisconsin Press, 1993.

Breines, Paul. *Tough Jews: Political Fantasies and the Moral Dilemma of American Jewry.* New York: Basic, 1990.

Breslin, James E. B. *From Modernism to Contemporary: American Poetry 1945–1960.* Chicago: University of Chicago Press, 1983.

Brod, Harry, ed. *The Making of Masculinities: The New Men's Studies.* Boston: Allen and Unwin, 1987.

Bromfield, Louis. "The Triumph of the Egghead." *Freeman* (Dec. 1, 1952): 155–58.

Brooks, Cleanth, and Robert Penn Warren. *Understanding Poetry.* New York: Holt, Rinehart and Winston, 1950.

Brooks, Richard. *The Brick Foxhole.* New York: Harper, 1945.

Brown, Kenneth. *The Brig: A Concept for Film or Theatre.* New York: Hill and Wang, 1965.

Brown, Norman O. *Life against Death: The Psychoanalytical Meaning of History.* Middletown, Conn.: Wesleyan University Press, 1959.

———. *Love's Body.* New York: Random House, 1966.

Brustein, Robert. *Revolution as Theatre: Notes on the New Radical Style.* New York: Liveright, 1971.

———. *The Third Theater.* New York: Knopf, 1969.

———. "The Third Theater Revisited." *New York Review of Books* (Feb. 13, 1969): 25–27.

Burgam, Edwin Berry. "Three Radical English Poets." In *Proletarian Literature in the United States: An Anthology*, ed. Granville Hicks et al. New York: International Publishers, 1935.

Burroughs, William S. *Naked Lunch*. New York: Grove, 1959.

———. *The Soft Machine, Nova Express, The Wild Boys*. New York: Grove, 1980.

Cain, James. *Double Indemnity*. 1936. New York: Vintage, 1992.

———. *The Postman Always Rings Twice*. 1934. New York: Vintage, 1992.

———. "Preface." In Cain, *Three of a Kind*. New York: Knopf, 1944.

———. *Three by Cain: Serenade, Love's Lovely Counterfeit, The Butterfly*. New York: Vintage, 1989.

Cantor, Harold. *Clifford Odets: Playwright-Poet*. Lanham, Md.: Scarecrow, 2000.

Capote, Truman. *Other Voices, Other Rooms*. 1948. New York: Vintage, 1994.

Carnegie, Dale. *How to Win Friends and Influence People*. 1936. New York: Pocket, 1994.

Carpenter, Frederic. "The Genteel Tradition: A Re-interpretation." *New England Quarterly* 15 (Sept. 1942): 427–43.

Carter, Julian B. *The Heart of Whiteness: Normal Sexuality and Race in America, 1880–1940*. Durham, N.C.: Duke University Press, 2007.

Castonovo, David. *Thornton Wilder*. New York: Ungar, 1986.

Chambers, Whittaker. *Witness*. Chicago: Regnery, 1952.

Chauncey, George. *Gay New York: Gender, Urban Culture, and the Making of the Gay Modern World 1890–1940*. New York: HarperCollins, 1994.

Chesser, Eustace. *Salvation through Sex: The Life and Work of Wilhelm Reich*. New York: Morrow, 1973.

Clark, Suzanne. *Sentimental Modernism: Women Writers and the Revolution of the Word*. Bloomington: Indiana University Press, 1991.

Cleaver, Eldridge. *Soul on Ice*. New York: Dell, 1968.

Clurman, Harold. *The Fervent Years: The Group Theatre and the Thirties*. New York: Knopf, 1945.

Cohan, Steven. *Masked Men: Masculinity and the Movies in the Fifties*. Bloomington: Indiana University Press, 1997.

Combahee River Collective Statement: Black Feminist Organizations in the 70s and 80s. Boston: Kitchen Table/Women of Color, 1986.

Connell, R. W. *Gender*. Cambridge: Polity, 2002.

———. *The Men and the Boys*. Berkeley: University of California Press, 2000.

Corber, Robert J. *Homosexuality in Cold War America: Resistance and the Crisis of Masculinity*. Durham, N.C.: Duke University Press, 1997.

Corrington, Robert. *Wilhelm Reich: Psychoanalyst and Radical Naturalist*. New York: Farrar, Straus and Giroux, 2003.

Costigliola, Frank. "'Unceasing Pressure for Penetration': Gender, Pathology, and Emotion in George Kennan's Formation of the Cold War." *Journal of American History* 83.4 (Mar. 1997): 1309–39.

Cowley, Malcolm, ed. *After the Genteel Tradition*. 1936. Carbondale: Southern Illinois University Press, 1964.

———. "Foreword: The Revolt against Gentility." In Cowley, *After the Genteel Tradition*. Carbondale: Southern Illinois University Press, 1964.

Crow, Barbara, ed. *Radical Feminism: A Documentary Reader*. New York: New York University Press, 2000.

Croyden, Margaret. *Lunatics, Lovers, and Poets: The Contemporary Experimental Theatre.* New York: McGraw-Hill, 1974.

Cuordileone, K. A. *Manhood and American Political Culture in the Cold War.* London: Routledge, 2005.

———. "Politics in an Age of Anxiety: Cold War Political Culture and the Crisis in American Masculinity, 1949–1960." *Journal of American History* 87 (Sept. 2000): 515–45.

Davidson, Michael. *Guys Like Us: Citing Masculinity in Cold War Poetics.* Chicago: University of Chicago Press, 2004.

Dearborn, Mary. *Mailer: A Biography.* Boston: Houghton Mifflin, 1999.

Dekoven, Marianne. *The Sixties and the Emergence of the Postmodern.* Durham, N.C.: Duke University Press, 2004.

D'Emilio, John. *Sexual Politics, Sexual Communities: The Making of a Homosexual Minority in the United States, 1940–1970.* Chicago: University of Chicago Press, 1983.

De Mille, George E. *Literary Criticism in America: A Preliminary Study.* New York: Russell and Russell, 1931.

Denning, Michael. *The Cultural Front.* New York: Verso, 1997.

Dickstein, Morris. *Dancing in the Dark: A Cultural History of the Great Depression.* New York: Norton, 2009.

———. *Double Agent: The Critic and Society.* New York: Oxford University Press, 1992.

———. *Gates of Eden: American Culture in the Sixties.* New York: Basic, 1977.

Duberman, Martin. *Stonewall.* New York: Plume, 1993.

Dvorsin, Andrew. "Introduction." In Rahv, *Essays on Literature & Politics 1932–1972.* Boston: Houghton Mifflin, 1978.

Echols, Alice. *Daring to Be Bad: Radical Feminism in America 1967–1975.* Minneapolis: University of Minnesota Press, 1989.

———. *Shaky Ground: The Sixties and Its Aftershocks.* New York: Columbia University Press, 2001.

Edel, Leon. *Henry James: A Life.* New York: Harper and Row, 1985.

Ehrenreich, Barbara. *Hearts of Men: American Dreams and the Flight from Commitment.* Garden City, N.Y.: Anchor/Doubleday, 1983.

Eliot, T. S. "Tradition and the Individual Talent." In his *The Sacred Wood: Essays on Poetry and Criticism.* 1920. London: Methuen, 1928.

Ellmann, Maud. *The Poetics of Impersonality: T. S. Eliot and Ezra Pound.* Cambridge, Mass.: Harvard University Press, 1987.

Elton, William. *A Glossary of the New Criticism.* Chicago: Modern Poetry Association, 1949.

Eng, David. *Racial Castration: Managing Masculinity in Asian America.* Durham, N.C.: Duke University Press, 2001.

Epstein, Leslie. "Walking Wounded, Living Dead." *New American Review* (Apr. 1969): 230–51.

Espana-Maram, Linda. *Creating Masculinity in Los Angeles's Little Manila: Working Class Filipinos and Popular Culture in the United States.* New York: Columbia University Press, 2006.

Farrell, James T. *Studs Lonigan.* Urbana: University of Illinois Press, 1935.

Faludi, Susan. *Stiffed: The Betrayal of the American Male.* New York: Perennial, 2000.

Feingold, Michael. "Interview with Eric Bentley." *Yale Theater* (Sept. 1968): 106–11.

Feuer, Lewis. *The Conflict of Generations: The Character and Significance of Student Movements.* New York: Basic, 1969.

Fiedler, Leslie. *Being Busted.* New York: Stein and Day, 1969.

———. *The Collected Essays of Leslie Fiedler.* 2 vols. New York: Stein and Day, 1971.

———. "Come Back to the Raft Ag'in, Huck Honey!" *Partisan Review* 15.6 (June 1948).

———. *Cross the Border—Close the Gap.* New York: Stein and Day, 1972.

———. *Love and Death and the American Novel.* New York: Dalkey Archive Press, 1998.

———. "The New Mutants." *Partisan Review* 32.7 (Fall 1965): 507–25.

———. *Waiting for the End: The American Literary Scene from Hemingway to Baldwin.* London: Penguin, 1964.

Field, Douglas. "Looking for Jimmy Baldwin: Sex, Piracy, and the Black Nationalist Fervor." *Callalo* 27.2 (Spring 2004): 457–80.

Firestone, Shulamith. *The Dialectic of Sex.* New York: Morrow, 1970.

Forter, Greg. *Murdering Masculinities.* New York: New York University Press, 2000.

Freeman, Joreen. "The Bitch Manifesto." In *Radical Feminism: A Documentary Reader,* ed. Barbara A. Crow. New York: New York University Press, 2000.

Freud, Sigmund. *Civilization and Its Discontents,* trans. James Strachey. 1930. New York: Norton, 1961.

———. *Das Unbehagen in der Kultur.* Wien, Germany: Internationaler Psycho-analytischer, 1930.

Friedan, Betty. *The Feminine Mystique.* New York: Norton, 1963.

Gathorne-Hardy, Jonathon. *Sex and the Measure of All Things: A Life of Alfred C. Kinsey.* Bloomington: Indiana University Press, 1998.

Genet, Jean. *The Thief's Journal,* trans. Bernard Frechtman. New York: Grove, 1964.

Gilbert, James. *Men in the Middle: Searching for Masculinity in the 1950s.* Chicago: University of Chicago Press, 2005.

Ginsberg, Allen. *Collected Poems 1947–1980.* New York: Perennial Library, 1988.

———. *Gay Sunshine Interviews,* ed. Winston Leyland. San Francisco: Gay Sunshine, 1978.

———. *Howl and Other Poems.* San Francisco: City Lights, 1956.

Gitlin, Todd. *The Sixties: Years of Hope, Days of Rage.* New York: Bantam, 1987.

Gold, Michael. "America Needs a Critic." In *Mike Gold: A Literary Anthology.* New York: International Publishers, 1972.

———. "Hemingway—White Collar Poet." In *Mike Gold: A Literary Anthology.* New York: International Publishers, 1972.

———. *Jews without Money.* New York: Liveright, 1930.

———. "Proletarian Realism." In *Mike Gold: A Literary Anthology.* New York: International Publishers, 1972.

———. "Towards Proletarian Art." In *Mike Gold: A Literary Anthology*. New York: International Publishers, 1972.

———. "Wilder: Prophet of the Genteel Christ." In *Mike Gold: A Literary Anthology*. New York: International Publishers, 1972.

Goldman, Eric F. *The Crucial Decade—and After: America, 1945–1960*. New York: Vintage, 1961.

Goldsmith, Arnold L. *American Literary Criticism: 1905–1965*. Boston: Twayne, 1979.

Goodman, Paul. *Growing Up Absurd: Problems of Youth in Organized Society*. New York: Vintage, 1960.

Gordon, Lyndall. *T. S. Eliot: An Imperfect Life*. New York: Norton, 1999.

Grant, Michael, ed. *T. S. Eliot: The Critical Heritage*. London: Routledge and Kegan Paul, 1982.

Greer, Germaine. *The Female Eunuch*. New York: McGraw-Hill, 1970.

Halberstam, Judith. *Female Masculinity*. Durham, N.C.: Duke University Press, 1998.

Hall, G. Stanley. *Adolescence: Its Psychology and Its Relations to Physiology, Anthropology, Sociology, Sex, Crime, Religion and Education*. 2 vols. New York: Appleton, 1904.

Hansen, Craig. "The Fairy Princess Syndrome." In *Out of the Closets: Voices of Gay Liberation*, ed. Karla Jay and Allen Young. New York: New York University Press, 1992.

Harper, Phillip Brian. *Are We Not Men? Masculine Anxiety and the Problem of African-American Identity*. New York: Oxford University Press, 1998.

Harrison, Gilbert. *The Enthusiast: A Life of Thornton Wilder*. New Haven, Conn.: Ticknor and Fields, 1983.

Hay, Harry. *Radically Gay: Gay Liberation in the Words of Its Founder*, ed. Will Roscoe. Boston: Beacon, 1997.

Hayden, Tom. *Reunion: A Memoir*. New York: Random House, 1988.

Henry, George W. *Sex Variants: A Study in Homosexual Patterns*. 2 vols. New York: Harper, 1941.

Herr, Christopher J. *Clifford Odets and American Political Theatre*. Westport, Conn.: Praeger, 2003.

Herring, Scott. *Queering the Underworld: Slumming, Literature, and the Undoing of Lesbian and Gay History*. Chicago: University of Chicago Press, 2007.

Hicks, Granville, et al., eds. *Proletarian Literature in the United States: An Anthology*. New York: International Publishers, 1935.

Hiss, Alger. *Recollections of a Life*. New York: Seaver, 1988.

Hoffman, Abbie. *The Autobiography of Abbie Hoffman* (originally titled *Soon to Be a Major Motion Picture*, 1979). New York: Four Walls Eight Windows, 2000.

———. *Revolution for the Hell of It*. New York: Dial, 1968.

Hofstadter, Richard. *Anti-Intellectualism in American Life*. New York: Knopf, 1963.

Homberger, Eric. *American Writers and Radical Politics, 1900–1939*. New York: St. Martin's, 1986.

Hoopes, Roy. *Cain: The Biography of James M. Cain*. New York: Holt, Rinehart and Winston, 1982.

Howe, Irving. *The Margins of Hope*. New York: Harcourt Brace, 1982.

——. "New Styles of Leftism." In *Beyond the New Left*, ed. Irving Howe. New York: McCall, 1970.

——. "The New York Intellectuals." In Howe, *Selected Writings 1950–1990*. New York: Harcourt Brace Jovanovich, 1990.

——. *Selected Writings 1950–1990*. New York: Harcourt Brace Jovanovich, 1990.

Howells, William Dean. *My Literary Passions; Criticism and Fiction*. New York: Harper, 1910.

Isaacs, Edith J. R. *Theatre Arts Monthly* (Apr. 1935).

Jancovich, Mark. *The Cultural Views of the New Critics*. Cambridge: Cambridge University Press, 1993.

Jay, Karla, and Allen Young, eds. *Out of the Closets: Voices of Gay Liberation*. New York: New York University Press, 1992.

Jeffords, Susan. *Hard Bodies: Hollywood Masculinities in the Reagan Era*. New Brunswick, N.J.: Rutgers University Press, 1994.

——. *The Remasculinization of America: Gender and the Viet Nam War*. Bloomington: Indiana University Press, 1989.

Johnson, David K. *The Lavender Scare: The Cold War Persecution of Gays and Lesbians in the Federal Government*. Chicago: University of Chicago Press, 2004.

Johnson, Joyce. *Door Wide Open: A Beat Love Affair in Letters, 1957–1958*. New York: Viking, 2000.

——. *Minor Characters*. New York: Anchor, 1983.

Johnson, Ronna C., and Nancy M. Grace, eds. *Girls Who Wore Black: Women Writing the Beat Generation*. New Brunswick, N.J.: Rutgers University Press, 2002.

Joyce, James. *Ulysses: A Critical and Synoptic Edition*, ed. Hans Walter Gabler. 3 vols. New York: Garland, 1984.

Kaplan, Harold I., and Benjamin Sadock, eds. *Modern Synopsis of Psychiatry*. Baltimore, Md.: Williams and Wilkins, 1981.

Kaye, Richard. "A Splendid Readiness for Death: T. S. Eliot, the Homosexual Cult of St. Sebastian, and World War I." *Modernism and Modernity* 6.2 (1999): 107–34.

Kazan, Elia. *A Life*. New York: Knopf, 1988.

Kennan, George. "The Long Telegram." In *Origins of the Cold War: The Novikov, Kennan, and Roberts "Long Telegrams" of 1946*, ed. Kenneth M. Jensen. Washington, D.C.: United States Institute of Peace, 1993.

Kermode, Frank. "Introduction." In T. S. Eliot, *The Waste Land and Other Poems*. New York: Penguin, 2003.

Kerouac, Jack. "Belief and Technique for Modern Prose." In *The Portable Jack Kerouac*. New York: Penguin, 1996.

——. *On the Road*. 1957. New York: Penguin, 1976.

——. *The Subterraneans*. New York: Grove, 1958.

Kimmel, Michael. *Guyland: The Perilous World Where Boys Become Men*. New York: Harper, 2008.

——. *Manhood in America: A Cultural History*. New York: Free Press, 1996.

Kinsey, Alfred. *Sexual Behavior in the Human Male*. New York: Random House, 1948.

Kissack, Terence. "Freaking Fag Revolutionaries: New York's Gay Liberation Front, 1969–1971." *Radical History Review* 62 (Spring 1995): 105–34.

Klein, Marcus. *Foreigners: The Making of American Literature 1900–1940.* Chicago: University of Chicago Press, 1981.

La Cela, Franco. "Rough Manners." In *Material Man: Masculinity, Sexuality, Style,* ed. Giannino Malossi. New York: Abrams, 2000.

Lahr, John. "The Living Theater: Return to Eden." In Lahr, *Up Against the Fourth Wall.* New York: Grove, 1970.

Laing, R. D. *The Politics of Experience.* New York: Pantheon, 1967.

Laity, Cassandra, and Nancy Gish. *Gender, Desire, and Sexuality in T. S. Eliot.* Cambridge: Cambridge University Press, 2007.

Lamos, Colleen. *Deviant Modernism: Sexual and Textual Errancy in T. S. Eliot, James Joyce, and Marcel Proust.* Cambridge: Cambridge University Press, 1999.

Laurents, Arthur. *Home of the Brave.* New York: Dramatist Service, 1945.

Leary, Timothy. *Flashbacks: A Personal and Cultural History of an Era/An Autobiography.* 1983. New York: Tarcher, 1990.

———. *High Priest.* Berkeley, Calif.: Ronin, 1995.

———. *The Politics of Ecstasy.* 1968. Berkeley, Calif.: Ronin, 1990.

Lee, Martin A., and Bruce Shlain. *Acid Dreams: The Complete History of LSD: The CIA, the Sixties, and Beyond.* New York: Grove, 1985.

Leitch, Vincent. *American Literary Criticism from the 30s to the 80s.* New York: Columbia University Press, 1988.

Levine, Martin. *Gay Macho: The Life and Death of the Homosexual Clone.* New York: New York University Press, 1998.

Levy, Peter. *The New Left and Labor in the 1960s.* Urbana: University of Illinois Press, 1994.

Lewis, Sinclair. "The American Fear of Literature." In *A Sinclair Lewis Reader: The Man from Main Street: Selected Essays and Other Writings, 1904–1950,* ed. Harry E. Maule and Melville H. Cane. New York: Random House, 1953.

Lilly, Mark. "Tennessee Williams: *The Glass Menagerie* and *A Streetcar Named Desire.*" In *Lesbian and Gay Writing: An Anthology of Critical Essays,* ed. Mark Lilly. Philadelphia: Temple University Press, 1990.

Lorenz, Konrad. *On Aggression,* trans. Marjorie Kerr Wilson. New York: Bantam, 1966.

Lowell, Robert. "Visiting the Tates." *Sewanee Review* 67 (1959): 558.

Lundberg, Ferdinand, and Marynia F. Farnham. *Modern Woman: The Lost Sex.* New York: Harper, 1947.

Macdonald, Dwight. "Masscult & Midcult." In Macdonald, *Against the American Grain.* New York: Random House, 1962.

Madden, David, ed. *Proletarian Writers of the 1930s.* Carbondale: Southern Illinois University Press, 1968.

———. *Tough Guy Writers of the Thirties.* Carbondale: Southern Illinois University Press, 1968.

Mailer, Norman. *Advertisements for Myself.* New York: Putnam, 1959.

———. *The White Negro.* San Francisco: City Lights, 1957.

Malina, Judith. *The Enormous Despair*. New York: Random House, 1972.

Malvasi, Mark G. *The Unregenerate South: The Agrarian Thought of John Crowe Ransom, Allen Tate, and Donald Davidson*. Baton Rouge: Louisiana State University Press, 1997.

Manso, Peter. *Mailer: His Life and Times*. New York: Simon and Schuster, 1985.

Mantegna, Gianfranco. *We, the Living Theatre*. New York: Ballantine, 1970.

Marcuse, Herbert. *Eros and Civilization: A Philosophical Inquiry into Freud*. New York: Beacon, 1956.

Maxwell, William. *New Negro, Old Left: African-American Writing and Communism between the Wars*. New York: Columbia University Press, 1999.

May, Elaine Tyler. *Homeward Bound: American Families in the Cold War Era*. New York: Basic, 1988.

McBride, Dwight. *Why I Hate Abercrombie & Fitch: Essays on Race and Sexuality*. New York: New York University Press, 2005.

Mendelsohn, Michael. *Clifford Odets: Humane Dramatist*. Deland, Fla.: Everett/Edwards, 1969.

Miles, Barry. *Ginsberg: A Biography*. New York: Simon and Schuster, 1989.

Miller, Arthur. *Death of a Salesman*, ed. Gerald Weales. 1949. New York: Penguin, 1996.

Miller, Gabriel. *Clifford Odets*. New York: Continuum, 1989.

———. *Critical Essays on Clifford Odets*. Boston: Hall, 1991.

Miller, Henry. *Sexus*. New York: Grove, 1965.

Miller, James. *"Democracy Is in the Streets": From Port Huron to the Siege of Chicago*. New York: Simon and Schuster, 1987.

Millett, Kate. *Sexual Politics*. Garden City, N.Y.: Doubleday, 1970.

Mills, C. Wright. *White Collar: The American Middle Classes*. New York: Oxford University Press, 1953.

Minton, Henry L. *Lewis M. Terman: Pioneer in Psychological Testing*. New York: New York University Press, 1988.

Morgan, Robin. *Going Too Far*. New York: Random House, 1977.

Morgan, Ted. *Literary Outlaw: The Life and Times of William S. Burroughs*. London: Pimlico, 1983.

Mosse, George L. *Nationalism and Sexuality: Respectability and Abnormal Sexuality in Modern Europe*. New York: Fertig, 1985.

Mulvey, Laura. "Visual Pleasure and Narrative Cinema." *Screen* 16.3 (Autumn 1975): 16–18.

Neff, Renfreu. *The Living Theatre: USA*. New York: Bobbs-Merrill, 1970.

Nietzsche, Friedrich. *The Birth of Tragedy and the Case of Wagner*, trans. Walter Kauffmann. New York: Vintage, 1967.

Oates, Joyce Carol. "Man under the Sentence of Death: The Novels of James M. Cain." In *Tough Guy Writers of the Thirties*, ed. David Madden. Carbondale: Southern Illinois University Press, 1968.

———. "Raymond Chandler: Genre and 'Art.'" In Oates, *Where I've Been, and Where I Am Going*. New York: Plume, 1999.

Odets, Clifford. *Six Plays of Clifford Odets*. New York: Grove, 1979.

Paller, Michael. *Gentleman Callers: Tennessee Williams, Homosexuality, and Mid-Twentieth-Century Drama*. New York: Palgrave Macmillan, 2005.

Parsons, Talcott. "Certain Primary Sources and Patterns of Aggression in the So-
    cial Structure of the Western World." *Psychiatry* 10 (1947): 167–81.
Parsons, Talcott, and Robert F. Bales. *Family, Socialization and Interaction Pro-
    cess.* Glencoe, Ill.: Free Press, 1955.
Partridge, Eric. *Dictionary of Slang.* London: Macmillan, 1961.
Peter, John. "A New Interpretation of *The Waste Land.*" *Essays in Criticism* 2
    (July 1952): 242–66.
Pleck, Joseph. "The Theory of Male Sex-Role Identity: Its Rise and Fall, 1936 to
    the Present." In *The Making of Masculinities,* ed. Harry Brod. Boston: Allen
    and Unwin, 1987.
Podhoretz, Norman. *Breaking Ranks.* New York: Harper and Row, 1979.
———. *Doings and Undoings.* New York: Noonday, 1964.
———. "The Know-Nothing Bohemians." *Partisan Review* 25 (Spring 1958):
    305–16.
———. *Making It.* New York: Random House, 1967.
Polan, Dana. *Power and Paranoia: History, Narrative, and the American Cinema
    1940–1950.* New York: Columbia University Press, 1986.
Rabinowitz, Paula. *Labor & Desire: Women's Revolutionary Fiction in Depression
    America.* Chapel Hill: University of North Carolina Press, 1991.
Rahv, Philip. *Essays on Literature & Politics 1932–1972.* Boston: Houghton Mif-
    flin, 1978.
———. *Literature and the Sixth Sense.* Boston: Houghton Mifflin, 1969.
———. *Myth and the Powerhouse.* New York: Farrar, Straus and Giroux, 1965.
———. "Paleface and Redskin." In Rahv, *Literature and the Sixth Sense.* Boston:
    Houghton Mifflin, 1969.
Ransom, John Crowe. *The New Criticism.* New York: New Directions, 1941.
———. *The World's Body.* Port Washington, N.Y.: Kennikat, 1938.
Reeves, Thomas C. *The Life and Times of Joseph McCarthy: A Biography.* Lanham,
    Md.: Madison, 1982.
Reich, Wilhelm. *Character Analysis.* New York: Farrar, Straus and Giroux,
    1972.
———. *The Function of the Orgasm.* 1942. New York: World Publishing, 1971.
Reid-Pharr, Robert. *Once You Go Black: Choice, Desire, and the Black American
    Intellectual.* New York: New York University Press, 2007.
———. "Tearing the Goat's Flesh: Homosexuality, Abjection, and the Produc-
    tion of a Late Twentieth Century Black Masculinity." *Studies in the Novel*
    28.3 (Fall 1996): 372–94.
Richards, Ian. *The Meaning of Meaning.* New York: Harcourt Brace, 1923.
Riesman, David. *The Lonely Crowd.* 1950. New Haven, Conn.: Yale University
    Press, 1961.
Robinson, Sally. *Marked Men: White Masculinity in Crisis.* New York: New York
    University Press, 2000.
Rogin, Michael. "Kiss Me Deadly: Communism, Motherhood and Cold War
    Movies." *Representations* 6 (Spring 1984): 1–36.
Roscoe, Will. "Introduction." In Hay, *Radically Gay: Gay Liberation in the Words
    of Its Founder.* Boston: Beacon, 1997.
Rosenthal, M. L. "Poet of New Violence." In *On the Poetry of Allen Ginsberg,* ed.
    Lewis Hyde. Ann Arbor: University of Michigan Press, 1984.

Roszak, Theodore. *The Making of a Counter Culture.* Garden City, N.Y.: Double-day, 1968.

Rubin, Jerry. *Do It: Scenarios of the Revolution.* New York: Simon and Schuster, 1970.

———. *Growing (Up) at Thirty-Seven.* New York: Evans, 1976.

Russo, Vito. *The Celluloid Closet: Homosexuality in the Movies.* New York: Harper and Row, 1987.

Sarotte, Georges-Michel. "Fluidity and Differentiation in Three Plays by Tennessee Williams: *The Glass Menagerie, A Streetcar Named Desire,* and *Cat on a Hot Tin Roof.*" In *Staging Difference: Cultural Pluralism in American Theatre and Drama,* ed. Marc Maufort. New York: Lang, 1995.

Savran, David. *Communists, Cowboys, and Queers: The Politics of Masculinity in the Works of Arthur Miller and Tennessee Williams.* Minneapolis: University of Minnesota Press, 1992.

———. *Queer Sort of Materialism: Recontextualizing American Theater.* Ann Arbor: University of Michigan Press, 2003.

———. *Taking It Like a Man: White Masculinity, Masochism, and Contemporary American Culture.* Princeton, N.J.: Princeton University Press, 1998.

Schechner, Richard, ed. *Dionysus in '69.* New York: Farrar, Straus and Giroux, 1970.

———. *Environmental Theater.* New York: Applause Books, 2000.

———. *Performance Theory.* London: Routledge, 2003.

Schlesinger, Arthur M., Jr. *The Vital Center: The Politics of Freedom.* Boston: Houghton Mifflin, 1949.

Searle, Leo F. "New Criticism." In *Johns Hopkins Guide to Literary Criticism,* ed. Michael Groden and Martin Kreiswirth. Baltimore, Md.: Johns Hopkins University Press, 1994.

Sedgwick, Eve Kosofsky. *Between Men: English Literature and Male Homosocial Desire.* New York: Columbia University Press, 1985.

———. *Epistemology of the Closet.* Berkeley: University of California Press, 1990.

Sengoopta, Chandak. *Otto Weininger: Sex, Science, and Self in Imperial Vienna.* Chicago: University of Chicago Press, 2000.

Shank, Theodore. *American Alternative Theatre.* New York: Palgrave Macmillan, 1988.

———. *Beyond the Boundaries: American Alternative Theatre.* Ann Arbor: University of Michigan Press, 2002.

Shaw, Peter. "The Tough Guy Intellectual." *Critical Quarterly* 8.1 (Spring 1966): 13–29.

Sherry, Michael. *Gay Artists in Modern American Culture: An Imagined Conspiracy.* Chapel Hill: University of North Carolina Press, 2007.

Simon, John. "Two Camps." *Partisan Review* 32.1 (Winter 1965): 156–57.

Sinfield, Alan. *The Wilde Century: Effeminacy, Oscar Wilde and the Queer Moment.* New York: Columbia University Press, 1994.

Smith, Wendy. *Real Life: The Group Theatre and America, 1931–1940.* New York: Grove, 1990.

Solanas, Valerie. "SCUM (Society for Cutting Up Men) Manifesto." In *Radical Feminism: A Documentary Reader,* ed. Barbara A. Crow. New York: New York University Press, 2000.

Solomon, Jeff. "Capote and the Trillings: Homophobia and Literary Culture at Mid-Century." *Twentieth Century Literature* 54.2 (2009): 129–65.

———. "Young, Effeminate, and Strange: Early Photographic Portraits of Truman Capote." *Studies in Gender and Sexuality* 6.3 (2005): 293–326.

Sontag, Susan. "Against Interpretation." In Sontag, *Against Interpretation.* New York: Anchor, 1966.

———. "Notes on 'Camp.'" In Sontag, *Against Interpretation.* New York: Anchor, 1966.

———. "On Culture and the New Sensibility." In Sontag, *Against Interpretation.* New York: Anchor, 1966.

———. "Two Camps." *Partisan Review* 32.1 (Winter 1965): 157–58.

———. "What's Happening in America." In Sontag, *Styles of Radical Will.* New York: Picador USA, 1969.

Spender, Stephen. "Remembering Eliot." In *T. S. Eliot: The Man and His Work,* ed. Allen Tate. New York: Delacorte, 1966.

Spurlin, William J., and Michael Fischer, eds. *The New Criticism and Contemporary Literary Theory: Connections and Continuities.* New York: Garland, 1995.

Stouffer, Samuel A., et al. *The American Soldier.* 4 vols. Princeton, N.J.: Princeton University Press, 1949–1950.

Strecker, Edward. *Their Mothers' Sons: The Psychiatrist Examines an American Problem.* Philadelphia: Lippincott, 1946.

Summers, Claude J. *Gay Fictions: Wilde to Stonewall: Studies in a Male Homosexual Literary Tradition.* New York: Continuum, 1990.

Szalay, Michael. *New Deal Modernism: American Literature and the Invention of the Welfare State.* Durham, N.C.: Duke University Press, 2000.

Tanenhaus, Sam. *Whittaker Chambers.* New York: Random House, 1997.

Teal, Donn. *The Gay Militants: How Gay Liberation Began in America, 1969–1971.* New York: St. Martin's, 1995.

Terman, Lewis, and Catharine Miles. *Sex and Personality: Studies in Masculinity and Femininity.* New York: McGraw-Hill, 1936.

Terry, Jennifer. *An American Obsession: Science, Medicine, and Homosexuality in Modern Society.* Chicago: University of Chicago Press, 1999.

Theweleit, Klaus. *Male Fantasies,* trans. Stephen Conway. 2 vols. Minneapolis: University of Minnesota Press, 1987.

Thorp, Charles P. "I.D., Leadership and Violence." In *Out of the Closets: Voices of Gay Liberation,* ed. Karla Jay and Allen Young. New York: New York University Press, 1992.

Trilling, Lionel. *E. M. Forster.* Norfolk, Conn.: New Directions, 1943.

———. "Freud and Literature." In Trilling, *The Liberal Imagination: Essays on Literature and Society.* New York: Scribner's, 1950.

———. "The Kinsey Report." In Trilling, *The Liberal Imagination: Essays on Literature and Society.* New York: Scribner's, 1950.

Tytell, John. *The Living Theatre: Art, Exile, and Outrage.* New York: Grove, 1995.

Wald, Alan. *Exiles from a Future Time: The Forging of the Mid-Century Literary Left.* Chapel Hill: University of North Carolina Press, 2002.

Weales, Gerald. *Clifford Odets: Playwright.* New York: Pegasus, 1971.

Weatherby, W. J. *James Baldwin: Artist on Fire.* New York: Fine, 1989.

Weaver, Neal. "Mirror, Mirror, on the Wall, Who's the Avantest Garde of All."
    After Dark (December 1968): 52–56.

Weininger, Otto. *Sex and Character.* Authorized translation from the 6th German ed. New York: Putnam, 1906.

Weinstein, Allen. *Perjury: The Hiss-Chambers Trial.* New York: Knopf, 1978.

Whyte, William H. *The Organization Man.* New York: Simon and Schuster, 1956.

Wilder, Thornton. *The Bridge of San Luis Rey.* New York: Boni, 1928.

Willett, John. "UGH . . ." [Review of *Naked Lunch, The Soft Machine, The Ticket That Exploded,* and *Dead Fingers Talk*]. *Times Literary Supplement* 3220 (Nov. 14, 1963): 919.

Williams, Tennessee. *The Glass Menagerie.* New York: Dramatists Play Service, 1945.

Wilson, Edmund. "The Economic Interpretation of Wilder." In Wilson, *The Shores of Light.* New York: Farrar, Straus and Giroux, 1952.

———. "The Literary Class Struggle." In Wilson, *The Shores of Light.* New York: Farrar, Straus and Giroux, 1952.

Wimsatt, W. K., and Monroe Beardsley. "The Affective Fallacy." In *Critical Theory since Plato,* ed. Hazard Adams. New York: Harcourt Brace Jovanovich, 1971.

———. "The Intentional Fallacy." In *Critical Theory since Plato,* ed. Hazard Adams. New York: Harcourt Brace Jovanovich, 1971.

Wolfe, Tom. *The Electric Kool-Aid Acid Test.* New York: Bantam, 1968.

Wright, Richard. "Blueprint for Negro Writing." In *The Norton Anthology of African American Literature,* ed. Henry Louis Gates et al. New York: Norton, 2004.

———. "How 'Bigger' Was Born." In Wright, *Native Son.* New York: Harper, 2008.

Wylie, Phillip. *Generation of Vipers.* New York: Holt, Rinehart and Winston, 1942.

Van Dyke, Henry. *The Man behind the Book: Essays in Understanding.* New York: Scribner's, 1929.

Van O'Connor, William. *An Age of Criticism: 1900–1950.* Chicago: Regnery, 1952.

Veblen, Thorstein. *The Theory of the Leisure Class.* 1899. New York: Penguin, 1988.

Vidal, Gore. *The City and the Pillar.* New York: Dutton, 1948.

———. "Introduction." In Vidal, *The City and the Pillar.* New York: Vintage, 1995.

———. *Palimpsest.* New York: Random House, 1995.

Index

JAMES PENNER is an assistant professor of English at the University of Puerto Rico, Rio Piedras.

This book was designed by Jamison Cockerham and
set in type by Tony Brewer at Indiana University Press
and printed by Integrated Book Technology, Inc.

The text face is Arno Pro, designed by Robert Slimbach,
and titles are set in Conga Brava, designed by
Michael Harvey, both issued by Adobe Systems.